Jazz Italian Style

Jazz Italian Style explores a complex era in music history, when politics and popular culture collided with national identity and technology. When jazz arrived in Italy at the conclusion of World War I, it quickly became part of the local music culture. In Italy, thanks to the gramophone and radio, many listeners paid little attention to a performer's national and ethnic identity. Nick LaRocca (Italian American), Gorni Kramer (Italian), the Trio Lescano (Jewish Dutch) and Louis Armstrong (African American), to name a few, all found equal footing in the Italian soundscape. The book reveals how Italians made jazz their own, and how, by the mid-1930s, a genre of jazz distinguishable from American varieties and supported by Mussolini began to flourish in Northern Italy and in its turn influenced Italian American musicians. Most importantly, the book recovers a lost repertoire and an array of musicians whose stories and performances are compelling and well worth remembering.

Anna Harwell Celenza is the Thomas E. Caestecker Professor of Music at Georgetown University, where she teaches courses in music history, radio journalism and the music industry. She is the author or editor of several scholarly books, and has published numerous articles on composers and musicians, from Franz Liszt and Gustav Mahler to Duke Ellington, Billy Strayhorn, Louis Armstrong and Frank Sinatra.

Jazz Italian Style

From its Origins in New Orleans to Fascist Italy and Sinatra

ANNA HARWELL CELENZA

Georgetown University, Washington DC

CAMBRIDGE
UNIVERSITY PRESS

CAMBRIDGE
UNIVERSITY PRESS

University Printing House, Cambridge CB2 8BS, United Kingdom

One Liberty Plaza, 20th Floor, New York, NY 10006, USA

477 Williamstown Road, Port Melbourne, VIC 3207, Australia

4843/24, 2nd Floor, Ansari Road, Daryaganj, Delhi – 110002, India

79 Anson Road, #06-04/06, Singapore 079906

Cambridge University Press is part of the University of Cambridge.

It furthers the University's mission by disseminating knowledge in the pursuit of education, learning, and research at the highest international levels of excellence.

www.cambridge.org

Information on this title: www.cambridge.org/9781107169777

DOI: 10.1017/9781316755228

First published 2017

Printed in the United States of America by Sheridan Books, Inc.

A catalogue record for this publication is available from the British Library.

ISBN 978-1-107-16977-7 Hardback

Cambridge University Press has no responsibility for the persistence or accuracy of URLs for external or third-party Internet Web sites referred to in this publication and does not guarantee that any content on such Web sites is, or will remain, accurate or appropriate.

To my loving husband, Chris.

Contents

Illustrations

Cover: Tristano Pantaloni, cover illustration for *Aria di jazz. Parole in libertà* by Vladimiro Miletti (1934)

Acknowledgments

It was in the fall of 2010 when I got the idea to write this book. My husband, Christopher S. Celenza, had recently been appointed Director of the American Academy in Rome, an assignment that happened to coincide with my own year-long sabbatical leave from Georgetown University. My original plan for that research year had been to begin work on a book about Duke Ellington. But upon arriving in Rome, I became intrigued with the local jazz scene and quickly discovered a story about the links between American and Italian jazz that surprised me. I have often joked with friends and family that I should have titled this book: "What I Did for Four Years While My Husband Served as Director of the American Academy in Rome." But all joking aside, working on this book was one of the most fulfilling experiences of my scholarly career, and not just because of the music I encountered, but even more so for the wonderful scholars and musicians I met in Italy and the new friendships that formed along the way.

As readers will discover, for this study, I am deeply indebted to the groundbreaking archival work of several Italian scholars, most notably Adriano Mazzoletti, Marcello Piras and Angelo Zaniol. Mazzoletti's work is especially important, not only because of his meticulous documentation of performers, venues, recordings and reviews in his multivolume *Jazz in Italia*, but also for the invaluable contribution that he and his wife, Anna Maria Pivato, have made toward the preservation of this music through their record label, Riviera Jazz. Their thoughtful curation of historic recordings has insured that this music will remain accessible to listeners for generations to come. I will be forever indebted to Adriano, not only as a scholar, but also as a mentor and friend. He generously gave of his time, offering encouragement and critiques in equal measure. But even more importantly, he single-handedly constructed a scholarly foundation that I and countless other scholars have relied upon in our explorations of Italian jazz. Special thanks also go to Marcello Piras, who welcomed me into the realm of jazz studies and happily shared his in-depth knowledge of African American music. Marcello offered advice during the early stages of this project, often pointing me in directions that proved beneficial. As I completed the project, he read excerpts of the book and offered helpful advice. With regard to Angelo Zaniol, I have not yet had the pleasure of meeting him in person, but we have communicated via email on several occasions, and I have avidly followed his postings on the *Ricordando Il Trio Lescano* website. I am especially indebted to Professor Zaniol for assisting me in transcribing the lyrics for several obscure jazz ballads and putting me in contact with other Italian scholars conducting research related to the Trio Lescano and Alberto Rabagliati.

One of the wonderful things about my time in Italy was being at the American Academy in Rome, with its mix of world-renowned scholars and artists. I spent many an afternoon and evening in Rome, listening to shoptalks and interacting with fellows and visiting artists/scholars working on projects that intersected with my own. The insight these exchanges brought to my research was invaluable, and I would especially like to thank Corey Brennan, Maurizio Campanelli, Lucy Corin, Michele D'Ambrosio, Dan Hurlin, David Kertzer, Ruth Lo, Christia Mercer, Emily Morash and Dominique Reill. Very special thanks also go to Tamzen Flanders, who offered support and insight as I worked through the early stages of my research. I miss our long walks through the Villa Doria Pamphili Park and our shared pursuit of Italian proficiency. Thanks also to the staff at the American Academy in Rome who facilitated my research, most notably Giulia Barra, Gianpaolo Battaglia, Anne Coulson, Sebastian Hierl, Karl Kirchwey, Marina Lella and Cristina Puglisi.

Georgetown University was very generous in its support of my research, and for that I owe a debt of gratitude to Chet Gillis, Dean of Georgetown College, and Jim O'Donnell and Robert Groves, who served as provosts during my time abroad. Together, they offered me what is most valuable to a scholar in the humanities: research time. I was able to spend several semesters in Italy by banking courses and teaching at Villa le Balze, Georgetown's study abroad program in Fiesole, Italy. At Villa le Balze, I taught an undergraduate seminar on Italian jazz. Many thanks to Katie Collins and my students of that semester. Thanks also to my research assistants at Georgetown, Christina Piazza and Jackson Sinnenberg and my colleagues in the Americas Initiative. Their enthusiasm for the subject kept me motivated. Thank you also to the faculty of the Department of Performing Arts, especially Anthony DelDonna, whose generosity and flexibility facilitated my time abroad.

As I worked on this book, I was given the opportunity to share my research with students and scholars in various Italian Studies and Music programs. My warmest thanks to Stefano Baldassarri (International Studies Institute – Florence), Victoria de Grazia (Columbia University), Wendy

Heller (Princeton University), Simon Martin (American University of Rome), Franco Piperno (Sapienza – Università di Roma) and Ramie Targoff (Brandeis University) for organizing these colloquia.

Working with Cambridge University Press has been a rewarding experience, and this is largely due to the wonderful support and encouragement I have received from my editor, Kate Brett. She has been in my corner every step of the way, cheering me on. My gratitude also goes to Lisa Sinclair and Siva Prakash Chandrasekaran for the final copyediting and production of this book. As this project drew to a conclusion, five outside readers read my work closely and offered critiques that proved immensely helpful. My deep appreciation to David Beard, Mervyn Cooke, Katherine Williams, Carl Woideck and Ed Green. I also want to thank Bruce Boyd Raeburn, Lynn Abbott and Alaina Hébert at the Hogan Jazz Archive in New Orleans, and Gerry Gross, in Baltimore. Gerry offered invaluable insights as I worked through the early drafts of several chapters. He was an incredibly generous friend and scholar, and he is deeply missed.

Finally, I would like to thank my husband, Chris, for the many years of love and encouragement. You listened attentively as I talked through ideas, helped me conquer abstruse Italian passages and read through numerous drafts. Thank you for everything, especially for all those hugs you supplied just when I needed them. I couldn't have written this book without you. And to be completely honest, I wouldn't have wanted to. For these reasons, and a thousand more, I dedicate this book to you.

Prologue

On September 8, 1935, a nineteen-year-old Frank Sinatra made his radio debut on the *Major Bowes' Amateur Hour* as the tenor in an all-male vocal quartet called the Hoboken Four.[1] Sinatra was new to the group – the trio had previously been called The Three Flashes – and legend has it that it was his mother, Dolly Sinatra, who persuaded them to add her son shortly before the competition. Only recently released commercially, the recording of this debut is generally only known by the most die-hard Sinatra fans and scholars.[2] The performance is far from remarkable. Still, it offers a window on a period of music unfamiliar to many listeners today.

Typical for the era, the recording begins with a bit of jaunty banter. The Major himself, Edward Bowes, serves as the show's master of ceremonies, and as he notes in his introduction: "We have now The Hoboken Four. They call themselves the singing and dancing fools."

When Bowes asks who serves as spokesman for the group, Sinatra jumps in, "I will. I'm Frank. We're looking for jobs. How 'bout it?" he asks charismatically in a thick, New Jersey accent.

The studio audience laughs, but Sinatra isn't deterred. "Everyone who's ever heard us, liked it," he declares, and to prove his point the quartet breaks into a rendition of "Shine," a tune made famous by Louis Armstrong:[3]

'Cause, my hair is curly
'Cause, my teeth are pearly
Just because I always wear a smile
Like to dress up ...

Bing Crosby and the Mills Brothers, an African American vocal quartet, recorded a jazz rendition of "Shine" in 1932 that clearly served as the model for The Hoboken Four's performance.[4] Sinatra often claimed that hearing Crosby on the radio in the early 1930s influenced his own early attempts at singing, and one can clearly hear it on this recording. Sinatra's voice, like Crosby's, floats above the others. He sings separately from his three colleagues, mimicking their lyrics and singing smart-aleck remarks after each line. His voice is high and vibrant, and his phrasing clipped. Only at the bridge, when he breaks into a brief passage of spirited scat singing influenced by the Mills Brothers' style, does a sense of rhythmic finesse and vocal virtuosity break through. It's not the Frank Sinatra so easily recognizable today – not the iconic singer millions eventually grew to know and love. Instead, we hear an inexperienced kid trying to imitate both Bing Crosby and the Mills Brothers – performers he'd heard on records, on the radio and in the cinema. Crosby's performance drew attention to an African American jazz sound made famous by performers like Louis Armstrong and the Mills Brothers. Sinatra's performance was little more than an imitation of Crosby imitating African American jazz.

Four years passed before Sinatra was recorded again: first on a demo recording of "Our Love" with the Frank Mane Orchestra, and then a few months later on a string of recordings with the Harry James Orchestra. These performances feature a markedly different sound – the warm, lyrical voice and nuanced phrasing we all readily recognize as the young Frank Sinatra. There is little trace of Crosby or the Mills Brothers. No more clipped phrases or driving scat solos. Instead, one hears the Sinatra whose meteoric rise as "The Voice" made him an essential element in the soundscape that defined World War II America. Hearing these recordings, one cannot help but ask: What happened in the four years between The Hoboken Four and Harry James? Where did Sinatra find his iconic sound? Who influenced him, and why? What cultural phenomena, if any, played a role in the creation of a musical style that so many today describe as emblematically American? Teasing out the answers to these questions was the first step in my journey of doing research for this book; and like much research, the answers I found were rarely the ones I expected. Indeed, three and a half years in Italy and the sources I encountered there caused me to stray from my original path of mid-century American culture and venture into the broader, less-trodden realm of transnational jazz.

I should confess from the beginning that this book is not about Frank Sinatra, at least not specifically. Rather, it is an exploration of a musical world that deeply influenced Sinatra but was largely erased from memory after World War II. This book is about Italian jazz, from its origins in New Orleans, to Fascist Italy and beyond. In this book, I take a wide view of jazz, from turn-of-the-century genres like the cakewalk and ragtime to the later arrival of big band swing. In short, the concept of jazz, as discussed in this study, encompasses not only improvised music played by small ensembles, but also dance music and popular songs that incorporated the syncopated rhythms and characteristic performance styles most commonly associated with jazz. *Jazz Italian Style* introduces readers to a genre of vocal swing that evolved in Italy and emerged out of a rich texture of transatlantic experiences. This was a style of music markedly different in its orchestration from American models. It was a style of music that filtered the influences of American jazz through a prism of highbrow Italian lyricism and lowbrow North Italian folk music. And perhaps most surprising to Anglo American readers, it was a style of music that eventually influenced singers in the United States.

Italian jazz found its voice in the 1930s, and by the middle of the decade its influence had reached across the Atlantic. In fact, the iconic American sound we now associate with performers like the Andrews Sisters and Frank Sinatra clearly arose in dialogue with innovative performances by the most famous singers in Italy under Mussolini's watch, namely, the Trio Lescano and Natalino Otto.

The year 2015 marked the centennial of Frank Sinatra's birth, and over the course of those twelve months, countless new documentaries and publications appeared exploring the allure of the Sinatra sound. Missing from those discussions, however, was a description of the soundscapes that characterized the Italian American communities that Sinatra would have known during the first half of the twentieth century, and the ways in which recorded sound facilitated a constant interaction between these communities in the United States and the music and film industries in Fascist Italy. Jazz played an important role in the culture of Italy's greater diaspora, and Italians on both sides of the Atlantic, including Sinatra, were swept up almost immediately by its dynamic sounds and the symbols it appeared to offer. Nowhere is this more clearly demonstrated than the release in 1917 of what most American scholars and musicians now reluctantly acknowledge to be the first commercial jazz recording: "Dixie Jass Band One-Step" and "Livery Stable Blues" by the Original Dixieland Jazz Band. The lack of enthusiasm behind the scholarly world's acceptance of the Original Dixieland Jazz Band has little to do with the ensemble's performance or talent. Rather, the reluctance concerns the race of these musicians: all five were white, and two of them – the band's founder and trumpeter, Nick LaRocca and drummer Tony Sbarbaro – were of Italian origin. For many scholars, the inconvenient truth of this milestone in the history of jazz is understandable. Jazz grew out of African American culture, and the honor of being "first" should have gone to a black ensemble. In later years, LaRocca only made matters worse by repeatedly declaring, in disturbingly racist language, that jazz was not indebted to African American culture at all. Let me be clear on this point: LaRocca was wrong. At its core, jazz is an art form that originated in America in the hands of African American musicians. There is no disputing this fact. But what originally made jazz so appealing to so many people around the globe was the mesmerizing synthesis of *all* its musical characteristics, the genesis of which could be linked to various ethnicities, including Italian.

As jazz developed in New Orleans during the 1910s, listeners became captivated by its upbeat, syncopated energy, which in turn made it ripe for commercialization via the latest recording technologies. Nick LaRocca didn't invent jazz, but he was the first to capitalize on the fact that it was a financially profitable, popular art form that could cross various ethnic and national borders with relative ease. False though it was, LaRocca's claim that he invented jazz played an influential role in Italy's early embrace of the music. And as the decades progressed, developing a distinctive genre of Italian jazz became important to many artists and political leaders in Italy. Even when Italy and the United States found themselves on opposite sides during World War II, jazz remained an important element in the Italian consciousness on both sides of the Atlantic. Consequently, a central goal of this book, and one of the things that makes it distinct from other jazz histories, is its exploration of these transnational connections. Most importantly, I am interested in investigating how "extra-musical" phenomena – politics, immigration patterns, economics and technology – influenced both the development of Italian jazz and its eventual demise.

Over the last decade, numerous studies have appeared describing the early reception of jazz in various European countries.[5] In England, France and Germany, jazz was defined as a "foreign" art form, "exotic" in nature, with indelible connections to African American culture. In the case of Germany specifically, jazz was eventually banned by the Nazi regime, which labeled it a "degenerate" and corrupting cultural force. *Jazz Italian Style* offers the first Anglo American study of Italian jazz, and until now, most scholars have simply assumed, due to the political alliances of World War II, that the reception of jazz in Fascist Italy mirrored what happened in Germany. Not so. Jazz flourished in Italy thanks to Mussolini's support, and the story of its development there is no less fascinating or important than the histories of jazz in other European nations. That said, I must admit that telling the story of Italian jazz can be difficult and even painful at times.

When jazz arrived on Italian shores at the conclusion of World War I, it was embraced, at least in part, as a "native" art form. The Futurists praised its "virile energy," Mussolini described it as "the voice of Italian youth," and musicians, mesmerized by its "progressive" sounds, left the conservatories and flocked to dance halls and nightclubs. Of course, jazz had its early detractors in Italy, just as it did in the United States, but in Italy, the music was embraced early on as a sign of youth and modernization. In Italy, the gramophone and radio served as modern-day messengers, and thanks to this technology, most Italian listeners could enjoy the music without having to contemplate the ethnic identities of its performers or composers. Consequently, Nick LaRocca (Italian American), Gorni Kramer (Italian), the Trio Lescano (Jewish Dutch) and Louis Armstrong (African American), to name just a few, all found their place in the Italian soundscape.

Mussolini's alliance with Hitler and the devastating civil war that erupted in Italy shortly thereafter led to a conscious erasure after World War II of this era in jazz history. Although several Italian scholars have worked hard to preserve the music and describe the performances of its greatest singers and instrumentalists, few have focused on the importance of Italy/US relations during this era, and none have confronted the uncomfortable fact that many jazz musicians contributed to the Fascist cause by supplying a soundtrack that endorsed Mussolini's government. Instead, previous scholars have tended to describe Italian jazz as a failed experiment whose practitioners were apolitical and whose influence ended with Mussolini's implementation of Italy's race laws in 1938. The present study offers a markedly different point of view: Italian jazz flourished until the end of World War II because Mussolini supported it. And when he was executed, many Italian musicians began rewriting their own stories in an effort to forget the uneasy relationships that they had forged with Fascist policies and practices.

I should note that the story of jazz in Italy is filled with dark moments and disconcerting events that at times reflect unflattering images of both American and Italian culture. Looking back on these episodes can be distressing and even shocking at times. This is no doubt the primary reason why the cultural history of Italian jazz has been overlooked for so many years. In Italy, hindsight and a sense of national remorse over the legacy of Mussolini have minimized the desire among scholars and musicians to dredge up the uncomfortable connections between jazz and the Fascist regime.[6] Similarly, the Cold War cultural propaganda that promoted jazz as a symbol of democracy in the United States left no room for discussions concerning Italian influences, especially those associated with the cultural policies of Fascism.

I realize that in many ways I am coming to this topic as an outsider, and perhaps that's a good thing. I did not witness the historical era under discussion, and despite my last name, I did not grow up in an Italian American family. So I do not have a stake in the game other than as a musicologist. My grandfather worked briefly as a jazz musician, and he and my mother instilled in me a love of big band swing. That's how I got started on my quest for the origins of the Sinatra sound. What I found along the way was the narrative presented in the chapters of this book.

Jazz Italian Style explores a complex era in music history, when politics and popular culture collided with national identity and technology. The book recovers a lost repertoire and an array of musicians whose stories and performances are compelling and well worth remembering. This is why, in addition to the book, I have compiled a set of playlists titled Listening to *Jazz Italian Style*, which is available on the book's Resources page at www .cambridge.org/9781107169777.

1 | Italians and the Origins of Jazz

The story of Italian jazz begins, interestingly enough, with a description of the American music industry penned by an Italian diplomat. In August 1919 Chevalier Bruno Zuculin published a somewhat glib, yet telling, description of the New Orleans jazz scene in *La Lettura*, a monthly illustrated supplement to *Corriere della Sera*, Italy's most widely read newspaper at the time.

There are two categories of jazz bands: those that are mostly black, which perform in the hotels, restaurants, dance halls and social clubs; and those, often Italian, that play in the cinemas, in variety shows and in those numerous theaters where the most genuine theatrical product of North America flourishes, namely the entertaining productions called "Musical Comedies" or "Girls and Music Shows," wherein the plot, if it exists at all, is of little importance to anyone, and the success of the performance is based primarily on the quality of the music and the beauty of the girls.[1]

Zuculin was reporting directly from New Orleans, where he had been serving as Italy's Consul General for just over a year.[2] Although the above quote is only a small excerpt from his lengthy "Musiche e danze americane" (American Musics and Dances), it serves as a useful point of departure for this chapter's discussion of Italy's contributions, both real and perceived, to the origins of jazz.

Zuculin's description of New Orleans has been largely overlooked by previous scholars, who generally refer to Ernest Ansermet's "Sur une orchestra nègre" as the first overview of American jazz written by a European.[3] Yet Zuculin's article predates by two months Ansermet's description in *La revue romande* of Will Marion Cook's Southern Syncopated Orchestra. Even more importantly, whereas Ansermet describes a concert in Switzerland performed for a European audience by a traveling ensemble, Zuculin offers an on-the-spot report of the music scene in New Orleans. He was the first to state, quite emphatically, that Italian immigrants played a role in the genesis of jazz in the United States, and it was this belief, perhaps more than anything else, that later drove many Italians, including Mussolini, to embrace the music as a "native" art form.

Zuculin identified two types of jazz bands in New Orleans, each of which could be distinguished from the other in three distinct ways: by race, by nationality, and by the various venues that hosted their performances. While he linked the American "black" bands to the city's "hotels, restaurants, dance halls and social clubs," where they were expected to supply traditional dance music, he associated the white, "often Italian," bands with the commercialization of jazz as found in the cinema and music halls, where success was linked not just to the music, but also to film and the draw of "beautiful girls." Zuculin described Italian bands as pushing jazz toward modernity. In their hands, the music mixed with technology and beauty to the joy and titillation of seated spectators. "Black" jazz was for dancing. "Italian" jazz was the new listening music of the modern age.

Where did this distinction between American tradition and Italian modernization come from? Was Zuculin disingenuous in his description of Italians' activities abroad, or was there some truth in his assessment that has since been overlooked or cast aside by historians? The answers to questions such as these begin to emerge when we step back in history several more decades and examine the social and cultural interactions that took place between Italians and other ethnic groups in various cities in the United States – namely, New Orleans, New York, San Francisco and Chicago – during the late nineteenth and early twentieth centuries.

New Orleans

New Orleans is the birthplace of jazz – most scholars and fans agree on this point – and since the city's founding by the French in 1718, it has served as an ethnic melting pot. Today one often speaks of the city's Creole and Cajun cultures and the strong presence of African Americans, be they former slaves, the descendants of free men of color or emigrants from the Caribbean and Latin America. But during the nineteenth century, New Orleans also welcomed a vast array of European emigrants – Irish, Germans, Slavs, Italians – and it was out of this cultural mix of African American, Caribbean and European, at the dawn of the twentieth century, that jazz as we know it evolved.

One issue that complicates descriptions of early New Orleans jazz is the shifting parameters of race designations during the second half of the nineteenth century. Before the Civil War, race was not polarized into black and white in New Orleans. The term "creole," for example, was originally used to identify individuals (be they of mixed race or white) who were born in

Louisiana but descended from colonial French or Spanish settlers. After the Civil War, however, legislative efforts to clarify various racial categories led to the eventual practice of using the word creole to refer exclusively to people of wholly European descent, and describing all others as creoles of color.[4] The division of race was further polarized in 1896, when the Supreme Court decision *Plessy v. Ferguson* categorized all African Americans, including creoles of color, under the singular designation of "Negro." Consequently, many historians have described the formative years of early New Orleans jazz in terms of black and white, dividing ensembles along strict racial lines into those made up of African American performers and those limited to white musicians. But in truth, Jim Crow laws and the new legal designations did not racially divide the New Orleans music community right away. Prior to 1900, those who had been designated as creoles of color moved easily between the realms of black and white, often performing in ensembles of both racial distinctions. In short, the makeup of many early New Orleans brass bands included musicians from a variety of racial and ethnic backgrounds.

Italy's link to New Orleans dates back to the seventeenth century, when explorers like Henri de Tonti took part in the early European settlement of the region.[5] But the contributions of Italians to the city's musical culture did not begin in earnest until the nineteenth century, when singers and instrumentalists were recruited to perform in the city's newly constructed French Opera House, which opened in 1859 and stood at the corner of Bourbon and Toulouse Streets in the French Quarter.[6] Few in number, these Italians tended to be conservatory trained. Most arrived in New Orleans via South America and the Caribbean, and although they generally only remained in the city for several months at a time, they nonetheless participated in the practice of racial integration that characterized the New Orleans music scene. At the French Opera, which served as a destination for tourists until it burned down in 1919, European musicians performed side by side in the orchestra pit and on the stage with professionally trained creoles of color. Although these Italian musicians likely had little direct contact with the genesis of jazz, the local creole musicians who remained in New Orleans embraced Italian music, taking pride in the fact that their opera company was one of the finest in the country and the site for numerous US premieres of works by Rossini, Bellini and Donizetti. This appreciation for Italian opera was passed on to their children and grandchildren, who later performed in the city's earliest ragtime bands.[7] By the time the first major wave of Italian immigrants began arriving in New Orleans after the Civil War, popular arias from Italian opera had become part of the city's cultural fabric and, consequently, served as some of the most common tunes "ragged" by New Orleans brass bands. Even Louis Armstrong was known to use quotes from Italian opera arias in the solos of some of his earliest recordings.[8]

Between 1880 and 1920, over four million Italians immigrated to the United States, and the majority came from Italy's southern regions – Sicily, Campania, Abruzzi and Calabria – areas that were largely agricultural, impoverished and overpopulated at the time. New Orleans served as a preferred destination for this large wave of immigrants, who differed in many ways from the trained musicians who had arrived in the city several decades earlier. Poor and often illiterate, the majority of this second wave arrived on the cargo boats out of Naples and Palermo that transported foodstuffs to the United States and shipments of cotton and tobacco back to Italy. According to the US census, roughly 950 Italian immigrants lived in New Orleans in 1850. By the 1890s as many as 30,000 Italians were living and working in the city, and 90 percent of these were from Sicily.[9] The population continued to grow through the turn of the century, so that, by 1910, a walk through the French Quarter revealed a veritable Italian colony, where upward of 80 percent of the neighborhood was Italian.

What drew these immigrants to New Orleans? More than anything, it was the promise of economic reward. Italy's southern regions had suffered centuries of economic hardship, and the unification of Italy in 1861 brought the implementation of new economic measures to the South, which impoverished the region even further. The heavy taxes needed to balance the national budget created enormous discontent and division among the populations of Italy's northern and southern regions. While the wealthy industrial cities of Milan, Turin and Genoa expanded substantially after unification, the agricultural centers in the South, and most noticeably Sicily, remained economically disadvantaged. By the 1880s, these dire economic circumstances were exacerbated even further by a global depression. As Mark Choate explains in his compelling history of Italian emigration, this is when the Italian government began to mount an active campaign to encourage its poorest citizens to move to the United States. The goal of this mass emigration was to relieve the overpopulation and unemployment in Italy's southern regions and thus simultaneously improve the economic prospects of Italians both at home and abroad. By 1900, the Italian government "had developed a flexible set of programs to establish a network of culture, trade, and exchange with Italians outside of Italy's territory and legal reach."[10] Emigration was not perceived as a sign of disloyalty, national abandonment or economic failure, but instead was viewed as a public service of sorts. As Choate explains, toward the end of the nineteenth century, "the Italian word *colonìa* meant not only overseas possessions, but also settlements of emigrants in foreign countries." Based on this definition, Italians viewed emigration itself as "a type of colonial expansion, though tenuous and unpredictable."[11] Consequently, those who left were praised as patriotic Italians making personal sacrifices for the betterment of their families and the new Italian state. Offered travel assistance by various religious and government agencies, they were encouraged to remain in close contact with family in Italy while simultaneously forging new financial prospects abroad. Emigration was indeed promoted as a form of colonization – a chance to promote Italian industriousness and culture. Religious and cultural associations were established in the host cities, and the Bank of Naples opened foreign branches to facilitate the transfer of hard earned funds back to Italy.

During the final decades of the nineteenth century, waves of immigrants entered New Orleans, where they served as manual laborers side by side with the city's black population. Be it working in the fields of local farms, selling fruits and vegetables in the French Quarter or loading ships at the docks, first-generation Italian immigrants generally maintained an economic and social status that was at par with or below that of African Americans. To be more specific, they were often cast as inferior to creoles of color and at the same social and education level of black field hands and former slaves. Consequently, these newly arrived Italians, "classified by many Americans (including members on Congress)" as "non-white," suffered many of the same injustices and persecutions as their African American neighbors.[12] One of the most horrific mass lynchings in US history occurred in New Orleans in 1891, when eleven Italian immigrants were shot and strung up by an angry mob after a jury found them innocent of assassinating the local police chief, David Hennessey. It was in the news reports surrounding this trial that the term "mafia" was first used to stigmatize Italian immigrants from Sicily as untrustworthy and criminal to the core.[13]

Prior to 1900, New Orleans was not a fully segregated city. Italian Americans lived side by side with African Americans, both former slaves and creoles of color, in some of the city's poorest neighborhoods – near the docks, in the French Quarter and Tremé neighborhoods and uptown – in rooming houses and clapboard duplexes. Living in such close proximity, the two populations could not help but be exposed to each other's cultures. The smells of the food and the sounds of the music wafted across the shared porches and balconies and permeated the thin wooden walls. Even Louis Armstrong, who grew up in one of the poorest neighborhoods in New Orleans, remembered eating spaghetti as a child in the home "of an Italian white boy."[14]

With regard to the development of jazz during the early decades of the twentieth century, numerous scholars have noted the undeniable influence on early jazz of West African musical characteristics brought to the United States through slavery. The assumption is often made that only former slaves could have been familiar with such rhythmic characteristics, but such was not the case. The folk dances of Southern Italy carried African influences as well.

Sicily is only 125 miles from North Africa, and as historian Robert C. Davis has noted, for well over two centuries, the Barbary Pirates captured thousands of Italians in towns along the coasts of Sicily and Campania and sold them as slaves in Tunisia.[15] When slavery in Tunisia ended in 1816, many of these ex-slaves returned to Italy. Further interactions between Italy and North Africa occurred half a century later, when Italy established a colony in Eritrea. Consequently, elements of traditional North African music found their way into the traditional music of Southern Italy, and when Italians from these regions immigrated to New Orleans, they brought their traditional music with them. Although we have no recordings of Italian folk music prior to the Italians' arrival, elements of North African influences were still audible in rural Italy when Alan Lomax traveled there and spent six months recording the music he encountered. For example, in Pagani, a small village in Campania, he came upon an Italian ensemble that he described as a "genuine North-African orchestra composed of drums, scrapers, rattles, clappers and tambourine" performing the Tarantella, a popular dance of Southern Italy. These shared links with African culture may be one of the reasons Italian Americans adapted so quickly to the emerging musical trends coalescing into jazz in turn-of-the-century New Orleans.[16] The various cultures of New Orleans's natives and immigrants mixed with great ease. Thus it should come as no surprise that the earliest founders of ragtime and jazz included both African Americans and Italians.

One of the "fathers" of early jazz in New Orleans history was George Vetiala Laine, better known by his stage name, "Papa Jack" Laine. Various Italian scholars have claimed Laine was of Italian heritage, mistakenly listing his middle name as Vitale.[17] But Laine was a third-generation American, the son of François Laine (whose parents emigrated from France) and Bernadine Wink (a second-generation American of German stock). Laine spent his entire life in New Orleans's 8th Ward, in close proximity to both the French Quarter and Tremé neighborhoods. He founded the Reliance Brass Band, one of the first bands noted for "ragging" marches and popular tunes, and was one of the first in New Orleans to take up the role of impresario in the realm of popular music. As Arnold "Deacon" Loyocano, an Italian American musician who played in Laine's band, later explained, Laine served as a pivotal figure in the development of jazz in New Orleans.

Can't truthfully say who had the first white jazz band in New Orleans. Don't know. But I do know that Jack Laine had the most popular band at the time. He was more in demand, around 1900, and he developed fellows like Nick LaRocca, Tom Brown, Raymond Lopez. They all played with him. In Laine's own words, he put a horn in their hands! He had two or three bands at that time, so popular that he couldn't fill all the dates. Many times, Bud, my brother, and I subbed for him.[18]

Laine got his start in "spasm" bands with other neighborhood boys, playing homemade instruments in various New Orleans parades. By age sixteen, he had become an accomplished drummer and bandleader of several string and brass ensembles. He also led a large drum and bugle corps during the Spanish American War. Laine's importance lies in the fact that he served as the first formal link between Italian-immigrant and African American musicians. He regularly employed a variety of new immigrants and creoles of color in his ensembles. His goal was to create numerous ensembles of varying size and instrumentation to fill the music requirements of New Orleans's growing entertainment industry, be it a parade, a wedding, an outdoor excursion on the shores of Lake Pontchartrain or a society ball. Laine's musicians offered audiences a diverse range of music, from traditional schottisches, quadrilles and waltzes to brass band marches, vaudeville tunes and ragtime. Through these ensembles, the membership of which was in constant flux, Laine brought together various segments of New Orleans's music community.

The earliest known photograph of Laine in a musical context, and there are many, dates from 1894, when he and several New Orleans colleagues traveled to Chattanooga, Tennessee with a bandleader named Siegfried Christiansen. Included in this group was euphonium player Dave E. Perkins, a creole of color who later played in bands led by Buddy Bolden, and several Italians, among them the trombonist Angelo Castigliola and tuba player Giuseppe Alessandra, better known by his Anglicized name, Joe Alexander. Whereas Castigliola was born in New Orleans, Alexander emigrated from Palermo in the early 1890s, and, consequently, would appear to be the first Italian-born musician to play jazz on American soil.[19] He remained active in New Orleans music for several decades, both as a performer and a bandleader, and was considered by many in the community to be an important link to the "Old Country."[20] One cannot help but wonder if the protagonist of Irving Berlin's "Alexander's Ragtime Band" (1911) – a tune which sold over one million sheet music copies within a year – might have been inspired by the New Orleans musician. The cover of the original music shows a white band similar to those led by Alexander and Laine, with a mix of brass and string players. Although one will likely never know for sure the inspiration behind Berlin's tune, it is nonetheless telling that when Berlin was asked by Twentieth-Century Fox to supply a storyline for the film *Alexander's Ragtime Band* in the mid-1930s, he proposed basing the plot on a white New Orleans bandleader named Alexander, who rises to fame playing Berlin's music.[21]

But to return to the topic at hand, the integration of immigrant musicians like Joe Alexander into New Orleans's native music scene was clearly facilitated by Jack Laine. One of Laine's early specialties was organizing ensembles to play for funerals, and it was likely in this capacity that he first recruited Italian musicians. For immigrants arriving from Sicily and Naples, the New Orleans tradition of brass band funeral processions must have seemed familiar. In Southern Italy, funerals often served as a time of community gathering, and it was common practice for those in attendance to follow the body to the graveside, walking behind the casket, which was carried in a horse-drawn carriage and accompanied by a somber brass band.

Laine organized a wide range of ensembles, including his famous Reliance Brass Band, which he led for nearly twenty years. By 1900, the market demand for music was so great that he divided the Reliance Band into separate units, each of which was prepared to play for a wide variety of events, from weddings and funerals, to public concerts, society club dances and parades. The demands of these events required him to expand the instrumentation of his ensembles, and by 1900 he had begun to add clarinetists, string players (e.g. violin, banjo, mandolin and guitar) and pianists to his traditional brass and percussion mix. Most importantly, Laine brought musicians from New Orleans's various ethnic groups together. Although segregation laws at the turn of the century prohibited blacks and whites from performing together, Laine often ignored such prohibitions if a musician could "pass" for another racial group. His bands included immigrants of various nationalities as well as creoles of color. In addition to Perkins, Laine regularly offered employment to clarinetist Achille Baquet, who also performed regularly in the Excelsior Brass Band, founded in 1879 by his father Théogène Baquet, who also conducted the Lyre Club Symphonic Orchestra.

The musical training and experiences of Laine's musicians ran the full gamut. While some had received formal training and could read music, others played by ear. This cultural and musical mix reportedly imbued his bands with a sense of energy and spontaneity that enabled them to perform successfully a wide repertoire, from traditional standards to the newest vaudeville and ragtime tunes. In 1904, Laine took his New Orleans musicians to the St. Louis Exposition in Missouri, where audiences from across the country were exposed, for the first time, to the boisterous brass band sound that roughly a decade later evolved into the New Orleans Dixieland style.

As Samuel Charters notes in his history of New Orleans jazz, "the over-whelming presence of Italian names among the lists of early New Orleans bands confirms that the beginnings of jazz in the city included a much wider range of music than simply small instrumental ensembles playing ragtime melodies."[22] The first generation, composed mostly of immigrants recently arrived from Naples and Sicily, included, in addition to Joe Alexander and Angelo Castigliola, Lawrence Veca, whom Laine once described as "a master on cornet,"[23] pianist Johnny Provenzano, bass player John "Bud" Loyocano, clarinetist Leonardo (Leon) Roppolo,[24] Vincent Barocco on baritone horn and trumpet player Pete Pellegrini. Like Joe Alexander, many of these musicians Anglicized their names after coming to America.

The next generation of Italian musicians, most born and raised in New Orleans, included Arnold "Deacon" Loyocano, Nick LaRocca, Joe Loyocano, Tony Giardina, Salvatore Castigliola, Anthony Sbarbaro, Joseph "Wingy" Manone, Leon J. Roppolo and Santo Pecoraro. Almost to a man, this second generation of musicians got their early training in one of Laine's many ensembles. And as we shall see later in this chapter, the majority of these musicians, like many of their African American colleagues, traveled north to Chicago and New York during the early years of World War I in search of new performance opportunities.[25]

Italian Americans enjoyed growing prestige in New Orleans as the century progressed, and with each generation, financial prospects improved. A contributing factor to this development was the establishment of various Italian American societies, which contributed in various ways to New Orleans's cultural scene. For example, the Italian Union Hall, located at 1020 Esplanade Avenue in the French Quarter, became one of the city's finest performance venues during the 1920s. The hall served as home to twenty-seven different organizations – some political, others cultural, educational and/or religious in focus. Built originally in 1835 as a private mansion, the building was purchased by a cooperative of various Italian societies in 1912 and turned into a cultural community center. Extensive renovations, paid for by the Italian Chamber of Commerce, included, among other things, the addition of a spacious dance hall on the second and third floors and classrooms for language training and music lessons. John Francis Spriccio was one of the most popular teachers.[26] His grandfather was an opera musician, who emigrated from Italy in the 1850s. The younger Spriccio was a talented violinist, who taught his students both classical music and ragtime. Various music ensembles – both African American and white – rehearsed and performed regularly at the Italian Union Hall.[27]

The solid establishment of New Orleans's Italian American community by the second decade of the century is evidenced by the numerous accolades that were bestowed on them by city officials. A case in point is the speech made by New Orleans Mayor Martin Behrman in 1913 at the anniversary banquet of the Giovanni Bersaglieri Benevolent Association. Behrman began his speech by offering a "cordial invitation to all law-abiding citizens of Italy to come to Louisiana and help develop the rich lands abounding in the state." He praised Italian Americans for their sense of community and loyalty to family and faith, and he assured those in the audience who had witnessed anti-Italianism in the past that times had changed: "I know the Italian colony of New Orleans," he declared, "while they cling to the traditions of the old country, they also revere the Stars and Stripes" and can be counted as "among the best citizens in America."[28]

As Italians began their ascent in New Orleans society, the barriers separating African American musicians and their white counterparts grew more impenetrable. The *Plessy* v. *Ferguson* decision, discussed above, clearly contributed to this phenomenon, but an even more notable event, economically at least, was the creation of New Orleans's first musicians union.[29] When Local 174 of the American Federation of Musicians (AFM) was founded on January 14, 1902, its charter stated that membership was strictly reserved for "white musicians of southeastern Louisiana."[30] Several months later, African American musicians established AFM Local 242 under the leadership of Théogène Baquet. But this second union was short lived. By 1905 Local 242 was no longer registered, and efforts to reinstate it were denied repeatedly. The result of all this was an acute disparity in the employment opportunities offered to white musicians and those available to African Americans. AFM Local 174 became a powerful political and economic force in New Orleans's burgeoning music scene. Since most large-scale venues, like musical theaters and cinemas, appreciated the regularized payment rates established by the unions, they tended to hire bands staffed by unionized musicians, and Italians lost no time in becoming card-carrying members. The unionization of music in New Orleans offered many first- and second-generation Italians the chance to build careers in the concert hall and recording studio. Unfortunately, this meant that one man's gain was another man's loss, and during the early decades of the twentieth century, the man on the losing end was most often black. Indeed, African Americans would have to wait until June 1926 for the successful establishment of their own union, Local 496.[31]

New York

The great influx of Italian immigrants into the United States between 1880 and 1924 affected central port cities up and down the East Coast, from New Orleans and Baltimore to Philadelphia, New York and Boston. New Orleans had been the initial destination of choice for those arriving in the early years, but in less than two decades, New York rose to the top. The Federal Census reported more than 175,000 Italian immigrants living within the city's five boroughs by 1900, and like New Orleans, the majority of them had arrived in cargo boats from Naples and Palermo.[32] One of the most notable in the realm of Italian jazz was Jimmy Durante, the son of Italian emigrants from Salerno. Durante dropped out of school in seventh grade to work as a ragtime piano player. He worked Manhattan's piano bar circuit, where he quickly earned the moniker "Ragtime Jimmy."[33]

A look at Italian Americans' contributions to the various pre-jazz genres that flourished during the first decade of the twentieth century reveals that, more than any other genre, they composed and performed ragtime. The heyday of classical ragtime, as defined by the works of Scott Joplin, occurred during the peak of Italian immigration during the early 1900s.[34] Purely instrumental at first, this classical form of ragtime was a written tradition, distributed primarily through sheet music and player piano rolls. As ragtime grew in popularity during the 1910s, it became more commercialized, which led to a subgenre: the syncopated novelty tune. Novelty tunes could be purely instrumental, making use of various special effects on an array of instruments, or written for voice with instrumental accompaniment. In the latter case, these were generally little more than ragtime tunes reissued with humorous lyrics that promoted many of the same negative ethnic stereotypes associated with the earlier coon song. For musicians like Durante, these novelty songs offered an entrance into New York's popular music scene.

A cosmopolitan financial center with burgeoning construction and textile industries, New York attracted emigrants from across Europe who, like the Italians, participated in a wide range of professions, including entertainment. The music industry, especially, offered numerous opportunities for advancement. Although the recording industry was only in a nascent stage during the first two decades of the century, the practice of marketing to niche audiences was not uncommon. Realizing the large profits to be made in the creation of "ethnic" and "race" records, labels like Columbia, Victor, Brunswick, Okeh and Gennett developed specialized series of recordings for various populations. In addition to records for African Americans, Germans, Hungarians and Irish, these companies produced music designed to appeal to the growing number of Italian immigrants. Beginning as early as 1910, discs featuring Italian musicians were marketed to select audiences in the United States. These recordings, produced primarily in New York, were distributed nationwide and sold selectively in record and tobacco stores within established Italian American communities.

The music represented on these early recordings basically broke down into three distinct categories: opera excerpts, traditional folk music and contemporary vaudeville and ragtime tunes. In the case of opera excerpts and folk songs, the singers' names were generally identified on the disc labels. This was also true for recordings featuring solo instrumentalists on traditional instruments like the mandolin or accordion. When it came to music performed by ensembles, however, the identities of the individual musicians were rarely noted. Instead, only the ensemble names were given, as in recordings of "I Cinque Abruzzesi" (The Five Men from Abruzzi), "I Suonatori Ambulente" (The Buskers or Street Musicians), "Orchestra Coloniale" (the Colonial Orchestra) or "I Cinque Siciliani-Americani" (The Five Sicilian Americans). Some of these band names reveal the racism many Italian immigrants encountered during the early twentieth century. This is most clearly seen in "I Quattro Buffoni" (The Four Idiots) and "I Sei Mafiusi" (The Six Mafiosi), a group that also recorded under the less offensive name "I Sei Siciliani" (The Six Sicilians). One wonders, however, if all of the instrumentalists who performed in ensembles such as these were actually Italian. A case in point is "I Sei Mafiusi," who also released records under the name "Banda Columbia" for German immigrant audiences. Similarly, the "Banda del Villagio" (Village Band) made numerous recordings as "The Victor Band" under the direction of the German American bandleader Nathaniel Shilkret.[35]

The burgeoning recording industry called for a continuous supply of new repertoire, making the publishing of sheet music a multimillion-dollar business. On Tin Pan Alley, the industry's epicenter, various Italian American composers found their entry into New York's music scene. Among those who left a lasting impression on American popular music were Domenico Savino, Donato Casolaro, Joseph Albert Piantadosi and Bob Yosco.

Domenico Savino was born near Taranto, in southern Italy, and immigrated to the United States at age twenty-eight after completing his studies in composition and orchestral conducting at the Royal Conservatory of Music in Naples. He published under the name D. Onivas (note that his pen name was simply his family name spelled backward), and one of his biggest hits was a fox-trot tune called "Indianola." Numerous ragtime orchestras performed this piece, the most famous being James Reese Europe's Harlem Hellfighters Band, the African American ensemble who fought in France during World War I and are rightfully credited with bringing ragtime to Europe. Upon returning to New York, Reese's group recorded a series of tunes for the Pathé label, including "Indianola," in spring 1919.[36]

Casolaro spent his formative years in Naples, much as Savino did, but at age 17 he immigrated to New York, where he quickly Anglicized his name to Dan Caslar. He must have received some musical training before traveling to the United States, since shortly after his arrival he enrolled at the New York Conservatory of Music and secured work as a piano player in various restaurants, among them the prestigious Café de Paris. After completing his studies, Caslar was hired by Florenz Ziegfield as a composer and conductor. In addition to composing his own works for the popular musical theater productions, he created orchestral arrangements of various ragtime tunes by Ford Dabney, Will Marion Cook, Joe Jordan and other African Americans employed by the Ziegfield Follies.[37] Between 1913 and 1915, Caslar published a handful of tunes with the Harry von Tilzer Music Company, the most prominent being the "Honeybunch Fox Trot" (1913). An advertisement appearing in *Billboard* magazine in 1914 declared that "the five most prominent dance orchestras in New York" were being "provided by Dan H. Caslar." In addition to the Café de Paris, he was by that point conducting ensembles at the City Athletic Club, Ciro's, Jardin de Danse and the Criterion Club.[38] Yet, despite these prestigious engagements and his new Fifth Avenue address, Caslar's success in New York was short lived. Like many young immigrants, he returned to his homeland in 1915 and served in the Italian military during World War I.

Unlike the Tin Pan Alley composers discussed so far, Al Piantadosi did not enter the United States as an immigrant. Instead, he was born in New York to Joseph Albert and Rose Piantadosi, who had traveled from Pietrastornina, Italy (in Campania), in 1880 in search of a more stable economic situation. After graduating from the St. James School, Piantadosi attended medical school for a year, but quickly abandoned his studies when offered the chance to tour as an accompanist for Anna Chandler on the vaudeville circuit. Once back in New York, Piantadosi quickly established a reputation as a ragtime piano player and songwriter. He often performed in resorts and nightclubs, like Callahan's Bowery Saloon, where he gained notoriety in 1906 for the novelty song "My Mariuccia Take a Steamboat."[39] According to a short feature article that appeared in *Billboard* in 1949, it was this tune's "melodic departure" back to "the old country" and the audiences' joy in imitating the steamboat whistle of the chorus that first convinced Irving Berlin to try his hand at composing ethnic-themed novelty songs.

Berlin at the time was working as a singing waiter at Mike Salter's Pelham Café, which was losing trade to Callahan's and Piantadosi's toot-toot song. So Salter decided to fight melody with melody, and talked Berlin and another of his singing waiters, Nick Michaelson, into turning out a tune that would bring his fickle customers back into the fold. This they did with "Marie From Sunny Italy," and thus two Italian gals of song, Piantadosi's *Mariuccia* and Berlin's *Marie* were the Lady Lucks that put their creators in the hall of fame.[40]

Indeed, Piantadosi's early fame as a composer and lyricist came from his specialization in ethnic tunes, among them "That Dreamy Italian Waltz" (1910), "I'm Awfully Glad I'm Irish" (1910), "That Italian Rag" (1911) and "On the Shores of Italy" (1914). Piantadosi was a staff composer for the Leo Feist publishing house when he published "That Italian Rag." Subtitled a "wiggy waggy, jiggy jaggy ragtime march," it was published simultaneously in both an instrumental version and as a novelty song with lyrics by Edgar Leslie that mimic an Italian American dialect:

Hey! Jim-mie come on and gim-me some Rag-time.
I'm a fall for what you call-a da Jag-time.
Make a jig, a nice-a wig-a-da wag-time,

And we do da "Kee-gar-e-kee-gar-e koo." (Hey! Shut up)
Hur-ry up and nun-ga stop-a da dance-a.
If I break da leg I take-a da chance-a.
Hey! Wal-jo be-fore I go in a trance-a,
You play da "Ric-cio, Ric-cio La-ri-o-la." Oh!

Like his early rival Berlin, Piantadosi was a charter member of the American Society of Composers, Authors, and Publishers (ASCAP), and his talent as a songwriter earned him work as a staff musician for various Tin Pan Alley publishers before he formed his own publishing house, Al. Piantadosi & Co., in 1917.

Bob Yosco, born Rocco Giuseppe Iosco in the south central Italian town of Castemezzano, arrived in New York with his parents, Domenico and Maria Antonia, in 1877. Yosco is best known today as one of America's first ragtime mandolin players. He probably learned the instrument from his older brother, Lawrence, who made a living building mandolins and banjos and who, by 1900, had founded the Yosco Manufacturing Company in New York.[41] Thanks in no small part to the massive influx of emigrants from Southern Italy, the mandolin had become phenomenally popular by this point, and mandolin ensembles sprang up all over the United States: in social clubs, high schools and universities. The popularity of the instrument soon earned it a place on stage – most notably vaudeville. Bob Yosco was a true virtuoso on the instrument, and he teamed up with another Italian, harpist George Lyons (born Dominic Martoccio), and went on the road as Yosco & Lyons. Like minstrelsy before it, early vaudeville depended heavily on ethnic stereotypes and self-deprecating humor. Yosco & Lyons supplied both in their performances of newly composed songs and comedy routines that referenced their Italian heritage. Their biggest hit was "Spaghetti Rag," which they published with Maurice Shapiro in 1910 and which was released on disc by Victor in 1912.[42]

The Orpheum Vaudeville Circuit, which featured performers like Yosco & Lyons in the United States, spread westward to cities like Chicago, Saint Louis and San Francisco during the first decade of the twentieth century. Wherever there was burgeoning industry, entertainment followed and embraced the latest cultural trends and music technology. For many Italian immigrants arriving after 1900, California became a popular destination. But not all immigrant communities in the United States were the same. Whereas the Italians who settled along the East Coast (namely, New Orleans, Baltimore, Philadelphia and New York) tended to come from Italy's southern regions – Sicily, Campania, Abruzzi and Calabria – the majority of the Italian immigrants who arrived in California were from urban centers north of Rome and generally came from a higher economic bracket. Consequently, they were better educated than the wave of emigrants from Sicily who had arrived in New Orleans in the 1880s and 90s.

San Francisco

San Francisco, in particular, served as the destination of choice for Northern Italians in the late nineteenth and early twentieth centuries. Similar to other ethnic groups, the first significant wave of Italians arrived in response to the Gold Rush of 1849. Drawn to the region's expanding construction, banking and entertainment industries, the majority of these Italians avoided work in the mines and instead set themselves up as artisans and proprietors in the burgeoning service industries. By 1860, the largest number of Northern Italians outside of Italy lived in San Francisco, where over the course of a single decade they had established an Italian Opera company (1851), created numerous mutual aid societies, founded San Francisco University (1856) and published several Italian language newspapers: *La Voce del Padrone* (1859), *La Scintilla Italiana* (1877) and *L'Italia* (1887). At their inaugural Columbus Day celebration in 1869, San Francisco's Italian community hailed the famous explorer as "the first Italian American" and took special pride in the fact that, like many of them, he had come from Genoa, a wealthy port city in the North.[43] All of this is to say that San Francisco's Italian population viewed themselves as distinct from the impoverished Sicilians and other "Southerners" who had settled in the urban centers along America's East Coast. Although the unification of Italy in 1861 had legally joined the two groups under a single national identity, differences in dialect, cuisine, cultural heritage, wealth and social status kept the two groups distinct from one another, both in Italy and in the United States.

Numerous musicians settled in San Francisco during the first decade of the twentieth century, and by far the most influential was Guido Pietro Deiro, a young nobleman who had abandoned the family estate near Turin in 1908 and traveled to the United States in an effort to escape an arranged marriage and his father's wish that he become a lawyer. Deiro quickly became one of the most noted musicians in California, and as a vaudeville performer, he traveled up and down the West Coast and across the Midwest. His first documented performance in the United States was at the Alaska-Yukon-Pacific Exhibition in Seattle in 1909. Deiro had been dispatched to the event by the Ronco-Vercelli accordion company, which had hired him to introduce their new instrument, the piano accordion, to American audiences. Like the mandolin, the piano accordion was an instrument popularized in the United States by Italian immigrant musicians, and in Seattle, Deiro caught the attention of a talent agent who promptly recruited him to perform as part of the Orpheum Vaudeville Circuit. Earning upward of $600 a week, Deiro became one of the highest paid musicians in the United States, and much of his success came from his virtuosic abilities, good looks, winning onstage personality and the breadth of his repertoire. He settled in San Francisco, where he received regular sponsorship from the Guerrini Musical Instrument Manufacturing Company, and by 1911 he was making recordings for Columbia Records.[44] He composed a series of hit songs, including "Kismet" (1911), which served as the theme song to a popular Broadway musical the same year, and "Deiro Rag" (1913),

published by Jerome H. Remick & Co. in New York. It is interesting
to note that Deiro's rags differed markedly from those created by Bob
Yosco and Al Piantadosi. Whereas musicians from Southern Italy readily
embraced ethnic-themed novelty rags, Deiro and other musicians from
the North tended to produce works in the classical ragtime vein, with
Scott Joplin as a model.

Deiro's approach to ragtime as a serious instrumental genre is clearly displayed in "Deiro Rag," which was recorded in 1912 for the Columbia label.
As Deiro explained to a reporter for the *San Francisco Chronicle* in 1917,
he preferred Columbia to Victor, because Columbia distributed his music
in both the United States and Italy.[45] Deiro's recordings were enormously
popular, and, along with his vaudeville stardom, they helped to propel him
to the status of a minor celebrity.[46] In both the United States and his homeland, Deiro bridged the gulf between "high" and "low" culture and transformed the accordion into "an instrument for all."[47]

As Deiro's fame grew, countless American newspapers published articles about him including interviews, wherein he often talked about his
Italian origins. He was regularly described as "a fine looking, well-built
young Italian" with a mastery "of half a dozen languages" including "perfect" English. One article, published in the *Cleveland Plain Dealer* in 1915,
included Deiro's own description of how he came to play the accordion:

It happened in Germany… My father and I were on a tour of that country, and while
we were there I bought a little accordion… There wasn't then, and there isn't now,
any school for accordion instruction. I had to learn the instrument myself and play
it myself. Later I had to improvise on it, and as I progressed I secured increasingly
better instruments.[48]

Improvisation was an important element of Deiro's style. Be it an opera aria
or a Tin Pan Alley song, Deiro made the tune his own by adding ornamen-
tal flourishes and syncopated rhythmic patterns. He eventually opened a
large music studio in San Francisco, where he offered private lessons and
sold instruments and sheet music. In 1913 he married Mae West, his partner in vaudeville and later one of America's most enduring movie stars.[49]
They were married for seven years, and during that period West traveled
to Chicago, where she encountered a provocative new dance called the
"shimmy" being performed in local dance halls by African American entertainers. West quickly mastered the dance, and in 1918 she introduced it to
audiences in New York along with a new song, "Ev'rybody Shimmies Now."[50]
Deiro's connection with West during this period is important. The shimmy,
along with the various jazz tunes that accompanied it, soon found their way

into the nightclubs and dance halls of Northern Italy, where avant-garde artists like the Futurists embraced their invigorating rhythms.

Futurism and Jazz

The Italians who settled in San Francisco did more than simply adopt the popular cultural practices of their new home. Well educated and financially independent, they brought with them recent trends in Italian art and literature, the most prevalent being Futurism. Although Futurist paintings and sculptures would not appear in America until 1915, when they were displayed as part of the Panama Pacific Exposition in San Francisco, the earliest manifestations of Italian Futurism, namely, aesthetic theories and avant-garde poetry, made a mark on American audiences as early as 1909. The movement's founder, F. T. Marinetti, advocated for new forms of poetry he called "versi liberi" (free verse) and "parole in libertà" (liberated words), both of which emphasized the importance of rhythm and improvisation. Marinetti's literary style was largely performative in nature; he regularly dispensed with syntax to experiment with disjunctive words, onomatopoeia, signs, symbols, sounds, colors and shapes. Marinetti published his first Futurist Manifesto – there would be many more to come – in the Parisian newspaper *Le Figaro* on February 20, 1909 and almost overnight sparked an artistic revolution that quickly reached across Europe and into the Americas. The basic tenets of Futurism included a fascination with speed, urbanism, modern industry and electricity. Futurism called for a rejection of the past in favor of embracing all that was new, mechanized and shocking. In studying the arrival of Futurism, it is helpful to reflect for a moment on the etymological origins of the name Marinetti chose. Though native English speakers might assume that the term Futurism simply refers to an interest in "the future," Marinetti's choice of nomenclature derived from the Latin word *futurus* – the future participle of the verb *esse* (to be). This distinction from the English noun "future" is important, for it reveals that the Futurists saw themselves as being equally engaged with both the present state of things and "that which is to be hereafter."[51]

In the mind of Marinetti and his followers, the essence of Futurism was not to prophesize about the future, but rather to experience the "present in motion" as it moved forward through time. Consequently, they were obsessed with recent innovations in the speed of transportation (steam engine, automobiles and airplanes) and methods of communication (gramophone, telephone, radio and film). One of their earliest heroes was the

Italian inventor/physicist Guglielmo Marconi, who garnered international fame in 1894 for his invention of an apparatus capable of transmitting electromagnetic waves, i.e. the prototype of the modern radio. Ten years later Marconi established the first transatlantic wireless news company, coining the phrase "World-Wide Wireless" (the initial www in communications), and almost overnight his name became an international brand.

The rise of Marconi is important to the history of Futurism in America, especially regarding the music industry and its eventual commercialization of jazz. In 1906 Columbia Records sponsored Marconi and his family on an all-expenses-paid visit to New York. As newspaper reports from the time explained, Marconi was given a whirlwind tour of Columbia's Bridgeport plant before he and his family were feted at a banquet at Manhattan's Waldorf-Astoria Hotel.[52] The motivation behind Columbia's invitation, however, was far from altruistic. As a short notice in the *New York Times* revealed, Marconi had just "joined the experimental staff of the Columbia Phonograph Company," for whom he would "endeavor to further develop the science of recording and reproducing sounds."[53] Columbia was hoping to profit from Marconi's international reputation, whose official title at the company was "consulting physicist," and the trip to New York was the first step in a publicity campaign for a new line of high-end gramophone discs called the Marconi Velvet Tone Series. Advertised as "Wonderful as Wireless," these semiflexible, laminated celluloid discs first appeared on the market in 1907 with a label bearing Marconi's portrait and facsimile signature. The fact that Marconi did not submit the patent for the disc – its design was actually the work of a Columbia engineer named Thomas H. McDonald – was of little consequence to the company.[54] Marconi was the face of modernity – his name, a watchword for the newest innovations in sound. Perhaps more than anything else, it was the importance of Marconi as an Italian brand that interested industry leaders in America and drew the admiration of Marinetti and his followers back in Italy.

The Marconi Velvet Tone Series flopped on the American market, primarily because few consumers could afford the hefty price tag or the gold-plated needles required to play the discs. Production ceased within two years, and by 1910 the discs were being remaindered in American department stores. But this had little effect on Marconi, who was awarded the Nobel Prize in Physics in 1909, a fact that the Futurists did not miss when they launched their own modernist campaign the same year.

Although Americans first began reading about Futurism shortly after the movement was launched, exposure to the Futurists' activities came mostly through secondhand descriptions in the popular press. As readers in America soon learned, the literary movement launched by Marinetti had branched out into other fields: painting, sculpture, architecture, politics, theater, music, advertising and even cooking.[55] Americans were exposed to Futurism through a series of op-ed articles, press releases and reviews of Futurist events in Europe. Consequently, many of the descriptions of Futurism published in the American press during the early years of the movement were filled with misconceptions. For the current study, the factual inaccuracy of these early reports is inconsequential. What is important here is the early perception of Futurism in the minds of American journalists and readers as being connected to the origins of jazz.[56]

As early as 1909, excerpts of Marinetti's founding manifesto were published in translation by various American news outlets. New York's *The Sun* appears to have been the first to introduce American readers to the concept of "Futurism."[57] As art historian John Hand explains, this short article explained to Americans "Marinetti's desire to have Italy recognized as a modern nation and not merely as a land of ruins and museums."[58] The call was for a new age of modern art, and the United States was identified as a helpful role model for the Italian avant-garde. Discussion of Futurism increased in 1911, when several American newspapers and magazines began covering the movement's latest activities. An anonymous article titled "The Futurist Movement in Italy," which appeared in the August issue of *Current Literature*, described Futurism as a multifaceted movement, intent on destroying the traditions of the past:

A militant association of Italian politicians, sociologists, writers, painters and musicians, organized under the banner of "Futurism," has lately made its appearance. It is bent, apparently, on revolutionizing everything, yet its creed cannot be defined in the terms of any existing revolutionary school.[59]

After describing the movement's latest appearance in the news – Marinetti had recently been acquitted on charges of being "offensive to the manners and morals of the community" in a Milanese court[60] – the article's author wonders how it could be that there might still be someone in America who had not heard of the new art movement:

If *The [New York] Times* or anyone else is uninformed about the tenets of Futurism, it is not the fault of the publicity department of the movement, which seems to be vested in the founder, Signor Marinetti, a young bilingual poet, critic, dramatist and novelist. It is he who conducts the organ of the movement, the massive review *Poesia*, emanating from Milan, … and it is he who wrote the lurid manifesto that appeared in the Paris *Figaro* in 1909.[61]

The author recites the core elements of the manifesto, once again, explaining that it "was sent to as many newspapers in Europe and North and South America as the Futurists could reach." He then goes on to explain how Futurism had caught the attention of America's literati, and like "the drumbeat of the Salvation Army," was successfully "drawing a crowd for subsequent education."[62] In response to the claim that Marinetti wished to "burn all the museums," the author of the article in *Current Literature* explains that it "is only a figure of speech." Indeed, "all he [Marinetti] wants is that artists and writers should use their own eyes and form their own standards for the generation of which they are a part." Marinetti firmly encourages his readers to stop looking at life "through a mist of souvenirs."[63]

On December 4, 1911 an article in *The Evening World* declared that the Futurists wanted society to "look ahead" and "abandon beauty" and "sentiment" for the "new cult in art."[64] Several weeks later, on Christmas Eve, the magazine section of the *New York Herald* printed a full-page, illustrated article declaring: "The New Cult of Futurism is Here." The main contributor to this article, an art dealer named André Tridon, who later made a name for himself as a translator of Sigmund Freud's writings, explained that Futurism had much to offer American culture.

Futurism believes in making the present an attribute of the future rather than of the past ... To forget convention as convention. To fit the present need to the present circumstance. To forget the past, which is wrong, which is dead. To knock convention – which is only the past crystallized into habit – out of painting and talking and everything we do.[65]

By way of illustration, the article contained images of all the art forms supposedly affected by Futurism: painting, sculpture, architecture, literature, fashion design, decorative arts and music. In the case of this latter art form, the accompanying image presented a pair of jovial dancers taking great pleasure in dancing the fox-trot, a popular new dance described as having Futurist associations. Although no Italians had linked the fox-trot to Futurism by the time this article appeared, such an association eventually became a commonplace that influenced composers on both sides of the Atlantic. This is perhaps most clearly seen in the creation of popular musical works like Otto Weber's *Futurismo Foxtrot* (1921) and Frank Signorelli's *Caprice Futuristic* (1927).

In general, American commentators characterized Italian Futurism as any art form or public activity that was "anti-traditional." Futurism became the watchword for all that was modern or experimental. It was the essence of speed, energy and noise. In the American press, the Italian Futurists were embraced as a new generation of European intellectuals who looked to America for inspiration. Thus it should come as no surprise that some of the earliest discussions of jazz in the American press made connections, although false, to the Italian Futurists.

Jazz: A "Futurist" Word

The etymology of the word jazz exists in a nexus of discourses that date back to the early twentieth century. As Krin Gabbard has noted: "Jazz is a construct," and the term "is routinely applied to musics that have ... little in common."[66] Countless scholars have attempted to trace the origins of the word, which has proven difficult, since its use in oral culture predated its first appearance in print, and its earliest meanings were not directly connected to music. With regard to the earliest musical links, many scholars have relied on oral history accounts when seeking the origins of jazz. Others have looked to homophones in foreign languages. For example, Clarence Major has proposed that the term is linked to an African term in Bantu dialect, *jaja*, which means to dance or make music, while Bob Rigter has proposed links to the French terms *jaser*, meaning to chatter or chat, and *chasse*, a chase or hunt.[67] New Orleans jazz musicians, interviewed in the 1950s and 60s, claimed the word came from a variety of sources: the name Jezabelle, a notorious New Orleans prostitute; or Jasmine, a perfume worn by the women who worked in Storyville, New Orleans's red light district, during World War I.[68] But these accounts only date back to around 1916. The etymology of jazz in print can be traced several years earlier, to California, where it appears to have first been used in connection to sports – specifically, baseball.[69]

The earliest known appearance of the word "jazz" in print occurred on April 2, 1912 in the *Los Angeles Times*, where a pitcher named Ben Henderson of the Portland Beavers was reported to have used the term to describe a newly invented baseball pitch:

BEN'S JAZZ CURVE. "I got a new curve this year," softly murmured Henderson yesterday, "and I'm goin' to pitch one or two of them tomorrow. I call it the Jazz ball because it wobbles and you simply can't do anything with it."[70]

On March 6, 1913 a reporter for San Francisco's *Bulletin* named E.T. "Scoop" Gleason used the term "jazz" extensively, again in connection with baseball. This time the term "jazz" served as a synonym for energy and excitement:

Everybody has come back to the old town full of the old "jazz" and they promise to knock the fans off their feet with their playing. What is the "jazz"? Why, it's a little of that "old life," the "gin-i-ker," the "pep," otherwise known as the enthusiasm.[71]

One month later a cultural editor for the *Bulletin* named Ernest Hopkins explained the supposed origins of the term "Jazz" in an article titled "In Praise of 'Jazz:' A Futurist Word Which Has Just Joined the Language." As Hopkins explained, Jazz was an example of "onomatopoeia" and a product of "Futurist language." Describing in detail the new linguistic craze, he praised "the sheer musical quality of the word" and claimed that just saying the word "jazz" (or "jaz" as it was sometimes spelled) had an electrifying effect. Hopkins's description of the word jazz, both its meaning and supposed origins, represents an important but often overlooked link between Italy and the earliest descriptions of a new American phenomenon called jazz. Hopkins opened his article by identifying a new linguistic craze that had taken San Francisco by storm:

This column is entitled "What's Not in the News" but occasionally a few things that are in the news leak in … This thing is a word. It has recently become current in the *Bulletin* office through some means which we cannot discover but would stop up if we could … This word is "JAZ." It is also spelt "Jazz," and as they both sound the same and mean the same, there is no way of settling the controversy.[72]

For those readers who were still not familiar with the term, Hopkins presented a loose definition:

"JAZZ" (We change the spelling each time so as not to offend either faction) can be defined, but it cannot be synonymized. If there were another word that exactly expressed the meaning of "jaz," "Jazz" would never have been born. A new word like a new muscle only comes into being when it has been long needed.

This remarkable and satisfactory-sounding word, however, means something like life, vigor, energy, effervescence of spirit, joy, pep, magnetism, verve, virility, ebulliency, courage, happiness, – oh, what's the use? – JAZZ.

Nothing else can express it.[73]

As Hopkins explained, jazz had a wealth of linguistic uses:

It is "jazz" when you run for your train; "jaz" when you soak an umpire; "Jazz" when you demand a raise; "jaz" when you hike thirty-five miles of a Sunday; "Jazz" when you simply sit around and beam so that all who look beam on you. Anything that takes manliness or effort or energy or activity or strength of soul is "jaz."[74]

Despite its diverse array of meanings, jazz is not a word to be taken lightly, claimed Hopkins. It is not mere street language. Rather it is a word of some importance that entered the English language through high art:

We would not have you apprehend that this new word is slang. It is merely Futurist language, which as everybody knows is more than mere cartooning.

"Jazz" is a nice word, a classic word, easy on the tongue and pleasant to the ears, profoundly expressive of the idea it conveys ... There is and always has been an art of genial strength; to this art we now give the splendid title of "jazz."[75]

Hopkins proposed that even the word's phonetic properties imbued it with a sophisticated artistic essence:

The sheer musical quality of the word, that delightful sound like the crackling of an electric spark, commends it. It belongs to the class of onomatopoeia. It was important that this vacancy in our language should have been filled with a word of proper sound, because "jaz" is a quality often celebrated in epic poetry, in prizefight stories, in the tale of action or the meditative sonnet; it is a universal word, and must appear well in all society. That is why "pep," which tried to mean the same but never could, failed; it was a rough-neck from the first, and could not wear evening clothes.

The term jazz fills a void in the English language, claimed Hopkins, who described it as a "universal word," implying that its origins might be foreign. Nonetheless, the word was here to stay, he explained: "Jazz is at home in bar or ballroom; it is a true American."[76]

Sentiments such as these help to explain the growing popularity of the term "jazz" within San Francisco's collegiate circles. From 1915 to 1918, students and faculty at the University of California, Berkeley and Stanford University used the term regularly in articles published in the *Daily Californian* and the *Daily Palo Alto*.[77] Jazz was never formally linked to music in San Francisco, but it appears a local banjo player, Bert Kelly, might have taken the term with him when he moved to Chicago in 1915 and formed the Bert Kelly Jazz Band.[78] It was during these years that the word became formally linked to music.

Chicago

Chicago was the second largest city in the United States when the word "jazz" arrived, with a population of nearly two million. Thanks to the transcontinental railway system, it had become a major transport center with a burgeoning economy. The city's rapid growth had attracted large numbers of fortune seekers, both black and white, from across the country. West Coast trends blended with East Coast trends in the Windy City, as musicians from various locales began to arrive. Thus it should come as no surprise that it was in Chicago where the musical trend that had been brewing in cities like New Orleans, New York and San Francisco was formally baptized in the press as "Jazz."

The first documented use of the term in reference to music appeared in an article by Gordon Seagrove titled "Blues is Jazz and Jazz is Blues" published in the *Chicago Daily Tribune* on July 11, 1915. Written as a descriptive piece capturing the atmosphere of a local cabaret, the article defined jazz as a new genre of music derived originally from the African American Blues, but now firmly linked to white musicians and dances like the fox-trot. The article opened by documenting an argument between a well-to-do woman with "snow white shoulders" and her husband. She wanted to dance, but he refused. Then the band began to play:

Suddenly from above the thread of the melody itself came a harmonious, yet discordant wailing, an eerie mezzo that moaned and groaned and sighed and electrified, a haunting counter strain that oozed from the saxophone (*sic*).[79]

The husband was transformed instantly. His once "tired eyes" now "shone with a wonderful light ... His mouth moved convulsively. The years fell away from his shoulders leaving only his frock coat." The husband had "turned to fox trotting. And the 'blues' had done it. The 'Jazz' had put pep into the legs that had scrambled too long for the 5:15."[80]

As Seagrove explained in the second half of the article, scenes such as these had recently become commonplace in Chicago, where "wailing syncopation is heard in every gin mill where dancing holds sway." For those who had not yet encountered the terms "blues" and "Jazz," Seagrove included a definition, conveyed to him by a "tall young man with nimble fingers" who had recently perfected the new musical style:

"A blue note is a sour note," he explained. "It's a discord – a harmonic discord. The blues are never written into music, but are interpolated by the piano player or other players. They aren't new. They are just reborn into popularity. They started in the south half a century ago and are the interpolations of darkies originally. The trade name for them is 'jazz.' "[81]

It is important to reflect on this passage a moment, for what Seagrove is describing is a new genre of music, which grew out of the African American genre called "the blues," but has now been transformed into a commercialized genre, with the new trade name of "jazz." Sidney Bechet, a native of

New Orleans who witnessed the birth of the genre, often commented that jazz was "a name the white people gave to the music."[82] In many ways, this first use of the word as a musical term gives validity to his claim. But even more importantly, one should note that the arrival in Chicago of the term "jazz" to identify a new style of popular music coincided with the arrival in 1914/15 of numerous musicians from New Orleans, both black and white, who had migrated to the city in search of work.

In Chicago, the geography of the city was markedly divided into black and white. Black musicians, who had been actively performing ragtime music on the city's South Side since the early 1900s, occupied a musical world of their own. By 1915, numerous well-known New Orleans musicians, including Jelly Roll Morton and Freddie Keppard, had made a name for themselves in the South Side cabarets. Chicago offered these musicians a better life than what was available in New Orleans. In addition to their own union (AFM Local 208), they enjoyed the security of regular engagements and better salaries. According to Keppard, he and his Original Creole Orchestra were even approached by the Victor Talking Machine Company in 1916 and invited to record for posterity their New Orleans sound. But Keppard turned them down, reportedly wary that recordings might facilitate players eager to imitate his performances.

Chicago's white musicians occupied the city's North Side, where they had their own venues, their own union (AFM Local 10) and their own audiences. In Chicago, black jazz and white jazz followed separate paths, so much so that the major cultural events of the South Side, which were regularly described in detail in a black weekly called *The Chicago Defender*, were rarely even mentioned in the white press. The North Side hosted countless high-end dance clubs, and one of the most famous, the Lamb's Café, was the first to host white musicians from New Orleans. Lamb's was an underground club, located in the basement of the Olympic Theater, on the corner of N. Randolph Street and W. Clark Street. Arnold "Deacon" Loyocano once described the venue as "a beautiful place, with tile floor and marble all around the sides." It was a far cry from many of the dance halls he had frequented in New Orleans, and he was mesmerized by the fact that "every note you'd hit would reverberate back about six times."[83]

The sound that reverberated off the marble walls of Lamb's Café must have been deafening. As another New Orleans musician, Raymond Lopez, noted, the first time a group of New Orleans musicians auditioned at Lamb's, the manager turned "white as a ghost" and then yelled: "What kind of noise is that! You guys crazy – or drunk?" But they got the gig anyway, and on May 17, 1915, a group of five white musicians named Tom Brown's Band from Dixieland opened at Lamb's Café. As Richard Sudhalter has noted, the New Orleans sound was not embraced right away. "The expected crowds did not materialize," and the venue's other ensemble, a string orchestra, "quit in protest at the new band's raucous sounds." But within a month "word started to get around ... and the public, ever curious, came to investigate."[84] As Lopez later explained in letters home, "customers lined up for nearly two blocks every night, clamoring for a chance to get in; guest celebrities dropped by, making sure they were seen."[85] The *Chicago Tribune* article published in July – the one mentioned above that first linked the term "jazz" to music – was almost certainly a description of the music played by Tom Brown's Dixieland Band at Lamb's Café. Over the next year, the word "jazz" spread like wildfire throughout the city, all the way down to the South Side. For example, on September 30, 1916, an article published in the *Chicago Defender* mentioned a black "jass band" led by H. Benton Overstreet, and in 1917 a band called the "Original Jazz Band" was advertised as playing at the Dreamland Café, one of the city's better-known South Side clubs.[86] The new jazz craze was so intense that Chicago's various promoters and club owners scrambled to import their own bands. A new wave of musicians from New Orleans, among them the aggressively ambitious cornet player Nick LaRocca and his friend, drummer Tony Sbarbaro, inundated the city. Both LaRocca and Sbarbaro had started out in Jack Laine's brass bands, and they stuck together as they established themselves in Chicago. Their first jobs were playing with Johnny Stein's Dixie Jass Band at Schiller's Café on 31st Street. But in May 1916 the band broke up, and LaRocca formed his own group, the Original Dixieland Jass Band (ODJB), with Sbarbaro and three other New Orleans musicians: Eddie Edwards (trombone), Henry Ragas (piano) and Larry Shields (clarinet). The ODJB played in countless venues, from Del'Abe's Café in the Hotel Normandy to the Casino Gardens just outside the loop. They even tried their hand at vaudeville, teaming up with Fogarty's Dance Revue, which earned a flood of praise from theater reviewers. A particularly colorful description of their theatrical debut appeared in the local press:

The Jass band was a hit from the start and offered the wildest kind of music ever heard outside of a Commanche massacre. There are five men in this band, and they make enough noise to satisfy even a north side bunch out for entertainment in the vicinity of Belmont Avenue and Racine.[87]

The band's loud, raucous style got the attention of a visiting talent agent, and by January 1917 they were performing in the Paradise Ballroom of the Reisenweber Hotel in New York, advertised as "the smartest, most beautiful

Figure 1.1 Victor Records promotional flyer for the Original Dixieland Jazz Band (1917).
Source: Eddie Edwards' scrapbook, The Hogan Jazz Archive, Tulane University, New Orleans, LA.

and most modern ballroom in America." LaRocca's "Jasz Band" was pro-moted as "the first sensational amusement novelty of 1917." Direct from "its amazing success in Chicago," the band was giving "modern dancing new life and a new thrill." It was described as "the latest craze ... sweeping the nation like a musical thunderstorm."[88]

Although countless musicians in Chicago and New York, both black and white, contributed to the development of the jazz during World War I, LaRocca and the ODJB stand out for their contribution to its rapid dissemination. LaRocca was a fine cornet player, but as the above advertisement reveals, his real talent lay in self-promotion. He had a driving ambition, and he realized early on the golden rule of publicity: the more people you can reach, the greater your chances of success. LaRocca did not invent jazz, as he would later claim, but he was the first to realize the importance of recording it. And on February 26, 1917, he and his band secured their place in music history when they entered a Victor recording studio and created the first commercially released jazz gramophone disc. Side A featured a tune called "Dixieland Jass Band One-Step," the B side was "Livery Stable Blues" (Figure 1.1).[89]

This gramophone disc launched the jazz age with all its accouterments, from flapper fashions to potent cocktails. By 1918 the band had sold over one million copies of the disc – a truly astounding number for the time – and listening to these tunes, one quickly realizes what made them stand out.

Novelty was a big part of the early Dixieland sound, both in the use of various percussion instruments and the special effects created by the brass and clarinet. In addition to a parade style bass drum and cymbals, Sbarbaro regularly used a large, fourteen-inch snare drum, two cowbells and a woodblock. The improvised counterpoint of the cornet, clarinet and trombone generally worked with the cornet playing melody, the clarinet noodling around the tune and filling gaps, complemented by the trombone, accenting the beat with deep, powerful tones. The piano, difficult to hear on the recordings, generally rumbled in the background, filling chords with a pounding, rhythmic pulse. "Livery Stable Blues" displayed the musicians at their best. LaRocca had developed a technique for imitating animal noises. By holding down the third valve and shaking the horn, he could produce a realistic "horse whinny." On "Livery Stable Blues" the breaks between choruses featured LaRocca's horse and a rooster crow played by Shields on clarinet. Effects like these garnered unending praise and unrivaled fame for the band, and within a year the ODJB became an international sensation. As Louis Armstrong noted in his autobiography *Swing That Music*, musicians back home in New Orleans took pride in the ODJB's success:

The first great jazz orchestra was formed in New Orleans by a cornet player named Dominick James LaRocca ... His orchestra had only five pieces, but they were the hottest five pieces that had ever been known before ... He had an instrumentation different from anything else before – an instrumentation that made the old songs sound new.[90]

Through the technology of recorded sound, the syncopated dance music of New Orleans was transformed into "jazz," the trade name for a new genre of commercialized music that had its roots in African American culture but was quickly being absorbed and transformed by other ethnic groups. It was this cultural transformation, and the important role played by Italian Americans, that greatly influenced perceptions of the genre as it reached beyond American shores.

LaRocca and his band set sail for England in March 1919 and remained there for a full year and a half. In 1919 and 1920 they recorded a series of tunes for Columbia UK. The discs were quickly distributed in countries across Europe, including Italy. Which brings us back to the article by Bruno Zuculin quoted at the beginning of this chapter. When the Italian consul to New Orleans wrote his description of "American Musics and Dances" in 1919, he was responding to the recent popularity of the ODJB's recordings in Italy. Zuculin felt the time had come to elucidate for Italian audiences what he believed to be the origins and cultural implications of the new musical phenomenon called jazz. Consequently, he began his article by offering a definition of the genre and describing its supposed link to Italy through Futurism and Italian musicians:

Now that the jazz bands have crossed the ocean and invaded Old Europe, scandalizing the traditionalist musicians and filling the Futurists with enthusiasm, everyone is wondering what jazz is. Many American journalists, confusing American dances with the music, have written that jazz is a new dance. Nothing could be more erroneous. Jazz is an orchestra, like any other, that has modern instruments added to the old ones and that plays all kinds of music. Of course, the rhythm is always the same; it is always that of ragtime or syncopated music, but really any melody can be played in that rhythm. In fact, I have often heard jazz bands playing "O sole mio," Neapolitan songs, and Viennese waltzes.[91]

Zuculin felt justified in telling his countrymen that jazz should be viewed as something of a native product. As he explained to readers, "New Orleans boasts of having created the first jazz band around twenty years ago," but since then, the music had undergone something of a transformation, from groups of rag-tag youth playing homemade instruments in the street, i.e. "spasm" bands, to more formal ensembles performing in dance halls. "The success of bands such as these" – which consisted of musicians playing "piano, guitar, trumpet, string bass and drums" – raised the music to a new level of "artistry," said Zuculin. And "this success rapidly spread from New Orleans to the rest of the United States." But then more changes occurred, some of which, Zuculin claimed, could be linked to the artistic influence of the Italian Futurists:

Along these lines, the orchestra was further perfected through the addition of various instruments that the Futurists call "intona-rumori" (noise intoners); and it was discovered that the jazz band lent itself better than any other type of music to [dances like] the two-step, the one-step and the fox-trot, and for this reason it took root in all the hotels and restaurants at night.[92]

In reference to what made the music different from previous styles, Zuculin did not hesitate to explain that originally, it was "[t]he black musicians" who "supplied these orchestras with the brio needed to give the prancing-dancing couples the excitement that the North Americans so avidly seek." But more recently, he continued, "another step forward has been taken as the old, traditional orchestras that were everywhere now begin to disappear." To return to the quote cited at the beginning of this chapter, Zuculin explained that the commercialization of jazz, as represented both in the dance hall and on recorded disc, had led to a division of the genre into two racial categories:

…those that are mostly black, which perform in the hotels, restaurants, dance halls and social clubs; and those, often Italian, that play in the cinemas, in variety shows and in those numerous theaters where the most genuine theatrical product of North America flourishes, namely the entertaining productions called "Musical Comedies" or "Girls and Music Shows."[93]

Of the Italian bands, he notes that the most outstanding performs in a Vaudeville venue: "the celebrated Pa[la]ce Theater in New Orleans, managed by the Italian Ben Piazza" and directed "by Maestro Guiseppe Fulcro" (Figure 1.2).[94]

With the history of the genre clarified, Zuculin dedicated the second half of his article to describing the special characteristics of contemporary jazz and the musical contributions that had been made by New Orleans's Italian musicians. In reference to the Futurist "intona-rumori," Zuculin went into greater detail about the various instruments involved and how they were usually played by the best performers, whom he referred to as "professors":

Figure 1.2 Caricature of the Italian Jazz Orchestra, directed by violinist Giuseppe Fulco, at the Pa[la]ce Theater in New Orleans.
Source: La lettura: Monthly supplement to the *Corriere della Sera* (August 1919): 599. Archive of Anna Celenza.

The bass drum player is the most important person in the jazz band, since in addition to the bass drum, plates, a tambourine, and cymbals he plays the tam tam, and Swiss bells, and hand bells, and cowbells, and the ratchet, and the car horn and the whistle, and the "baby cry" or crying baby, and woodblocks of various types and sizes, etc. etc.[95]

But it was not just the array of instruments that made these performances special:

The professors often try themselves to give color and animation to the arousing music. And this is why one sees bows that dance in the air and violins that spin around or are twirled on the neck and tambourines played with the head and with the knee, and so on *ad libitum* by the musicians.[96]

Zuculin explained that this commercialization of the music "happened during World War I."

But after the armistice we wanted something more exciting for the Americans. And just like that there it was, not a new music but a new dance – the Shimmie – that appears to have been invented specially for dancing to the sound of the *intona-rumori*.[97]

Zuculin did not mention Guido Deiro by name, but he linked the new dance to the Italian Futurists' *intona-rumori*, and he referred obliquely to Deiro's wife, Mae West, when he mentioned the tune she had recently premiered on the vaudeville circuit:

For the last few months the most popular song in America is the one titled: "Everybody Shimmies Now." And truly, everyone is dancing it, such that you will even see it being danced by one of the Southern Governors. And what exactly is this shimmie that has caused rivers of ink to flow both for and against?[98]

Zuculin answered his own question by explaining that "it is a dance derived from Negro dances that resembles the famous Spanish Rumba," which was popular at that time in Italy. Zuculin conveyed shock at the virulent reaction to the dance shown by many American Protestants and concluded his article by dismissing such prudish behavior. To those readers who agreed with him, he offered a humorous anecdote concerning "a group of female students at Louisiana State University" who "bombarded with smelly eggs a female director who wanted to prohibit all enrolled female students from dancing the shimmie and wearing backless dresses."[99]

This last point might seem quaint and inconsequential at first glance, but in 1919, Zuculin's comments carried weight. As Italy's consul to New Orleans – not to mention his status as a member of Italian nobility – Zuculin's ridicule of American morals, specifically its *Protestant* morals, set the stage for Italy's reception of jazz and all its accouterments: the clothes, the dances and even the cocktails. Although many of his claims concerning the origins of jazz are justly dismissed today, his desire to promote the role of Italian immigrants in the development of early jazz clearly influenced the music's reception across the Atlantic. We should remember that when Zuculin wrote his article, the genre was in its nascent stage, and the idea that one kind of jazz might be considered more authentic than another did not yet exist among New Orleans musicians and their listeners.[100] Although Zuculin clearly identified two distinct types of jazz in his article on the New Orleans scene – one connected to African American performers, the other to Italian immigrants – he never compared the two in terms of authenticity or superiority. Instead, he tried to explain to his readers back home how both groups had contributed to the genre's development. Zuculin was the first to state, quite emphatically, that Italian immigrants played a role in the genesis of jazz in the United States. It was this belief, perhaps more than anything else, that inspired many Italians, including the Futurists and Mussolini, to embrace the music as a "native" art form. As we will see in the chapters that follow, Zuculin's description of jazz set the stage for a dramatic era in Italian cultural history – an era defined by politics and musical innovation.

2 | Jazz Crosses the Atlantic

In most histories of jazz, the music's arrival on the European continent is commonly linked to the presence of African American soldiers, most notably the Harlem Hellfighters Band of the 369th Infantry Regiment. The syncopated "ragging" of marches and popular dances that these musicians performed under the baton of Lieutenant James Reese Europe invigorated France during World War I and contributed to a fascination with black culture among avant-garde artists and musicians.[1] The Parisian setting in which jazz first achieved notoriety has interested scholars for several decades, but as Jed Rasula has noted, "Paris is only one piece of the puzzle."[2] Although Lieutenant Europe's ensemble was by far the most distinctive, it was only one among many military bands, both large and small, that spread America's new music across the continent during World War I. The repertoire, musical training and cultural background of these military ensembles varied widely. Some bands were developed on an ad-hoc basis; others were formally organized and trained before deployment. Some were composed of black musicians; others, like the Scrap-Iron Jazzerinos and the 158th Infantry Band under the direction of Second Lieutenant Albert R. Etzweiler, were strictly white.[3] Most included male musicians only, but there were a few ensembles brought over to accompany theatrical entertainments organized by nonmilitary organizations like the Red Cross and YMCA that included women musicians too.[4] Not surprisingly, such a diverse range of ensembles meant that the early dissemination and reception of jazz in various parts of Europe differed markedly. In Britain, jazz received a mixed reception, where it was viewed as a product of American folk culture related to both black and white traditions.[5] And in France and Germany audiences embraced the music as an exotic, avant-garde art form performed almost exclusively by African Americans and rooted in a primitivist aesthetic.[6] In Italy, however, the early reception of jazz differed markedly. Many Italian listeners perceived jazz as a fully commercialized art form linked to wealth, modern technology and Italian American innovation.

Jazz made its inaugural entry into Italy on June 27, 1918 – the day 1,700 members of the US Army Ambulance Service (USAAS) arrived in Genoa aboard the S.S. Giuseppe Verdi, a luxury ocean liner supplied by the Italian government to assist in the efficient transport of American aid. In addition to 60 trucks, 30 cars, 360 ambulances and 30 motorcycles with side cars, the Americans arrived with enough musical instruments and sheet music to outfit three ensembles: two pit bands linked to the Kernell-Fechheimer shows *Good-Bye Bill* and *Let's Go*, and a smaller group referred to in military documents as the "American Jazz Band," also nicknamed Hamp's Jazz Band, after their bandleader, Charles W. Hamp, who played both piano and saxophone.[7]

The USAAS had been sent to assist the 332nd Regiment, the only US forces stationed in Italy during World War I. The regiment's principal mission was to build up Italian morale by showing that Americans had arrived and were finally engaged in protecting Italy's interests. Since the troops sent to Italy were far fewer in number than those delegated to France, they were advised to make themselves noticeable so that they might appear more numerous than they were. The USAAS bands, whose core duty was "propaganda and morale building," played a key role in creating this impression. Travel was encouraged, and the American Jazz Band, in particular, moved up and down the peninsula, from one locale to the next, performing "distinct American music" in public venues open to soldiers and Italian citizens alike.[8] In his study of USAAS activities during World War I, military historian John R. Smucker, Jr. included detailed descriptions of the American Jazz Band's six months of active service.[9] After the Armistice, the band's duties continued, and as one band member noted in a letter home, the YMCA took over management of the ensemble:

The problem of finances arose – who was going to foot the bill? This was solved in Treviso where … we met a YMCA secretary named Pepin from Detroit. Pepin called his headquarters in Paris, France, and secured permission to spend 20,000 Lire for our expenses.[10]

Additional on-the-spot descriptions of the American Jazz Band's experiences during this period were related in letters home written by musicians. As the following excerpts reveal, the band received a warm reception from locals as they completed their "Victory Tour" of Italy at the conclusion of the war:

We arrived in Milano on that fateful day, November 11, 1918 [the day Germany signed an armistice agreement with the Allies], and the people were mad with joy. None of us had a button on our tunics when we, in the wee small hours, finally made it to our hotel. We augmented our equipment in Milano as some of us played more than one instrument. We rehearsed some more and then played in the hospitals for

convalescents in the area around Lago Como and several very large charity bazaars
in Milano. Our own ambulance sections were first on the official tour. Every section
was visited and some had moved up pretty close to Trieste. We then had our only
chance to see Venice on this trip, and we played "Down in Honky Town," going
under the Rialto Bridge in two big gondolas tied together.[11]

A reporter for the Paris edition of the *New York Herald* described this
memorable Venetian performance, noting that the band's usual "penchant
for physical comedy" put them at some risk in the "picturesque setting."[12]
Like LaRocca's ODJB, the USAAS Jazz Band regularly included slapstick
physical antics in their performances: "Instead of sitting calmly on stage,"
noted a contemporary witness, they "dance, roll over, embrace each other
and do various acrobatic acts without missing a note, the whole effect
being whimsical and full of surprise."[13]

As one soldier noted in a letter home: after Venice, the band went
"back to Milano for some recordings for the Società Italiana di Fonolipia"
[*sic*].[14] Fonotipia was Italy's leading gramophone record label at the
time. Established in 1904 by the Anglo French composer Baron Frederic
d'Erlanger, Fonotipia's studios were located in Milan and generally hosted
recording sessions featuring celebrities, most notably the leading opera
singers of the day. For two weeks in December 1918, however, performers
from the "U.S.A. Army Ambulance Service" and the "Italian Army" came
together to record a commemorative set of forty gramophone discs, filling the Fonotipia studios with a markedly different sound.[15] "The biggest
phonograph concern in Italy offered to pay a high price for the records,"
reported one military official. "Owing to army regulations, however, the
contract was declined." But that didn't stop the musicians. They played for
free, and in 1921 the recordings were reportedly still "immensely popular
in Italy."[16]

Fonotipia's interest in documenting the performances of the USAAS Jazz
Band says a great deal about the music's early audience in Italy. From the
beginning, the jazz performed by American troops was associated with the
upper echelon of Italian society. Like the stars of Italian opera, American
bands were marketed to wealthy audiences, most notably those in the
North, who could afford a gramophone and were eager to learn the latest
dances being taught in the dance academies that sprang up in nearly every
urban center north of Rome.

A catalogue for the USAAS gramophone discs produced by Fonotipia
reveals that, from the beginning, the project was perceived as one that could
be marketed on both sides of the Atlantic. Prices were listed in both Italian

lire and US dollars, and the recommended price per disc – two dollars – was quite expensive. The catalogue also carried a dedication, written in both Italian and broken English, that reflected the record company's reverence for the US military's contributions:

The Società Italiana di Fonotipia begs to dedicate this catalogue of Italo-American Propaganda Programme to the US Army Ambulance Service with Italian Army in Italy as a slight mark of gratitude for the kind and valuable assistance obtained through the courtesy of Colonel E. Persons and Lt. Colonel C. Franklin, Chairman of Entertainment Committee.[17]

Unfortunately, there appears to be no extant complete set of these recordings.[18] Nonetheless, a photo of the "American Jazz Band" and a detailed list of the repertoire included in the catalogue, combined with the register of recording sessions preserved in the Fonotipia archives, reveal much about how these early performances must have sounded. The instrumentation on these recordings for the USAAS "American Jazz Band" included: piano, drums, saxophone, string bass, two violins, one viola, two banjos and a ukulele.[19] Their repertoire was a mix of popular dance tunes ("Hindustan" Fox Trot by Oliver Wallace and "Uncle Tom One Step" by Hugo Frey),[20] patriotic tunes ("Over There" and "[It's a long way to] Tipperary"), Broadway numbers (*"Good-bye Bill* Medley" and "Chinese Blues"), and contemporary jazz tunes ("Oriental Jazz" and "[Darktown] Strutters Ball"). The inclusion of these last two numbers is especially telling, since LaRocca and his ODJB had recently released the inaugural recordings with Columbia and Aeolian Vocalian.[21] By 1919, many of the tunes recorded by LaRocca's group had attained immense popularity in Italy, where the bandleader's Italian heritage was taken as a point of pride. Recognizing a profitable market when they saw one, American recording companies like Columbia and Victor regularly used their Italian affiliates to produce reprints of the ensemble's recordings shortly after their initial release in the United States. Although the ODJB never performed in Italy, the influence of their recordings had a telling effect on Italian musicians attempting to imitate their style. This is clearly heard in a rendition of "At the Jazz Band Ball," recorded by Nicola Moleti and the Orchestra del Trianon in Milan in April 1919 and released on the Grammofono label, an Italian affiliate of The Gramophone Company Ltd., which was based in the United Kingdom.[22] This recording doesn't swing with the same ease as the American original, and the Italian performers struggle in their attempts to replicate the collective improvisation made famous by the ODJB. Nonetheless, the influence of the American model is clear. Additional recordings by Moleti's band – most notably "Hindustan"

Fox-trot and the Tin Pan Alley song "Smiles" by Lee S. Roberts and J. Will Calahan – also appeared on Fonotipia's recordings of the "American Jazz Band."[23]

In addition to their studio work, the American Jazz Band continued to perform for a variety of audiences, large and small, across Northern Italy for several months after the war. Their concerts "amazed and delighted the Italians."[24] But as one band member noted, the most memorable interactions involved hobnobbing with Italian nobility, many of whom embraced the new dance music with great enthusiasm:

> It was on one of these trips into Milano that the band was invited to the home of La Contessa Jeannette dal Verme, where we played, danced, and drank through a very pleasant evening. I can't remember the names of the guests at the dance, but I do know one was a princess; and we all took a turn with her.[25]

The princess referred to here was Yolanda of Savoy, the eldest daughter of King Victor Emmanuel III of Italy and his wife Princess Elena of Montenegro. Princess Yolanda was an avid sportswoman, who took great pleasure in the athletic dances associated with the new American music. Yolanda served as a hostess and sponsor for the ensemble during their visits to Rome, as did Thomas Nelson Page, the American Ambassador to Italy during World War I.[26] As one band member noted:

> Our tour took us to Turino [*sic*], Firenze, (with a side trip for some to Pisa), and on to Rome where that lovable couple, Ambassador Page and his beautiful wife, took us under their wings and saw that every wish of ours was satisfied … In all these places we played to the convalescents, the poor, the opulent, young, old, and the nobility. The only one we missed was the Pope! This was a new experience for the Italian people with American dance and jazz music, and although many did not understand the words of the songs, they loved their rhythms, the humor, and the lonesomeness of a blues tune.[27]

After the Armistice, numerous American military bands, all of them white, appeared in celebratory performances in Italy highlighting the cooperation of Allied Forces. Some of these bands were sponsored by the YMCA, others by Italian government officials.[28] From 1918 until the spring of 1921 (when the final American troops went home), the YMCA maintained a series of relief centers in Rome, Venice, Genoa and Trieste that served the "sailors and marines from the Adriatic fleet" who remained in Italy "through the Fiume controversy."[29] These military personnel were drawn especially to Rome, where in addition to motorbus tours of the city's ancient monuments, they were treated to an array of musical entertainment. Vittorio

Spina, who later became a well-known Italian jazz guitarist, witnessed the arrival of these soldiers as a young boy. In a 1960 interview he looked back fondly on his first encounters with American jazz:

In Rome, the American troops had arrived, and these soldiers had formed an orchestra that rehearsed at the YMCA on via Francesco Crispi. The head of the orchestra was a sergeant named Griffith, who later married a girl from Rome.[30] In fact, I lived right behind there, and I always went to hear them play. In the orchestra there was an American soldier who played banjo. I wasn't familiar with the instrument, so I started to do a little investigation of those four strings. I thought to myself: "How is it tuned? If it's tuned like a guitar, then it would be easy to play," I told myself, since I already knew how to play [the guitar]. But I just couldn't figure it out. At a certain point I thought, "it's tuned the way it's tuned." I was a kid, a smart aleck. I went up to [the banjo player] and said: "You know, I also play banjo. Will you let me try it?" The bandleader said to let me try and asked me what tune I knew how to play. Since I had a good ear, I said right away: "That first one," and started to play, but nothing recognizable came out. At the end they asked me to play something I knew, and then things began to go better. This is how I entered into friendship [with them].[31]

The Americans in Rome offered Spina more than just friendship. The Spanish flu was ravaging Italy at this time. Food was scarce, and many families, like Spina's, found themselves in difficult circumstances.

They gave me chocolate, cigarettes; in short, they revived me a little! Meals were often skipped at my house. My father had recently died, and there was no money. In short, these Americans were my salvation, because a few days later they came to find me and invited me to work for them: to pick up the mail, do little odd jobs … And then, there was the orchestra, and I was always there listening, trying to figure out how to play the banjo.[32]

Photos from the period confirm Spina's story. One shows him sitting in a crowded hall, waiting for a concert to begin. The audience is mixed: Italian officials, American military, well-dressed young women. Italian and American flags hang along the back wall. Spina is sitting on the lap of an American soldier and grinning from ear to ear.[33] A second photo shows Spina, a bit older, playing mandolin while an American sailor (perhaps Sergeant Griffith) provides accompaniment at the piano (Figure 2.1). As Spina explains, he was eventually given a position in the band:

One fine day the banjo player was transferred, and Sergeant Griffith asked me if I wanted to play with them. Imagine that! They brought me my own instrument, and two times a week I played with the American orchestra, for dances at the Sala Pichetti on via del Bufalo. It was a real big orchestra: trumpets, trombones,

Figure 2.1 Vittorio Spina (mandolin) with American soldier, perhaps Sgt. Griffith (piano) in Rome, ca. 1918.
Source: Photographic archive of Adriano Mazzoletti.

saxophones; and they played all the pieces that were in vogue at that time: "Havana," "Ka-Lou-A" [*sic*], "Indianola," "Original Fox Trot." There was no talk of improvisation; it was all written stuff, American pieces that Griffith had transcribed.[34]

Enrico Pichetti, the owner of the hall rented by the YMCA during this period, included a description of these performances in his memoire *Mezzo secolo di danze* (Half a Century of Dance):

During the war, this form of entertainment needed by the young people that fought on the battlefield was offered in full form to the Americans. The YMCA rented the Hall three times a week to host dances for the Americans passing through Rome and those that belonged to the association. They played [the music] themselves and brought their own jazz-band instruments, from which they created furious rhythms and cadences, drawing out what seemed like discordant sounds and wild pitches, accompanied by singing. After a while, however, our ears became accustomed [to the music] and we realized that the syncopated beat added an overwhelming eagerness to the dance ... I wasn't stupid. When I heard their jazz band I realized that, justifiably, our music and our instruments could not satisfy them. Whenever the sailors of the Navy, who were anchored in Naples and Citavecchia, came to Rome, they flocked to my Hall, which was always crowded.[35]

Jazz drew more than just Americans. Pichetti's club quickly became a popular venue for Italians too. But as Spina explained, not everyone was welcome: "only someone with an invitation could enter: nobles, aristocrats, everyone from the upper class."[36] This is an important point: from the beginning, jazz was embraced by the Italians as an elite, modernist art form. It is worth remembering that the first US military jazz musicians to arrive in Italy did so aboard a luxurious ocean liner. In the early 1920s, jazz became a symbol of affluence among most young Italians, and as the music's popularity grew, exclusive nightclubs appeared in the upscale neighborhoods of large Italian cities. New dance schools sprouted like weeds across the urban landscape, promising step-by-step upward mobility for eager, aspiring socialites. Jazz was for the wealthy, and for those who aspired to be wealthy. Recognizing the profits to be made, Italian entrepreneurs began to invest heavily in jazz after the war, so much so that by 1924 a wide variety of venues geared towards the country's affluent and aristocratic youth could be found in Rome and all major cities north (Milan, Turin, Florence, Genoa, Venice, among others).

One of the most famous nightclub impresarios during these early years was Arturo Agazzi, known professionally as Mirador. Born and raised in Milan, Mirador moved to London in 1913, where he found work managing musical performances for private parties and small clubs before landing a job as manager of Ciro's, one of London's most prestigious clubs. This was where he first encountered American popular music. As soon as the armistice was announced in 1918, Mirador returned to Milan, where he set up his own club, aptly named Mirador's, which hosted Mirador's Syncopated Orchestra, the first native jazz band in Italy. Although Mirador was not a professional musician himself, his talent as an impresario led to the creation of an efficient nightclub circuit, which facilitated the employment of countless jazz musicians, both Italian and foreign, who toured in small combos from one venue to the next in all the major cities north of Rome.[37]

Southern Italy did not take to jazz in the early years, which is ironic, given the fact that the family of Nick LaRocca, the Italian American first credited with commercializing jazz, came from Sicily.[38] There are myriad social and cultural reasons why cities like Naples and Palermo were left out of the jazz circuit, as we shall see in later chapters. For the moment, it is enough to say that the region's poverty, high illiteracy rate and strong ties to provincial traditions cut it off from many of the cultural and technological innovations associated with jazz. Of course, there were some southern Italians, like the Neapolitan Futurist Francesco Cangiullo, whose variations on Marinetti's *parole in libertà* explored popular entertainment, including jazz, and the noise of urban life. But like other southern Italians, Cangiullo had to venture north to participate in modern Italian culture. Simply put, Italy's jazz awakening was regional, not national. Jazz was a phenomenon limited to the industrial north.

So far, I have discussed the presence of jazz in Italy as a predominantly "white" phenomenon. Although it is true that Italian listeners first experienced live jazz as the commercialized form of dance music performed by white military units, it would be mistaken to assume that Italians were unaware of the music's African American roots. When Bruno Zuculin published his article on "American Dances and Music" (discussed in the previous chapter), he was responding to Italy's growing fascination with the music being supplied by groups sponsored by the USAAS and YMCA. Jazz was not the first American genre to reach Italian audiences, but it was definitely the most influential, and Italians were curious about the links between the newest imported dances – the fox-trot and one-step – and earlier African American dances like the cakewalk, which had made a fleeting appearance in Italy before the war.[39] Not surprisingly, it was the Futurists who first discussed the African American art forms that fueled the birth of jazz in the United States and informed its reception in France.

The Futurists and Jazz in Italy

Marinetti and his colleagues viewed jazz and its associated activities – dance, fashion, cocktails and improvisation – as effective tools for Futurism, the movement designed to foster the political and artistic revival of Italy in the modern age. Recognizing that they lived in a world defined by technological progress, the Futurists strove to bring art closer to the new sensibility of modern life. As one scholar has noted: "They hailed the thrill of speed and wondered how human beings could embody the excitement they found in machines."[40] The Futurists were the first in Italy to adopt the aesthetic of "primitivism" and its links with African American culture. They eagerly embraced the beauty of primitivism as described by their avant-garde colleagues in France, and they looked to dances like the cakewalk as ideal sources for the development of a primitive aesthetic.

In their numerous treatises, the Futurists hailed the rejuvenating powers of primitivism and modernism, often linking their aesthetic qualities in effective and compelling ways. For example, in 1910 Umberto Boccioni wrote: "Our time initiates a new era naming us the primitives of a new, completely transformed sensibility."[41] He declared himself and his fellow Futurists as the "first people" committed to discovering "a totally new reality, a reality of the machine age, where industrial development, the expansion of big cities, and mass production" reflect "the spirit of modern times."[42] It is important to focus on Boccioni's understanding of the term "primitives," which at the time evoked a connotation different from how we might understand the term today. Boccioni and other Futurist artists embraced the label "primitive" as a positive attribute. To be a contemporary artist practicing "primitivism" meant that one appropriated into one's own modern art the ideas and characteristics of so-called primitive and exotic cultures of the past. Thus the jazz musician, like the Futurist painter, was simultaneously a primitive and a modernist. Both took the characteristics of earlier African American art forms and transformed them into a mechanized and modernist aesthetic. To borrow the language of John J. White, when the Italian Futurists embraced primitivism, they looked to American culture as a model. Theirs was "a modernist primitivism," which was not "backward-looking" but rather seeking "to create a new sensibility appropriate to its own culture, especially those elements of the modern world" that pointed "towards the future."[43]

Boccioni used the metaphor of the primitives as a way to link the world of contemporary American culture to his vision of a possible future for Italy. He defined the modern city as an "industrial jungle" full of machines. In his treatise *Pitture e scultura futurista* (1914) he depicted this "techno jungle" as full of "café-chantant, gramophone, cinema, neon signs, mechanistic architecture, skyscrapers [...] nightlife [...] speed, automobiles and airplanes."[44] In short, the Futurist concept of the urban, mechanistic landscape of the modern age was firmly grounded in the popular culture and technological advances of the United States. The "new and completely transformed sensibility" of the Futurist, as Boccioni described it, looked to the urban environment that cultivated and disseminated early jazz. As Przemysław Strozek describes it, "the rhythm of life and of new forms of popular culture were encompassed in the rhythm of an operating machine." This, above all else, was "the Futurist experience" of primitivism in "the industrial age."[45] More importantly, this was also what motivated the Futurists to embrace early on African American dance styles like the cakewalk, and later musical genres like ragtime and, eventually, jazz. "It is this passionate love of Reality," Boccioni wrote in 1914, "that makes us prefer an American cakewalk dancer to hearing the Valkyrie, that makes us prefer the events of a day caught on film to a classic tragedy."[46] As Boccioni explained, it was technology and its relation to contemporary popular music, above all else, that had the power to capture the modern Italian aesthetic:

The gramophone, for example … is according to us a magnificent natural element for bringing to life psychological realities. We enjoy it when its beautifully lucid metal trumpet sounds and blows in a nasal tone a little mechanized song that always extends beyond the musical art of the philistines' modest salon.[47]

One cannot help but wonder if Boccioni was being wholly sincere when he wrote these words. Did he truly embrace African American dance and its related music, or was he simply trying to shock partisans of traditional European culture? Either way, the outcome was the same: the cakewalk had captured the Futurist imagination. As Marinetti noted in *Il manifesto della danza futurista* (1917):

We Futurists prefer Loïe Fuller and the cakewalk of the Negroes ([for their] utilization of electronic light and mechanical movements). One must go beyond the current muscular possibilities in dance and aim for the ideal of the multi-part body of the motor, which we have so long dreamed about. Our gestures must imitate the movements of machines, assiduously paying homage to steering wheels, tires, pistons, and so preparing for the fusion of man with the machine, achieving the metallization of Futurist dance.[48]

This early fascination with the cakewalk, as shown in the writings of Boccioni and Marinetti, was likely sparked by their exposure to contemporary film. Although the origins of the cakewalk in the United States date back to the mid-nineteenth century, the dance did not make its mark on European popular culture until 1902, when it was performed in Paris by the Nouveau Cirque as part of a pantomime called *Les Joyeux Nègres*. This performance started a French craze, which was soon captured in films distributed across Europe. During the early decades of the twentieth century, film served as a powerful medium for lending meaning to various types of cultural phenomena. As Matthew Jordan has noted: "Several early filmmakers noticed how well film conveyed rhythm, and they turned to dance and the new rhythms of the Cake-Walk as subject matter for their short films."[49] It was likely through films such as these that the Italian Futurists first experienced the cakewalk. In 1903, several French films featuring the dance were screened in Milan and Rome; these included *Le Célèbre Cake-Walk per Elks* and *Dwarf's Cake-Walk* produced by Pathé Films, *Le Cake-Walk* released by Alfred Lubin, and most notably George Méliès *Le Cake-Walk infernal*, which presented a strangely captivating interpretation of the dance.[50]

In this rendition, the cakewalk undergoes a cultural transformation during a performance in Hades, under the watchful eye of Pluto (played by Méliès himself). The film is just over five minutes long, and as Méliès's plot summary reveals, his primary goal was to introduce viewers to the frenetic rhythms of dance and reveal its obliterating effect on traditional European culture:

> Pluto, having seen the world [above], comes back home amazed by the success of that popular dance, the Cake-Walk. He has brought back with him two well-known [African American] dancers, who begin to perform their favorite dance amidst the flames. A strange and ugly creature attempts to join in the dance, but his limbs break away and dance off on their own, far away from him. All the inhabitants of His Majesty's underground realm are seized with the irresistible mania for dancing and start performing an unbridled folk dance. When Satan sees this, he conjures up an enormous blaze, which annihilates everything around him. He then disappears among the flames.[51]

The visual effects of this short film are mesmerizing, especially when one considers the technical limitations of the time, and it was modern imagery such as this that led Marinetti to proclaim "the cakewalk of the Negroes" to be an art form similar in its innovative effects to the dances of Loïe Fuller. Fuller was not African American, but she was often paired with them in European descriptions of avant-garde dance, due to her captivating use on stage and screen of newly patented, multicolored lights and flowing, voluminous silk costumes. The films of both Fuller and various cakewalk dancers offered early-twentieth-century viewers a technological blending of light and frenetic movement, body and machine, that for Marinetti represented a clear embodiment of the modern age via art. Equally appealing must have been the implied message of Méliès's *Le Cake-Walk infernal*: Modern art requires an annihilation of the past. With his primitivist cakewalk, Méliès's Satan ignites the purifying inferno.

For the Futurists, film served as an important, although ultimately misguided, entry into African American culture. Through film, they found a persuasive blend of primitivism and modern technology that defined African American dance as a visually rhythmic phenomenon. That being said, it is important to remember that the Futurists' first impressions of the cakewalk were limited to the purely visual, and that their exposure to jazz as a sonic experience did not occur until later, when American troops reached Italian shores. Of course, ragtime music and dances like the foxtrot were not completely unknown before the war. There were a few dance instructors in Rome and Turin who posted notices in local newspapers offering lessons in "one-step, two-step and rac-time" [*sic*] as early as 1915.[52] In fact, the first documented Italian bandleader who tried to make a name for himself playing American dance music was Umberto Bozza. Today, Bozza is best known as Benito Mussolini's violin teacher – more about that in Chapter 3 – but long before he encountered his infamous student, Bozza served as one of the most respected performers of light, café music in Rome, where his performances of the fox-trot at the Apollo Club met with little resistance. Mixed among his repertoire of waltzes, polkas and mazurkas, the fox-trot entered his repertoire in 1915 and was embraced immediately as a civilized, energetic dance. I mention this because the lack of criticism early on was in stark contrast to the reception of another "New World" dance, the tango, which Bozza had attempted to incorporate into his repertoire a few years earlier. Whereas Italians originally embraced the fox-trot as a modern, "white" commercialized dance that had evolved from the "primitivism" of African American dances like the cakewalk, the tango, which arrived in Italy just prior to the war, was roundly criticized for its barbarity and overt sensuality. Pope Pius X publicly questioned the embrace of the tango by Italian youth, asking: "Why don't they dance the Furlana [a fast-paced North Italian folk dance in duple 6/8 meter], which is so much more beautiful?" The Archbishop of Ferrara's response was not as diplomatic. On January 24, 1914 he publically condemned the tango as "a manifestly obscene form of entertainment," which he described as being both "barbaric and detestable."[53]

Thanks to the arrival of American troops, dances like the fox-trot, one-step and two-step continued to fare well in Italian popular culture. As the extreme hardship of the immediate postwar period subsided and the economic life of Italy's major cities returned to normal, the nation's leisure activities experienced something of a revolution. As noted earlier, enthusiasm for all things American fueled the establishment of numerous Italian nightclubs during the early 1920s. Not surprisingly, the Futurists were involved.

The Rise of the Italian Nightclubs

Within the space of two years, four nightclubs designed and run by prominent Futurists opened in Rome: the Bal Tic Tac, the Gallina a Tre Zampe (The Hen on Three Feet), the Cabaret degli Independenti (Cabaret of the Independents) and the Cabaret del Diavolo (Devil's Cabaret). Giacomo Balla was the first Futurist to jump on board. His Bal Tic Tac began serving patrons in 1921, and as the bandleader Ugo Filippini noted, the club's jazz ensemble offered listeners something new:

The orchestra [at the Bal Tic Tac] was made up of two violins: me and [Pietro] Leonardi, who had been playing with the orchestra of Umberto Bozza. On banjo was Alfredo Gangi ... he had also cut his teeth with Bozza. On piano [Antonio] Jannone from Naples, and on drums Lorenzetti. To these was soon added a tenor saxophone. I got him from a [marching] band sponsored by the local police. This instrument also caused quite a sensation. It was the first time that one encountered a saxophone in a Roman nightclub.[54]

The underground location of the Bal Tic Tac also offered patrons a new experience, as Filippini explained:

The locale where we performed ... was not at street level. To enter one had to descend a staircase. There was a long corridor, enormous, then a large room. At the end of the corridor there hung an electric sign that said: "If you don't drink champagne, go away!"[55]

As to the music, the primary activity was dancing. Filippini continues:

The young aristocrats ... came to dance and dance. It was madness! The early American dances, the fox-trot, the one-step, the shimmy ... Ladies retained by older aristocrats, Luigi Medici del Vascello and others, spent the whole night dancing. They danced three, four hours straight. And they paid ten times the cost for a bottle of champagne ... and so we went down there to play. I remember the good tips that came. Yes indeed, one surely made good tips![56]

The Bal Tic Tac quickly became the place to be, and as a reporter noted a few weeks after the opening, the club's interior overwhelmed the senses almost as much as the music:

The hall's decoration is a triumph of skillful imagination, and the Futurist painter Balla is its ingenious creator. The very walls seem to dance: the great architectural lines appear to interpenetrate each other with their clear tonalities of light and dark blue. They create a luminosity that looks like a carnival in the sky ... Red, white and blue pillars exude the *bonhomie* of a convivial Bastille Day. The spiral staircase presents a joyful harmony of red and yellow, making it as appealing as a cheerful Hell. This inventiveness, together with the atmosphere of spontaneous joy that is totally suitable for the location, creates a perfect harmony out of the whole. It introduces a truly new character to avant-garde art, which previously irritated so many unsympathetic eyes with its clashing chords.[57]

An overview of the entertainment sections of local newspapers from this period reveals that performances at the Bal Tic Tac quickly set the tone

for other Roman nightclubs. By 1922, the spectrum of entertainment possibilities ranged from "Arabian belly dancing to Spanish flamenco, from
a *Patriotic Cotillon* to a *Grand 'Surprise' Show*, from a *Tea Dance* to the
Sound of the Jazz-Band."[58] And as one reporter noted, at the Bal Tic Tac,
one found "ladies in *décolleté* and gents in tails rubbing shoulders with the
sober blackshirts of the Fascists and the blue uniforms of the Nationalists."[59]

This reference to the Fascists and Nationalists is telling, for the rise of
jazz and the rise of Mussolini, though disconnected at first, happened
simultaneously. To give a quick overview: After being wounded in the war,
Mussolini moved to Milan, where he served as editor of his own newspaper, *Il Popolo d'Italia*. As a wartime editor, Mussolini no doubt encountered
notices about the new jazz clubs run by Mirador in Milan and the Futurists
in Rome. He also learned a great deal about the power of propaganda in
gaining the support of the masses. Mussolini ran for, and lost, a seat in
the Chamber of Deputies during the 1919 elections, but this did not deter
his efforts to strengthen the power of the Fascists. A turning point came
in December 1920 when D'Annunzio and his followers were driven from
Fiume, and the Italian nationalists turned to Mussolini as their new leader.
Championing economic liberalism and an improvement in the conditions
of workers, Mussolini formed the National Fascist Party (PNF) in 1921,
and finances began to pour in from industrialists, both Italian and foreign.
Membership in the PNF grew quickly, from 20,000 in 1920 to 300,000 in
1922. After much political turmoil, King Victor Emmanuel III granted
Mussolini control of the government on October 29, 1922, after 30,000
of Mussolini's supporters made their symbolic "March on Rome." As the
new Prime Minister of Italy, Mussolini formed a coalition government of
Fascists, Nationalists, Catholics and right-wing Liberals. Notably younger
than the politicians who preceded them, these "blackshirt Fascists and blue
uniformed Nationalists" proclaimed the promise of a modern, energetic
Italy – a state of being that seemed to come alive all at once in new nightclubs like the Bal Tic Tac.

The theme of the show at Balla's Bal Tic Tac changed every week, but this
appeared to have little effect on the "immense audience" that streamed in
night after night. As one reporter noted, by 1922, "the beautiful and characteristic venue" in the center of Rome had become "the preferred nightclub
of the better public, who find here every convenience and enjoy the comfort
of an elegant, fresh ambience."[60]

The success of Balla's club spurred other Futurists to follow suit. In
1922 Anton Giulio Bragaglia opened the Gallina a Tre Zampe and the
Cabaret degli Independenti, while Fortunato Depero founded the Cabaret

del Diavolo, which was laid out on three floors in imitation of Dante's *Divine Comedy*: "Paradise" on the top floor, "Purgatory" a level below, and "Hell" at the very bottom. These clubs became the favorite locales of Rome's avant-garde artistic community, and among the wide array of entertainment, which included theater, pantomime, dance, poetry readings, and so on, one found American jazz in its early guises (ragtime and Dixieland) mixed with the experimental "noise music" more commonly associated with Futurism. The general mood and atmosphere of the various Futurist clubs varied. Whereas Bal Tic Tac catered to a broad clientele with a popular, variety-style program, Bragaglia focused a bit more on avant-garde performances. Depero's club was the most exclusive. Resembling more a dining club than an American-style nightclub, it served as a meeting place for Rome's intellectual elite.[61] A review of a party hosted by Depero in his Casa d'Arte in Roverino in January 1923 gives us a sense of what his jazz-infused performances entailed. It begins with a description of the club's interior:

In the salon reserved for women, huge orange lampshades diffused an intense light. Dyed the same color were the scarlet wisteria [patterns] on the extremely original cabaret furniture from Rome.[62]

We then discover that the evening's activities had been meticulously orchestrated. Through a series of signals played by the orchestra, guests were told when to dance and when to sit quietly. A full cast of assistants had been employed to manage the events, and these "young friends of Depero, striped in red, bustled to and fro through the halls in a friendly, diligent manner."[63] After two sets of dance music, the evening's central spectacle began:

A young man with a trumpet passed through the halls and announced repeatedly: "Directly from Peking – Depero!" Meanwhile, another nice fellow striped in red and sitting at the drums, announced, with the help of a bell, the proximity of the train while other young Futurists bustled into the great hall yelling: Clear the track! Clear the track! Then the giant black machines arrived, puffing and whistling, heralded by a cannon shot. After a tour around the hall … with musical comments from piano and drums … they departed with the same serious rhythm, sustained and solemn, with which they had entered, saluted by intense and vigorous applause.[64]

But this was not the end of the evening: "Shortly thereafter, by now it was quite late, the same Depero re-entered, again from China, this time seated in a little yellow carriage." He pretended to read articles from a Chinese newspaper, much to the chagrin of his guests. And when it appeared the evening had begun to fizzle to a close, Depero presented his final delight:

The orchestra began to play again, but it was no longer the one from before. In fact, no one had suspected that Depero's young Futurist friends knew how to play. They prepared a surprise for us: the "Jazz-Band!" With great expansion of the drums (woodblock, gong, cymbals, castanets, drum, xylophone, whistles, triangles, milk bottles, etc.) and diminution of the strings, they played a rhythm of incalculable joy with a nonchalant precision that gave the party the ultimate finishing touch and defined the magical environment to perfection.[65]

This glowing description, which appeared in the Socialist newspaper *Il Popolo*, says much about the importance of jazz to the Futurists. As in all their performance art, they saw in this music a mechanized energy – luxurious and free from tradition – that explored a modernist aesthetic through spectacle, surprise and most importantly improvisation. The Futurists didn't simply host jazz performances, they evoked the essence of the music in countless other genres: paintings, poems, short stories, theater works and essays. In addition to supplying interiors for Italy's newest night-clubs, Futurist artists illustrated the sheet-music covers of jazz-inspired compositions (For example, Nino Formoso's *Ti-ta-tò. One Step*, 1918; Otto Weber's *Futurismo Foxtrot*, 1921; Virgilio Mortari's *Fox Trot del Teatro della Sorpresa*, 1921) and captured the "noise" of jazz in onomatopoeic texts, as heard in Ivan Jablowsky's "Jazz-tazzine-tazúm" (1923); Diavolo Mari's "Jazz Band" (1925); "Sensualità meccanica" (1926) by Fillia (Luigi Colombo); Vladimiro Miletti's "Jazz-impressioni" (1933); and "Newyorkcocktail" (1933) by Farfa (Vittorio Osvaldo Tommasini), to name just a few.[66] Futurist composers became equally enamored of jazz. In 1920, Alfredo Casella com-posed "Fox-Trot for Four Hands Piano" that he published in 1922 with a dedication to the French music pedagogue, Marthe Morhange. Similarly, his "Cinque Pezzi, Op. 34 for String Quartet" features a fox-trot. Casella also referred to jazz in his critical writings from this period. In 1921, he noted his recent discovery of several American gramophone discs, which introduced him to extraordinary performances by black jazz musicians:

Recently, I've had the opportunity to hear from abroad certain extraordinary American gramophone discs, in which one can hear some fantastic Negro jazz musicians improvise in an improbable way around the modest texture of certain fox-trots. And I thought, upon hearing such sumptuous rhythmic polyphony adapted to several well-known dances from the wonderful inventive genius of those performers, that one could indeed draw from a simple fox-trot a polyrhythmic, polyphonic monument that holds a candle to any Bach fugue.[67]

Where did Casella come across such recordings? Most likely the American Academy in Rome (AAR). Founded in 1894, AAR began offering prizes in music composition in 1921, and in its early years, Casella served as an important advisor to the fledgling music program. Leo Sowerby, a composer from the Midwest, who had studied in Chicago, was the first Rome Prize Fellow in musical composition. As Carl Engel noted in *The Atlantic Monthly* in August 1922, Sowerby had been "guilty of sounding the jazz note in his chamber music and in a piano concerto." Convinced that it offered "a more comprehensive expression of the *modern* American spirit," Sowerby no doubt picked up his abiding interest in jazz during his stint as a bandleader in France during World War I.[68] One can imagine that Sowerby might have brought some of his favorite gramophone discs with him when he moved to Rome. Perhaps he was the one who first exposed Casella to the wonders of American jazz. A perusal of the AAR Archives from this period reveals that Casella was the primary member of the institution's "Musical Circle" – a group of local Italian composers and musicians invited to participate in AAR events in order to expose American composers to Roman musical life. As the First Professor in Charge of the AAR Music Program, Felix Lamond later noted in a report on the Music Program's inaugural years, the participation of Italians like Casella in AAR activities was especially important since "the eager working out of theories of these modern composers was very instructive to our fellows; it was a lesson in what to imitate and what to avoid."[69]

In 1922, Casella's AAR contacts facilitated for him a trip to the United States, where he participated in a series of music concerts sponsored by Elizabeth Sprague Coolidge and sought out live performances of jazz. He reflected on the latter experience in articles published in both Italian and English shortly after his return to Italy:

Among all the sonorous impressions that a musician may have experienced in the United States, that which dominates every other by its originality, its force of novelty and even of modernism, its stupendous dowry of dynamics and of propulsive energy, is, without doubt, the Negro music called jazz.[70]

Casella attempted to define in his writing, although with some difficulty, what made jazz such an exceptional font of inspiration for modernist composers: "To explain what jazz is, is impossible with an ordinary vocabulary," he noted, because it is "an art made solely of continuous improvisations, of incessant rhythmic force, of constant energetic mobility."[71] Casella noted that the "occasional decadent examples of jazz," which he had encountered "here and there in Europe," did not give "even faintly, an idea of that most curious music." Although Casella continually defined American jazz as "Negro" music, he curiously offered the performances of a white Jewish musician, Ted Lewis,[72] as the epitome of the new modernist sound:

Hear, for example, the jazz of Ted Lewis ... If this instrumental technic is unusual and bewildering, not less so are the aesthetic values revealed through it. Art that is – art composed, first of all, of rhythm; of a brutal rhythm often; of a rhythm of other times sweet and lascivious; but always rhythm of a barbaric effectiveness which would raise the dead; rhythm, which, on account of its persistency, its tremendous motive force brings to mind not rarely, the more heroic pages of Beethoven or of Stravinsky.[73]

Casella's embrace of jazz's heroic, modernist qualities was not unique. Futurist composers like Franco Casavola wrote similar descriptions of the new music. For example, in his manifesto *La musica futurista* (1924), he described jazz as a fresh step forward for Italian Futurist composers:

The Jazz Band today represents the practical actualization, although incomplete, of our principles: the individuality of its instruments' singing brings together, for the first time, sonic elements of different character. And the bold and necessary persistence of its rhythms forms the basis of Futurist music.[74]

Casavola also praised jazz as a Futurist art form in his "Difesa del Jazz Band," published in *L'Impero* in 1926.

The Jazz Band is the typical product of our generation: heroic, violent, arrogant, brutal, optimistic, anti-romantic, unsentimental and ungraceful. Born of wars and revolutions. Deny it and you deny us![75]

Casavola claimed that "the principle features of jazz," which included "the obstinate rhythm, the tendency towards improvisation, the extravagant formation of the orchestra" and "the search for new and unusual sounds" belonged to "the folk heritage of all nations in general and Italy in particular." He even went so far as to declare: "To us Futurists it is given to foresee the early developments [of jazz] and then dictate the first laws."[76]

Casavola's earliest compositions making reference to his new aesthetic included: "Ranocchi al Chiaro di Luna" (Frogs in the Moonlight) on a text by A. G. Bragaglia and "La Danza delle Scimmie" (Dance of the Monkeys) from the ballet *Hop Frog* for the Teatro della Sorpresa, a touring, Futurist theatrical troupe. He also composed a tango for his Futurist ballet *Cabaret epileptic* (Epileptic Cabaret), an early advertising jingle "Campari" and the *Fox-Trot Zoologico*, all with popular influences.

The Italian fascination with jazz was not lost on foreign observers. Various European critics commented on the Futurists' connection to the music, although not always in the most positive light. For example, in 1921, the British journalist Clive Bell wrote:

The great modern painters – Derain, Matisse, Picasso, Bonnard, Friesz, Braque and so on – were firmly settled on their own lines of development before ever Jazz was heard of. Only the riff-raff has been affected. Italian Futurism is the nearest approach to a pictorial expression of the Jazz Spirit.[77]

And looking back in 1927, Piet Mondrian noted in an essay titled "Jazz and the Neo-Plastic:" "Many movements have … set out to abolish form and create a freer rhythm. In art, Futurism gave the major impulse."[78]

Of course, not everyone embraced the Futurists' avant-garde spectacles. A few articles denigrating jazz for its "primitive" origins and "immoral" tendencies appeared in the Italian press between 1919 and 1922, but they were few in number compared to those articles promoting jazz and the exciting, modernistic atmosphere it had engendered.[79] In fact, the only Italian contingency that appears to have had a consistent problem with jazz in the early years was the Catholic Church, whose representatives spoke out not so much against the music, but against the dances and scandalous ladies' fashions associated with them. In an article titled "Ballo, digiuno e astinenza" (Dance,Fasting and Abstinence) published in 1920, a reporter for *Corriere della Sera* drew attention to what local church leaders were saying about the behavior of young women during the season of Lent:

A respected archbishop, whose opinions appear in the latest issue of *Journal Diocesan*, has noted, among other things, the evil and danger facilitated by certain amusements, such as the dances currently being performed in theaters and other public and private places, which go beyond the limits of honesty and modesty. The Cardinal Archbishop speaks especially to Christian women, reminding them of Christ's word and … warning them that they should not consider lawful, the youthful entertainment that includes the forms of immorality found in some modern dances. Nor should they seek to excuse the pretext of all shame and scandal through charitable receipts.[80]

But warnings such as these were no deterrent to the spread of jazz in Italy. As the playwright Massimo Bontempelli noted in an essay titled "Roma sotterranea," by 1924 the proliferation of nightclubs featuring jazz and cocktails had insured that archeologists were no longer the only ones interested in underground Rome: "We, who feel as different as possible from the archeologist, have descended underground to find the most ultra-modern Rome" – i.e. the numerous nightclubs that now occupied the basements of Rome's finest theaters and hotels. Bontempelli's essay offered evocative descriptions of the modernist delights to be found in these underground locales: the music (mostly jazz), cocktails, dancing and fashion. In addition to the Futurist clubs, he described the Le Grotte dell'Augusteo (The Caves of the Augusteo [Theater]), La Falena (The Moth), and other "minor dens" like The Cozy Cottage. By the mid-1920s, numerous nightspots had taken root across central and northern Italy, and all of them featured jazz. There was the Tim Tum Bal, La Sala Umberto, La Bombonnière, L'Apollo, Il Salone Margherita and Ruel e Calore in Rome; Mirador's, the Ambassador's Club, Sporting Club del Casinò, Il Trianon, Dancing Monte Merlo, Sala Volta and Sala Orfeo in Milan; Rajola in Florence; Belloni, L'Olimpia, Verdi and Giardino d'Italia in Genoa; and Lo Stabilmento Romano, Clubbino, Sala Gay and Cinema Ambrosio in Turin, to name the most popular ones. And with each new club came the need for new bands, which quickly led to a seismic shift in Italy's music culture.

The most famous bands in the early years were Mirador's Syncopated Orchestra, Ambassador's Jazz Band, the Black and White Jazz Band, the Imperial Jazz Band and the Orchestra Di Piramo. The director of this last ensemble, Armando Di Piramo, began his career as concertmaster in the Orchestra of the Monte Carlo Opera, and his talent as a classical violinist can be heard on a pair of recordings made with Nicola Moleti (piano) in Paris for Pathé.[81] But upon his return to Italy in the early 1920s, Di Piramo chose the dance hall over the opera house and became a driving force in Genoa's burgeoning music culture, often connecting with musicians who worked on the luxury steam ships that crossed the Atlantic. Di Piramo was one of the first bandleaders in Genoa to organize dance bands specializing in the new music being imported from the United States.[82] Even more importantly, he was one of the first to record these dances in Italy, initially with the Orchestra Del Cova in 1924, then later as the Orchestra Di Piramo. At first, Italian recording companies, like La Fonotecnica (a label primarily known for recording opera singers), were wary of recording American dance music, believing that the listenership would be limited at best. But Di Piramo soon convinced them otherwise, explaining that his ensemble's prominent use of violins and focus on melody over rhythmic diversity would attract a broad commercial audience. A specifically Italian trait that could be traced back to Umberto Bozza, the jazz violin had only just been introduced in the United States by Joe Venuti. In the years to come, Venuti would serve as an important link between the developing swing traditions in the United States and Italy.

During the 1920s, there was little stability in the personnel playing in Italian ensembles. Bands formed, broke up, then formed again with new musicians. The demand for jazz raised the "value" of the musicians who could play it. Fees were high, and jazz offered many musicians the chance for social advancement. For example, in Turin, Cinico Angelini's Jazz Band Le Perroquet found themselves in a position most American performers would have envied. As Angelini himself explained: "It was during this period [ca. 1923] when [our] orchestra became the favorite of Prince Umberto of Savoy, who often called on us to play at the dances that were given at the Royal Palace."[83] With opportunities such as these, it is easy to understand why so many conservatory-trained musicians abandoned Italy's opera houses and concert halls for the chance to play jazz.

One of the most well-known musicians to follow this path was Amedeo Escobar, who resigned from his position with the Teatro dell'Opera in Rome after hearing a trio of American musicians – Mons Smith, piano; Eddie Solloway, violin; and a drummer named Harry – at the Hotel Excelsior in Rome.

The absolutely new and electrifying music played by this trio convinced me to give up classical music – I was a cellist – for syncopated music. I had never heard anything like it, and I was shocked.[84]

Escobar took up jazz piano and eventually joined the Black and White Jazz Band, organized by Filippini in 1922. Over the next few years, he established his reputation as a formidable jazz performer "with a ferocious memory," who "composed several hundred fox-trots."[85] He was the first in Italy to compose works for the standard jazz band configuration (piano, drums, saxophones, trumpets, trombones and bass), and during the 1930s and 40s he enjoyed even greater success as a composer of film scores. As Filippini recalls, Escobar's talent was augmented by his close connections with powerful figures in Italy's new political network, most notably Giacomo Acerbo, Baron of Aterno.[86] A Mussolini ally elected to the Italian Chamber of Deputies in 1921, Acerbo served as a link between the Fascists and King Victor Emmanuel III during the March on Rome in 1922. When Mussolini became Prime Minister, he appointed Acerbo his trusted undersecretary.

Another important Escobar connection, albeit from a different realm of society, was his friendship with Giacomo Puccini. According to Escobar, he first came in contact with the famous opera composer during a tour to Viareggio with the Imperial Jazz Band in 1924:

Every evening, while we played, Giacomo Puccini sat next to me. And he was always very interested in what I was doing. He would say to me: "What was that trick he just did on the trumpet? Will you write it down for me? That ending that the banjo just played, will you note it down on the staff?" Just like that, he took all these little pieces of paper, put them in his pocket and took them home. Sometimes I accompanied him, and we talked a lot. He told me that he wanted to compose a lyric opera using certain musical ideas that he had heard while listening to us play. He was very passionate [about it all]. There was one tune in our repertoire that he especially liked – it was called "Dumbell" – that I had transcribed from a disc by Zez Confrey.[87]

The Confrey tune mentioned here was first recorded for Victor in New York on December 26, 1922.[88] One year later it was repackaged with a Paul Whiteman tune, "Mr. Gallagher and Mr. Shean," and released in England by HMV, who then rereleased it in Italy under the Grammofono label.[89] All this is to say that, through the wonders of technology, Italian performers interested in jazz had easy access to recordings being made in the United States and released to an international market.

After Viareggio, Escobar and the Imperial Jazz Band traveled on to Florence, where they had an engagement at the Rajola. While in Florence, the Italians encountered Harl Smith's Lido-Venice Dance Orchestra, an American band that had been brought over by the nightclub's owner, Arturo Rajola. For several nights, the two bands played together, side by side – no doubt an eye-opening experience for both ensembles. For the Italians, hearing the improvised solos performed live by the Americans offered greater insight than any recordings had about how the music could change and evolve, organically, with each performance. For the Americans, there was surprise over how effectively the Italians had appropriated their music.[90]

The best-known figures from this first generation of Italian jazz musicians enjoyed a musical education markedly different from many Americans. With only a few notable exceptions, Vittorio Spina being one of them, the first Italian jazzmen received years of formal training, either in the conservatories or municipal bands, before converting to jazz and beginning their careers in Italy's nightclubs. In addition to Escobar, there was Cinico Angelini (violin, arranger, bandleader), Felice Barboni (saxophone), Pippo Barzizza (piano, composer, bandleader), Carlo Benzi (trombone, saxophone, bandleader), Sesto Carlini (clarinet), Giuseppe Cattafesta (clarinet, saxophone), Armando Di Piramo (violin, bandleader), Gigi Ferracioli (violin, bandleader), Giovanni Fusco (piano, bandleader, composer), Umberto Mancini (composer, bandleader), Luigi Mojetta (drums, trombone), Gino Mucci (drums), Gaetano "Milietto" Nervetti (piano, bandleader) and Potito

Simone (trombone). Simone once noted that it was his discovery of recordings from America, more than anything else, that had convinced him to
switch from classical to jazz:

In these years I played the trombone without vibrato, with a firm tone, as taught
in the classical school. It was only a few years later, when I began to listen to the
American discs, that I learned the vibrato, the phrasing and the jazz intonation of a
trombone player that I admired greatly: Miff Mole.[91]

From the beginning, this crossover from the classical realm to jazz, this
learning from recordings, engendered a subtle difference between the syncopated dance music that was being cultivated in Italy and the music that
was coming out of the United States. Almost to a person, the Italians sight-
read music fluently and knew music theory. Many had studied composition
in conservatory, which greatly facilitated their ability to transform popular
tunes from recordings or sheet music into their own fully orchestrated jazz
arrangements. No doubt the Italians copied some of the American playing
styles in the beginning, as Simone did with Miff Mole, but they never fully
abandoned the lyrical phrasing, complex harmonies and approach to large-
scale formal structures learned during their formative years in conservatory. Thanks to the archival work of Adriano Mazzoletti and Marco Pacci,
we now have an exhaustive discography of the music performed by Italy's
homegrown jazz bands during the 1920s.[92] Although many of the most
popular Italian performances from these years featured tunes imported
from the United States, by the second half of the decade, a surprisingly large
percentage of the music was not just arranged, but actually composed, by
native composers. In fact, it was jazz – more than any other genre – that
contributed to the growth of Italy's recording and radio industries during
the second half of the 1920s.

Recordings and Radio

From its beginning, the record industry in Italy was characterized by
fusions with, or takeovers by, foreign companies, all eager to import and
sell their own product to an Italian market and to record and export discs
featuring Italian singers, both operatic and popular, to a home market.[93]
Although several Italian companies had been founded in the early years
of the twentieth century – Fonodisco Italiano Trevisan (renamed Fonit in
1926), Fonotecnica and Fonotipia – their percentage of the Italian market
was small.[94] Simply put, the Italian record industry was primarily in foreign

hands prior to Mussolini's creation of the state-run label Cetra in 1933. More on that in the following chapter.

As in the United States, where New York served as a hub for the early recording industry, the production of recordings in Italy was centralized. Turin and Milan were the major locations for commercial recording studios, with Rome, as the center of the country's film industry, contributing some recording opportunities as well. In addition to this tripartite geography of record production should be added the major recording centers in other European countries, most notably those in Germany, England and France, where many Italian jazz musicians produced recordings distributed to markets both in Europe and the United States.

The United States was especially eager to capitalize on recording opportunities in Italy. Realizing the large profits to be made in "ethnic" and "race" records, labels like Columbia, Victor, Brunswick, Okeh and Gennett developed a series of specialized recordings for various populations during the early decades of the twentieth century. In addition to records for African Americans, Germans, Hungarians and Irish, these companies produced music, sometimes in collaboration with companies abroad, designed to appeal to the growing number of Italian immigrants in the United States. One of the Italian artists who had the most success recording music for the United States was Di Piramo. In 1926, Di Piramo signed an exclusive contract with Columbia for his Orchestra Italiana. Many of the recordings produced under this contract were intended for distribution in both Italy and abroad. In addition to tunes by Italian and American composers, Di Piramo's Orchestra Italiana recorded tunes in Yiddish ("In Chiedis," "Yahrzeit") and Hebrew ("Jeruscherlajim").[95] But Di Piramo's most influential recording with Columbia undoubtedly occurred in 1930, when a singer named Romiglioli joined his band for a tune titled "Gigolò." Written the year before by the Italian composer Leonello Casucci, "Gigolò" was first recorded under the title "Schöner Gigolo" in Germany, where Casucci was working as a pianist in a tango orchestra. Enrico Frati supplied the Italian lyrics, which revealed the tragic story of a once glorious soldier whose life had taken a humiliating turn for the worse.

Ridi Gigolò,
Danza Gigolò,
Che per questo sei pagato ...
Oggi non sei più
Quel che un giorno fu:
Il bell'ussaro adorato!

Tutto ormai crollò,
Lo splendor passò!
A che serve ricordare?
Taci a tutti il dolor
Che ti spezza in petto il cuor.
Sorridi ... e và a danzare!

Laugh Gigolo,
Dance Gigolo.
This is what you're paid for ...
Today you no longer are
What you once were:
The adored grand Hussar!
Everything has crumbled,
The splendor has passed!
What's the use of remembering?
Don't tell anyone of the pain
That breaks your heart into pieces.
Smile ... and go dance.

In 1931, this tune was published with a less tragic set of English lyrics (by Irving Caesar) and promptly recorded as "Just a Gigolo" by Louis Armstrong for Okeh records, then a subsidiary of Columbia. Bing Crosby also made a recording of the tune in 1931, thus making it the first Italian jazz tune to hit the top of the charts in the United States.

To get a sense of the numbers involved in the output of Italian music by American recording companies: Victor and Columbia produced just over eight thousand discs of Italian musicians (not counting opera) between 1910 and 1940. Although some of these recordings were distributed in Italy, most were sold selectively in record and tobacco stores within, or nearby, Italian American communities in the United States. With the increased popularity of jazz just after the war, American companies were eager to establish production studios and distribution offices in all the major European capitals. And in the case of Italy, that capital was Milan.

As far as quantity goes, Milan was the most productive center for recordings of popular music, due to the city's industrial and commercial status and its geographical location on Italy's northern border. Although World War I slowed production of gramophone discs for several years, companies like Pathè opened "listening halls" so that potential clients could still get access to the latest recordings. As the popular singer/songwriter Rodolfo

De Angelis later noted, these listening studios enabled up-and-coming musicians to hear their own performances:

You had just ten minutes to learn and record every song. The din of the orchestra was so loud, that the one who could cry out the loudest got to make the record. The microphones had low sensitivity back then. Fortunately, the Pathè patent allowed you to hear right away what you had just blasted out. But it wasn't very subtle. A few days after the recording session you could go to the listening hall in the Galleria, which was always packed with people, and listen to the disc through a set of head-phones, that is if you paid with a twenty-cent token. Once there, you sat down in front of the unit and requested a number, [which was sent] below, down to the base-ment, where the young ladies operating the large-horned gramophones played the disc. When the number requested was no longer in the catalogue, they made you listen to the song they wanted to hear.[96]

Milan was also the center of Italy's music publishing industry. Ricordi, Suvini, Zerboni, Curci, Monzino and Garlandini all eventually had their headquarters and central presses there,[97] which made it all the easier for songwriters like De Angelis to get their product out to consumers both as sheet music and recordings.

Although Italian Radio did not become an established industry in Italy until the mid-1920s, local stations, like Radio Araldo in Rome, had a slight impact on developing listener interest right after the war. In fact, the first documented transmission of a jazz performance in Italy was broadcast by Radio Araldo in October 1922. The ensemble was a sextet called Young Men Jazz, and as their bandleader Giorgio Nataletti later explained, even though they were inexperienced teenagers, the success of their first perfor-mance led to two years of regular employment:

We performed in the auditorium of the Piazza Poli, and the radio antenna was between the Palazzo Poli and the back of the pediment of the Santa Maria in Via Church. Our repertoire was made up of tunes like "Dardanella," "Ka-Lou-A" [*sic*], "Pretty Girl," "The Sheik of Araby," "Yes! We Have No Bananas," "Kitten on the Keys," "Tea for Two," "Shine," "Limehouse Blues," "Sugar Blues," a few rags and a few stomps. We were also paid: twelve lire per transmission. Maria Luisa Boncompagni [who was later nicknamed "Auntie Radio" and "the nightingale of the radio"] was entrusted with announcing the program. We remained on Radio Araldo from October 1922 until August 1924, when the band broke up.[98]

When Young Men Jazz concluded their broadcasts in 1924, the listenership of Radio Araldo was still no more than 1,300.[99] In fact, it was low numbers such as these – combined with the threat of foreign dominance in radio broadcasting – that led to the state's formation of Unione Radiofonica Italia (URI) on August 27, 1924. URI fulfilled two purposes: in addition to serving as a foundation for a national broadcasting system, it consolidated the various commercial factions willing to invest in it.

URI was not a state-run radio – that would come in 1927. Instead, URI was a private company formed by the union of the Società Italiana Radio Audizioni Circolari (SIRAC) and Radiofono, and given an "exclusive concession" (e.g. a monopoly) by Mussolini's government. Radio Araldo was intended to have a stake in URI as well, but eventually opted out, selling its shares to the other two stakeholders. SIRAC represented the major Italian and foreign interests in this sector. Radiofono had among its shareholders the major Italian production companies of telephone, telegraph and radio equipment, but also representatives of foreign industry such as Western Electric and Ericsson. Another company represented under the corporate umbrella of Radiofono was SISER, the company founded by Guglielmo Marconi, which was linked to his Wireless Telegraph Company.[100]

Marconi's involvement in URI was symbolically important, for it was his innovations in wireless communications that led Italy to declare him as the Father of Modern Radio. Using Marconi's ingenuity as proof of the nation's place at the forefront of communications technology, the Italian government instituted protectionist measures that kept the price of radios high, thus ensuring the continued perception of the radio as a sign of success and national pride and protecting the burgeoning recording industry, which had taken a hit in countries like the United States where the market had been flooded with affordable radios.

The invention of the gramophone and radio transformed modern culture and led to the quick dissemination of jazz, both in the United States and abroad. Recordings and radio transmissions transformed domestic life by bringing music into the home. While competitive markets in the United States made gramophones and radios affordable for a relatively large portion of the population, the high cost of such devices in Italy limited their use to businesses and the wealthy. For those families who could afford such devices, jazz introduced a completely new tradition of social interaction in Italy. Jazz energized the modern world, and as we will see in the chapter that follows, Mussolini noticed.

3 | Jazz and Fascism

On October 28, 1922, Mussolini orchestrated one of the most audacious performances in Italian political history – the "March on Rome." In later years, Mussolini would describe the event as a political coup, a spontaneous uprising of 300,000 citizens that led to the Fascist suppression of Italy's liberal and socialist parties. But in truth, no more than 10,000 poorly armed young men marched into the capital that day. Their leader, *Il Duce*, joined them briefly at various points along the route to pose for photographs that appeared in newspapers around the world in the weeks that followed. As one British observer noted, Italy's citizens were not alarmed by the uprising, but rather invigorated by the display: "Romans looked on, curious, chattering, gesticulating; the streets and squares were full, the cafés crowded."[1]

The purpose of Mussolini's March was to solidify, in the minds of Italian citizens, his triumphant takeover of the Italian state. For several months leading up to the March, Mussolini and his Blackshirt followers had been committing various violent acts of aggression across the peninsula in a push for political strength. Sensing the dark clouds of civil war looming on the horizon, Italy's King Victor Emmanuel III (a mild-mannered, petite man, wary of confrontation of any sort) begrudgingly appointed Mussolini his new Prime Minister. The King reasoned that it would be better to give the Fascist leader a position within government than to have him continue to cause unrest from the outside. The March on Rome represented a public confirmation of Mussolini's new appointment. It served as his grand premiere on the stage of international affairs, the opening scene of his political career. For the next two decades, Mussolini served as the self-appointed architect of Italian identity, the virile voice of a new, modern state.

Mussolini's March on Rome was a choreographed performance if ever there was one. More show than revolt, the demonstration impressed many of the bystanders who witnessed it, both Italian and foreign. For example, the US Ambassador to Italy at the time, Richard Washburn Child, was mesmerized by the display:

It was youth and the spirit of the crusades that came swinging down the Corso toward us in the Piazza Venezia. They came with the swinging glad melody,

"Giovinezza" [Youth], which was thrown back at them from the crowd, was echoed between buildings and filled the open piazza over the soil which once had felt the rumble of the triumphal cars of the Caesars.[2]

Child embraced the event as a great moment in Italian history – a triumph comparable to those witnessed in antiquity and the Middle Ages. Yet the March also elicited a modern euphoria, an excitement encapsulated within a single musical performance. The energy of Mussolini's young Fascists, marching along in step and singing the anthem "Giovinezza," confirmed, both politically and culturally, a generational shift in Mussolini's new Italy. As Ambassador Child keenly noted, Mussolini's strength lay in his ability to connect with his nation's "youth."

"Giovinezza" was a relatively new song. First sung by university students in Turin in 1909, the tune was adopted by Alpine regiments in the Italian army and became a victory tune for World War I veterans, of which Mussolini himself could be counted. The lyrics underwent various changes over the years, but the general message remained essentially the same: Italy's glorious young soldiers, strong and courageous, will lead the nation into a prosperous future.

Su, compagni in forti schiere,
Marciam verso l'avvenire.
Siam falangi audaci e fiere,
Pronte a osare, pronte a ardire.

Come on, comrades in strong armies,
Together we march into the future.
We are phalanxes bold and proud,
Ready to challenge, ready to dare.

Mussolini was so taken with the tune that after the March on Rome he commissioned the playwright and novelist Salvatore Gotta to write a fresh set of lyrics promoting the Fascist cause. In its renewed guise, verse one of the song defined Mussolini's Fascist youth as victorious heroes and virtuous innovators, whose valor in the March on Rome led to the strengthening of a united Italy, an ideal dating back to the musings of Dante:

Salve o popolo d'eroi!
Salve o patria immortale!
Son rinati i figli tuoi
Con la fede e l'ideale.
Il valor dei tuoi guerrieri,
La virtù dei tuoi pionieri,

La vision dell'Alighieri
Oggi brilla in tutti i cuor.

Hail, O population of heroes!
Hail, O immortal fatherland!
Born again are your sons
With faith and the idea!
The valor of your warriors,
The virtue of your pioneers,
The vision of [Dante] Alighieri
Today shines in every heart.

With Italy's reclaimed glory firmly established, verse two of "Giovinezza" proclaimed the importance of Mussolini, and by inference his Fascist ideology, in the reconstruction of modern Italian identity.

Dell'Italia nei confini
Son rifatti gli italiani;
Li ha rifatti Mussolini
Per la guerra di domani
Per la gloria del lavoro
Per la pace e per l'alloro,
Per la gogna di coloro
Che la patria rinnegar.

Within the borders of Italy,
The Italians are remade,
Mussolini has remade them
For the war of tomorrow,
For the glory of work,
For peace and for the laurel [of victory],
For the shame of those
Who denounce the Fatherland.

Verse three defined the inclusivity of Mussolini's new Italy, where artists and laborers, aristocrats and commoners, receive equal status in exchange for fidelity to *Il Duce*:

I poeti e gli artigiani,
I signori e i contadini,
Con orgoglio d'italiani
Giuran fede a Mussolini.
Non v'è povero quartiere

Che non mandi le sue schiere
Che non spieghi le bandiere
Del fascismo redentor.

Poets and artisans,
Noblemen and peasants,
With Italian pride
Swear allegiance to Mussolini.
There is no poor neighborhood
That does not send its troops,
That does not unfurl the banners
Of redeeming Fascism.

This verse was especially meaningful to Mussolini supporters, for it indoctrinated an ideal of inclusivity and took on a religious theme of end-redemption. Mussolini presented himself as Italy's twentieth-century Caesar, a savior figure who would lead his followers into the modern age. Consequently, the most important element of his new Fascist anthem was the refrain sung between each verse:

Giovinezza, giovinezza,
Primavera di bellezza
Per la vita, nell'asprezza
Il tuo canto squilla e va!

Youth, youth
Springtime of beauty,
Over the hardship of life
Your song forever rings!

Ubiquitous in Fascist Italy, "Giovinezza" emphasized the promise of youth, and this concept served as the symbol of Mussolini's new government: its vigor, optimism, hope and energy. After the March on Rome, foreign commentators noted the importance of music to Mussolini's political dominance. For example, Leonard Peyton wrote in *The Musical Times*: "Like most revolutions, the recent pacific – but nonetheless extraordinary – Fascist revolution at Rome has been accompanied by music, and what was at first a mere party song has been raised almost to the dignity of a national hymn."[3] "Giovinezza" was never a jazz tune, but its dotted rhythms, lilting melody and sanguine lyrics offered the same pep and mechanized energy that characterized the nation's newest trends, both musical and political.

The arts played a significant role in Mussolini's remaking of Italian identity. Unlike Hitler, who rejected avant-garde initiatives, Mussolini supported the newest trends in modernist art and architecture.[4] Within the realm of music, his interests ran the gamut, from opera and symphonies to fox-trots and jazz. He was not always consistent in his proclamations concerning music; like many of us, his tastes changed over time. That said, there was one style of Italian music he never fully embraced: the traditional folk music of southern Italy. As a native of the North, Mussolini consistently belittled the "old-world tenors and mandolin players" characteristic of Naples and the villages of Sicily,[5] and this regional preference affected the evolution of Italian jazz over the next three decades and its reception, in Italy and abroad, after World War II.

The key to Mussolini's takeover of the Italian government was his ability to tap into contemporary cultural currents dominating northern Italy and inspire, for better or worse, a sense of renewal and modernization among the nation's citizenry. Mussolini promised to bring Italy into the modern age, and he was quick to criticize those who clung to the past. "Most of the objections to technical progress lack justification," he claimed.

Where should we be without great ships, huge iron bridges, tunnels, airplanes? Is man to become retrogressive, to return to the bullock cart of antiquity, when he has the motorcar, which is so much quicker, more convenient, and more dependable?[6]

Beyond getting the trains to run on time and strengthening the nation's infrastructure and economic outlook, Mussolini embraced the entertainment technology of the new generation, namely, gramophones, radios and the cinema. He also implemented protectionist measures for these media, and through them jazz flourished in Italy, especially in Rome and all urban centers north of it. Thanks to Mussolini's initiatives, jazz became a symbol of national identity during his years in power. From 1922 until 1943, jazz served as the soundtrack for Italy's "Giovinezza" generation.

But why jazz, a style of music that the rest of the world firmly associated with American innovation? Simply put, jazz equaled modernization, technological innovation and a rejection of the past. The Futurists introduced this jazz aesthetic to the Italian consciousness, and as Mussolini welcomed them under the umbrella of Fascist protection, he adopted jazz for many of the same reasons they did. In fact, Casavola's defense of jazz in 1926 was embraced by Futurists and Fascists alike:

The Jazz Band is the typical product of our generation: heroic, violent, arrogant, brutal, optimistic, anti-romantic, unsentimental and ungraceful. Born of wars and revolutions. Deny it and you deny us![7]

For both the Futurists and Fascists, jazz offered a path towards modernity in the 1920s and served as a symbol of Italian influence abroad. Italy made room for "American" jazz, because many Italian artists and intellectuals hailed it as a worldwide musical revolution that never could have come into existence without the contribution of Italian innovation. Whether this is factually true or not is unimportant; it's what most Italians believed in the 1920s. Consequently, in many of the early discussions of jazz that appeared in the Italian press, the music was placed in a context of meaning and significance that eventually became seen as typically Italian.[8] Jazz served as the key to Italy's future, "the magic formula, so laboriously sought by the alchemists of art after an unconscious period of gestation," which had finally been "concretized in crude and embryonic form."[9] In the mind of Casavola, and Mussolini too, Italians "were the ones to foresee the early developments of jazz and then dictate its first laws."[10]

In assessing the role of jazz in Italy under Mussolini's rule, many post-World War II scholars have assumed, mistakenly, that Il Duce's attitude toward the music must have been similar to that of Hitler, who vehemently rejected jazz, especially when composed and/or performed by African American and Jewish musicians. But Mussolini and Hitler held contrasting opinions about contemporary culture, especially with regard to modern art. Although the two dictators joined forces during World War II, their motivations for doing so were markedly different. The core of Hitler's political agenda was his fundamental belief in the supremacy of the so-called Aryan race, and his central goal was to lead Germany in its domination of as much of the world as possible. Hitler's power as a leader lay in his ability to convince his followers that in order to succeed, they first had to eliminate those he defined as enemies of German culture: namely Jews, communists and capitalists. By contrast, Mussolini's deepest belief was in his own genius for governing. He was an inconsistent leader, and his policies on various topics – from economics and foreign affairs to Catholicism and race – fluctuated noticeably from one year to the next. Mussolini did not define Italy's enemies specifically by nationality or religion during the first decade and a half of his dictatorship. Instead, he described his nation's foes as those individuals, both in Italy and abroad, who refused to embrace what he defined as his own talent for leadership. Hitler was unswerving in his political dominance and beliefs.[11] Mussolini was more chameleon-like. A performer at heart, his power lay – at least during the first twenty years of his dictatorship – in his ability to adapt each spectacle and performance to the audience at hand.

Jazz thrived in Italy under Mussolini's leadership, and this was primarily because those he empowered through political appointments often shared his ideas about how to unify the Italian citizenry. For example, Mussolini's Undersecretary Giacomo Acerbo, his foreign minister and son-in-law Galeazzo Ciano and the Secretary of the PNF Achille Starace all recognized the symbolic importance of jazz and encouraged its presence in the nation's cafés and on the radio. Under Mussolini's leadership, jazz served as a recruitment tool, a symbol of what the modern state was willing to embrace. Yet it would be shortsighted to claim that Italy's fascination for jazz was simply a display of political bravura. In truth, the evolution of the music under Fascism was a complex process, influenced as much by Mussolini's personal interests and familial relationships as by the musical ambitions and tastes of Italian musicians and their fans.

Mussolini's Musical Interests

By all accounts, Mussolini was an avid supporter of music, and this artistic preference was disseminated widely via newspaper articles, photographs and newsreels during his years in power.[12] Within days of Mussolini's March on Rome, reporters stumbled over each other in an attempt to document his every cultural outing, be it a night at the opera, a gallery tour or a concert.[13] Although assessments concerning the extent of Mussolini's musical training varied widely during his dictatorship – with devotees praising his musical ability and detractors denigrating his talent and acumen – no one denied the symbolic importance music played in the creation of his public image. As Mussolini himself noted the year before his March on Rome: "Fascism is a grand orchestra, where everyone plays a different instrument."[14] Mussolini clearly saw his own role in this metaphor as that of the invincible conductor. The Italian composer Ottorino Respighi echoed this sentiment several years later in an interview with an American reporter:

Mussolini has a definite plan to unify the great cities of Italy, those with traditions to uphold, in a kind of artistic exchange, if I may use the term; ... He is truly and sincerely interested in music, and is happiest when with artists. A delightful comrade, ... Mussolini is doing for art, for Italy, what a great conductor does for an orchestra. There are no great orchestras, of themselves. A great performance is always just the greatness of the conductor manifested through a body of players.[15]

Mussolini's musical background became a popular topic in the propaganda machine that promoted his persona to an adoring public. In 1927, the well-known music critic Raffaello De Rensis published a booklet, titled *Mussolini musicista* (Mussolini the Musician), which presented an overview of the prime minister's musical training and interests. According to De Rensis, although Mussolini was "perturbed ... in a strange and indefinable way" by the "dragging cantilenas" he heard in church as a child, his reaction to outdoor band music was markedly different:

> When the gay, noisy Romagna bands arrived on religious holidays, little Benito was among the most assiduous listeners. He often followed them as they marched through the streets of the village; the crisp, bold rhythm stirred his instinctively war-like spirit.[16]

The symbolic significance of De Rensis's anecdote about "little Benito" embracing a marching band over church music is clear. Still, there is no reason to assume that the story is pure fiction. De Rensis interviewed Mussolini as part of his research, and it is possible that Mussolini shared this anecdote with his biographer. Such a musical preference seems likely given the dictator's lifelong enthusiasm for military rituals and broadly advertised anti-Clericalism – Mussolini even went so far as to write a bodice-ripping historical novel in 1909 about a philandering cardinal.[17] As to Mussolini's musical training, he was largely an autodidact, who only began formal music lessons late in life. His early school records reveal he had a commanding voice – his highest scores on final exams being in "History, Literature and Singing."[18] As an adolescent, Mussolini reportedly played trombone for several years in the school band in Forlimpopoli, but eventually switched to the violin, which remained his instrument of choice from that point forward.[19] There are no recordings of Mussolini performing, which leaves us with little more than the testimonies of friends and family as evidence of his musical facility and repertoire preferences. Mussolini's belief in the importance of music to Italian identity can be traced back as far as 1901, when, as a seventeen-year-old with a talent for public speaking, he gave an impromptu speech in the local theater commemorating the passing of Giuseppe Verdi, a musician he lauded as one of his nation's great heroes.[20] After the March on Rome, Mussolini often claimed Beethoven as his favorite composer. Testimonials from friends and family, however, reveal that in private settings he generally played folk dances from the Romagna region or improvisations of popular operetta tunes, and as a teenager, he could be counted on to supply the dance music at drinking parties in his father's tavern.[21] According to his longtime lover and biographer, Margherita

Sarfatti, Mussolini even tried his hand, although unsuccessfully, at writing song lyrics.[22]

Mussolini didn't begin formal violin lessons until 1909, when at age twenty-six he entered the studio of Archimede Montanelli in Forlì.[23] At the time, Mussolini was working as editor of the socialist weekly he had founded called *La Lotta di Classe* (Class Struggle). According to Montanelli, he and Mussolini discussed the state of Italian music on a regular basis over the next few months, and within a year, Mussolini began attending performances at the local theater and writing reviews. Not surprisingly, Mussolini's insights concerning the antiquated state of Forlì's music scene foreshadowed his later attitudes towards the need to modernize Italy's music repertoire. For example, on April 2, 1910 he declared:

We will not talk about the repertoire. Forlì – Because of its miserable theater one must almost always content oneself with works that are nothing more than musical exhumations. As to modern works, we get nothing, or very little ... From the point of view of musical culture, this is very lamentable.[24]

Mussolini's debut as a music critic coincided with the birth of his first child, a daughter named Edda. Of all his children, Edda had the closest relationship with her father.[25] She was his favorite, and according to Edda's mother, Rachele, Mussolini lulled his daughter to sleep each night by playing lullabies on the violin.[26] Even as a child, Edda was headstrong and opinionated like her father. She appears to have been the one who introduced jazz into the Mussolini household. In the early 1920s, when as an adolescent she became fascinated with American dance music, Mussolini bought Edda her first gramophone. And according to her younger brothers Vittorio and Romano, born in 1916 and 1927 respectively, Edda's immense record collection sparked their own fascination with American jazz. Vittorio learned to play banjo at a relatively early age, and in the mid-1930s he made a name for himself writing editorials and music reviews praising the "Hot" jazz coming out of the United States.[27] Romano's connection to the music was even stronger. After World War II, he became an internationally recognized jazz pianist, who maintained an active performance career that included collaborations with jazz legends like Chet Baker, Duke Ellington, Lionel Hampton and Dizzy Gillespie.

Both Vittorio and Romano published memoires about life with their father, and their depictions of Mussolini as a caring family man serve as a contrast to the more prevalent images of the infamous, Beethoven-loving dictator who enacted Italy's race laws and tied the nation's fate to Hitler's Germany.[28] Mussolini's private life differed markedly from his public persona. This is no excuse for the deaths and pain he inflicted during his twenty-three years in power, but it does help explain how jazz found a firm footing in Italy during the Fascist era. Like many fathers, Mussolini encouraged his children's musical interests, even when they differed from his own. As his sons later noted, music was a constant presence in the Mussolini household. Vittorio remembered his father playing gypsy dances and popular tunes on his violin.[29] "At home, everyone listened to music," said Romano:

My father preferred symphonic music, my brother Bruno [born 1918] opera, me and my sister Anna Maria [born 1929] loved all sorts of music, but especially jazz … My father, in his turn, was very content to listen to me play the piano: I played the blues and American standards, but also Italian songs. Although he wanted me to develop my sight-reading ability and learn to read music well – something that he was able to do – I never really did.[30]

The Mussolini family's connection to jazz was never hidden from the public. Photographs from the 1930s confirm that Mussolini invited jazz musicians home and introduced them to his sons (Figure 3.1). As Vittorio and Romano affirmed on countless occasions, their interest in jazz was not an act of teenage rebellion, but rather a natural part of growing up in their father's home. Which raises the question: Why is the topic of jazz so often omitted from discussions of Mussolini's private life? The answer lies partly in Mussolini's talent at constructing a public persona for himself early in his career.

Mussolini came from humble origins, and when he made his "premiere" in Rome as the nation's Prime Minister in 1922, he felt the need to prove himself not only as a formidable military figure and politician, but also as a well-educated cultural leader. Of the hundreds of publicity photographs taken of Mussolini during his early years in power, some of the most famous show him in his private living room, standing erect and staring into the camera, holding his violin and bow as though he is about to play. Taken shortly after the March on Rome, these images were the first step in the creation of his musical persona. The photos were published widely, in Italy and abroad, and described as a glimpse into the leader's private life, an image of him partaking in a favorite pastime outside the rigors of public service. Years later, Mussolini commented on the photos.

I have to laugh at those old photographs from 1922 that show me in a morning coat while I play the violin. That was the time of my earliest innocence. But even that caused a fuss. Hostile critics took advantage of the incident. After all, I wasn't playing the emigrants' harmonica or the beggars' barrel organ.[31]

Figure 3.1 Bruno and Vittorio Mussolini with the jazz pianist Gaetano "Milietto"
Nervetti at the seaside resort of Riccione, Italy (1931).
Source: Photographic archive of Adriano Mazzoletti.

With these photos, Mussolini's public musical identity became firmly
linked to the realm of classical music. But privately, he continued to pursue more popular fare. Shortly after his move to Rome, he engaged a new
violin teacher: Umberto Bozza, a dance band leader who had made a name
for himself during World War I playing fox-trots and tangos at the Apollo
Theater.[32] Mussolini did not broadly publicize the identity of his new
teacher; it would have clashed with his carefully constructed personal identity. But for many of the Italian musicians drawn to jazz, Mussolini's choice
of Bozza served as a tacit endorsement of their participation in the burgeoning dance music industry. When jazz arrived on Italian shores, Bozza was
one of the first to expand his repertoire to include it, and in the early 1920s,
his dance orchestra served as a training ground for a number of Italian jazz
musicians, most notably Alfredo Gangi (guitar, banjo), Armando Frittelli
(piano), Luigi Antoniolo and Armando Manzi (trombone), Gino Filippini
and Benedetto Cioppettini (violin), Giuseppe Zita and Vincenzo Spiotta
(saxophone).

Bozza has been left out of the Mussolini narrative, but his influence
on the dictator's musical taste was significant. Bozza's orchestra presented an international mix of popular music, from Viennese waltzes and

French chansons to Argentine tangos, improvisations on Romany tunes and American fox-trots. He imported much of his music from Paris, where he had spent his early career. Like many musicians at the time, Bozza straddled the worlds of classical music and jazz. Conservatory trained, yet also drawn to popular culture, he tried to find a musical middle-ground in Italy similar to that defined in the United States by Paul Whiteman and George Gershwin.[33]

Bozza's mixed musical interests influenced countless performers in addition to Mussolini, the most notable being his son, Eugène, who composed numerous jazz-infused concert works for trumpet during the 1930s while serving as a fellow at The French Academy in Rome and conductor of the Opéra-Comique in Paris.[34] For Bozza and his Roman fans, the jazz-infused popular music he imported from the United States and France, and then disseminated in Rome, was a symbol of sophistication, both cosmopolitan and aristocratic – a more measured and easily accessible alternative to the avant-garde take on jazz being sponsored by the Futurists at the same time.

When Mussolini came to power, he was an enthusiastic supporter of all things American, and the open environment he created for jazz led to a benefit concert on April 24, 1924, at New York's Carnegie Hall, organized by Paul Whiteman and George Gershwin. Their goal: to raise money towards the establishment of a "Fellowship in Jazz Composition" at the American Academy in Rome. Leo Sowerby, the first American Academy Fellow in Music, had just returned to the United States after three years in Rome. As evidence of the beneficial effects Italy offered to aspiring American composers, Whiteman commissioned from Sowerby two compositions: an overture titled *Synconata* and *Monotony*, a "jazz symphony" inspired by Sinclair Lewis's novel *Babbitt*.[35] These were performed at the Benefit Concert, which in truth was little more than an encore performance of the groundbreaking premiere of Gershwin's *Rhapsody in Blue*, which had taken place on February 12, 1924 – Lincoln's birthday. Titled an "Experiment in Modern Music," this concert had attempted to bring together the "white" realm of European concert music and the "black" realm of American jazz. As the critic Isaac Goldberg noted, the significance of Whiteman's "experiment" was as political as it was musical: "It was a birthday for American music, even an Emancipation Proclamation, in which slavery to European formalism was signed away by the ascending, opening glissando of the *Rhapsody*."[36]

Whiteman described the concert as an attempt "to justify jazz to the ways of the highbrows," a goal that Mussolini would have supported. The concert raised over $25,000 towards the endowment of an additional Composition Fellowship, but when the award was finally established, the Academy Board omitted "jazz" from the guidelines. Although many European intellectuals in the 1920s viewed jazz as America's greatest cultural product, the conservative protectors of US concert halls and conservatories were not yet convinced. Nonetheless, Mussolini's support for American jazz continued. He visited the American Academy on at least two occasions, and each time he was welcomed warmly by the fellows. Some even went so far as to greet the prime minister with the upraised arm of a Fascist salute. During Mussolini's first visit, in 1930, the director at the time, Gorham Phillips Stevens, praised "the marvelous progress" Italy had made under Il Duce's leadership.[37] During a second visit, in 1933, the fellows entertained Mussolini with a performance of Werner Janssen's "American Kaleidoscope," a chamber work incorporating an array of popular tunes, among them "Old Folks at Home" and "Dixie."[38] Pleased by this warm reception, Mussolini welcomed the transplanted American artists and scholars and encouraged them to continue their collaborations with musicians in Italy.

Mussolini never composed or performed jazz himself, but he embraced the music as a symbol for the Fascist regime. Jazz equaled modernism, and for this reason, perhaps more than any other, he incorporated it into Italy's cultural policy. Mussolini learned to adapt his definition of Italian culture according to the audience at hand. As far as music goes, this meant welcoming under the umbrella of Fascism a wide array of styles and genres, from opera and concert music to patriotic anthems and jazz. While Mussolini continued to claim Beethoven as a favorite composer, he also embraced the modernist attributes of contemporary popular culture and worked hard to strengthen the media that promoted it, namely, radio, the recording industry and film.

The Rise of Jazz on Italian Radio

Mussolini mediated the transition from traditional Italy to modern mass society by promoting technology, controlling the market and encouraging a new consumerist ethos. As the country became more industrial, especially in the North, foreign influences, most notably from the United States, began to pervade Italian culture. During his first five years in power, Mussolini gradually took control of Italian radio. The initial step in this process was to unify Italy's radio industry under a single commercial entity: the Unione Radiofonica Italiana (URI). Mussolini's interest in creating what amounted to a commercial monopoly of radio broadcasting and production was driven by two desires: (1) to protect Italian companies from foreign dominance, and (2) to build, using private instead of public funds, the infrastructure needed to support nation-wide broadcasts. This process of unification began in June 1924 when Mussolini's Minister of Communication, Costanzo Ciano, contacted the major producers of Italian radio – Radiofono and SIRAC – and informed them of the government's plan.[39] Radiofono had among its shareholders the major Italian production companies of telephone, telegraph and radio equipment; SISER (the company founded by Guglielmo Marconi and linked to his Wireless Telegraph Company); and representatives from Western Electric in the United States. SIRAC represented the interests of the major producers of Italian radio content and had close ties with various American interests, including RCA.[40] The unification under URI proceeded with little protest. Fascist officials saw it as an important first step in taking control of the nation's media, while private investors viewed the agreement as a means of eliminating future competition.[41] When URI transmitted its first broadcast several months later, it began with a performance of "Giovinezza," which Fascist officials later described as a turning point in the modernization of Italian society:

On the evening of October 6, the notes of "Giovinezza" were diffused for the first time from the station in Rome. Since then, the Fascist anthem has been repeated every evening as a reminder that Italian Radio, born and developed during the first decade of the regime, is an invaluable tool for the dissemination of new initiatives and every new conquest carried out by the regime itself.[42]

The development of jazz as an accepted art form was among the many initiatives of the new Italian state. Like the radio, it was often linked to Italian innovation. For example, during the first URI broadcast, Giacomo Acerbo, Mussolini's undersecretary and a jazz fan, praised the radio as a "new technological wonder" created by the "Italian Genius, Guglielmo Marconi" that would soon be "transmitting the Italian spirit through the airwaves."[43] On May 1, 1925 national legislation established the core programming for URI: concerts, theatrical works, talk shows and news;[44] and by December a new state-of-the-art station began transmitting from Milan. But what exactly was the content of these early broadcasts? What types of music could be heard during the initial years? The most accurate description comes from the pages of *Radiorario*, a weekly magazine tied to URI programming that hit newsstands in January 1925. As an editorial in this first issue explained, the purpose of *Radiorario* was to publicize the new technology among the Italian citizenry and to shape the tastes and opinions of a nascent audience.[45] Each issue featured short articles describing recent technological innovations and upcoming performances by popular artists. Advertisements for the radios and gramophones produced by URI's private investors were included too. But the most important component of each *Radiorario* issue was the daily program guide listing the broadcast schedule of various stations. Reading through the first few months of these programs, one quickly discovers the prominent position music held in URI broadcasts, with at least 12 percent of each daily broadcast dedicated to dance music and jazz. Jazz was also a conspicuous component of foreign radio broadcasts, and *Radiorario* provided listeners with the offerings of these stations too.

Fascist leadership understood the symbolic importance of URI broadcasts, and they encouraged URI's investors to create programming that would attract new listeners, most notably Mussolini's target audience, the nation's youth. This programming imperative not only affected the content of radio broadcasts, it also informed the earliest design of the *Radiorario* cover, which for fifty-four weeks carried the same set of four simple drawings. On the left were two "live" scenes, showing a couple dancing to jazz musicians playing banjo and saxophone (above), and a teacher lecturing to a group of students (below). These vignettes were linked, via radio wires stretching across the page, to similar images on the right showing radio listeners: a young couple dancing (above), and a group of school children taking notes (below). This simple framing device, displayed on each *Radiorario* cover, served as the government's visual declaration of radio's nascent audience: the "Giovinezza" generation defined in song at the beginning of each broadcast.

For URI's private investors, Mussolini's political goal of engaging the nation's youth could not be ignored. Yet as much as Il Duce's desire served as a programming incentive, it also presented URI management with an economic challenge. When URI began its broadcasts in 1924, Italian listenership was remarkably low in comparison to that in the United States, Germany, Great Britain and France. Radios were still exorbitantly expensive in Italy, and investors realized that to make Italian radio a commercial success, programming would have to be created that attracted not only the youth, of which Mussolini was so fond, but also the matriarchs and patriarchs who controlled the family finances. Consequently, during the first year of URI broadcasts, opera and symphonic works dominated the music programming. But beginning in 1926, URI became dual-funded. The general operating expenses for the broadcasting system were no longer solely paid for by advertising revenue from on-air ads and print advertisements in *Radiorario*. Radio owners were now also expected to pay a subscription fee (*abbonamento*) to the government through their local Post Office.[46] This expansion of revenue sources meant that in both its legal status and in its financial support, URI represented a mix of private and public interests. Not surprisingly, this mix created a tension between the economic strategies of private investors and the Fascist state's political goals. Because of its largely commercial interests, URI had to appeal to all listeners: young and old, conservative and moderate, nationalistic and cosmopolitan. This need to diversify, mixed with Mussolini's interest in youth culture and demand for a purely Fascist government, caused URI to put into circulation music, ideas and attitudes that slowly changed perceptions of acceptable behavior and "drove a wedge between generations."[47] It should be noted that as the government became more invested in URI broadcasts, the amount of jazz programming increased and even began to include live broadcasts from élite nightclubs.

The first live jazz broadcasts from URI stations that can be definitively documented occurred on February 1, 1926. That evening the Milan Station broadcast a ninety-minute program, from 4:30 to 6:00 P.M., featuring the "Jazz Band of Maestro Stefano Ferruzzi." This was followed shortly thereafter by an hour-long broadcast, beginning at 7:30 P.M., featuring the "Orchestra of Maestro Amedeo Escobar" from the luxurious Hotel De Russie in Rome.[48] We do not have the set list of what these ensembles performed, but if Ferruzzi's recordings from that year are any indication, the music was mostly popular dances (fox-trots and tangos) by Italian songwriters like Vincenzo Billi, Giovanni Castorina, Odoardo Spado and Sandro Manfrino (who also published in Paris under the name Jack Bill).[49] This interest in Italian jazz was confirmed several months later when Italy's "Association of Authors of Musical Comedies, Popular Music, Songs and Dances" met for the first time and voted to take steps to limit the import of "American jazz." Connected with this decision was the creation of an additional association known as "The Writers of Musical Scores for Moving Pictures," whose purpose was to offer equal protection for the film industry.[50]

The focus on Italian music during the first year of URI broadcasts had a noticeable effect in that the listenership in Italy more than doubled. That said, the audience was still conspicuously small in comparison to other countries of equivalent size. For example, in 1926, when Germany and England could boast of subscriber bases exceeding a million (1,022,000 and 1,230,000, respectively), Italy had attracted a meager 26,850 subscribers. In 1927, the number grew to 40,678 – a sizeable increase, but still paltry compared to the numbers in neighboring countries. The primary reason for Italy's low subscription numbers was the expense to Italian consumers: not just the cost of the radio itself, but also the annual subscription fee each household receiving a radio signal was required to pay to the state. Of course, less expensive, foreign-made radios could have been made available to Italian buyers, but that wasn't something that interested Mussolini. If Italians were going to listen to the radio, a technological wonder created by "Italian genius," they were going to listen to devices designed and constructed in Italy.[51] From the beginning, having a radio in Italy was a sign of prestige and fashion.

Mussolini's interest in radio and his desire to have more control over its programming became all the more obvious on January 15, 1928 when URI was transformed into Ente Italiano per le Audizioni Radiofoniche (EIAR). Although the group of major shareholders did not change, programming was placed under a new Broadcasting Supervisory Committee (Comitato superiore di vigilanza sulle radiodiffusioni) devised by Costanzo Ciano, one of Mussolini's trusted advisors. Because EIAR was state run, radio programming became more closely linked to Fascist interests and consequently a popular topic of political debate. The number of subscribers increased substantially under EIAR control, from 40,678 in 1927 to just under 100,000 in 1929. By 1937 there were as many as 800,000 subscribers.[52] One of the primary reasons for the increased subscriptions was the new branding of subscription fees. Upon payment of the fee, subscribers had the opportunity to become an "EIAR Pioneer." As an official announcement of this program explained, EIAR had created the designation "in an effort to expand the development and diffusion of radio." Each year, EIAR officials selected among the loyal subscriber base a "pioneer" from each municipality, "no matter how small," to serve as an official representative of the state. The task of these pioneers was "to quietly but effectively propagate the lofty educational, cultural, artistic and entertaining purposes of national radio, not only among current radio listeners, but also among the many who should be listeners."[53] Those who were selected as EIAR Pioneers were presented with an elegant certificate, appropriate for framing. Thus, what was previously perceived as an oppressive requirement (the paying of the subscription fee) was transformed into an act of arts patronage through the EIAR Pioneers program. Owning a radio was no longer just a symbol of prestige; it was now also an act of arts activism and Italian patriotism.

It is interesting to note that the founding of EIAR in 1928 coincided with the first appearance on the Italian market of recordings by African American musicians like Louis Armstrong and Duke Ellington. Imported by the Italian affiliates of foreign recording companies – most notably Columbia, Parlophon and Victor – these discs had a noticeable impact on many Italian musicians and their fans. But it wasn't just the recordings, black musicians also began to arrive in Italy.[54]

African American Musicians in Italy

When African Americans first ventured across the Atlantic as musicians and dancers in the late nineteenth century, they traveled the continent, sometimes for years at a time, exposing eager audiences to what was often described as the "exotic" music of the New World: namely "coon songs," spirituals and eventually ragtime. Italy was generally cut off from these tours, both for geographical and economic reasons. Although a handful of black musicians ventured south of the Alps between 1904 and 1910 (the most famous being Pete Hampton, Laura Bradford Bowman and Arabella Fields), their visits were brief and few in number when compared to other European countries.[55] African American performers did not begin to travel to Italy regularly until the second half of the 1920s.

Josephine Baker was one of the first black stars to visit Italy. In 1928 she arrived in Rome, where Mussolini charmed her instantly with his self-assured manner and interest in all things modern and American. In Paris, municipal labor laws had recently capped the employment of foreign musicians at 10 percent. Baker was pleased to see that Mussolini had not implemented such draconian limits in Italy … at least, not yet. With the limits in France, some African American musicians traveled farther afield in search of employment. Those who came to Italy often found work, but they also discovered how different life could be south of the Alps. There was no "Harlem" in Rome or Milan, as there was in Paris's Montmartre district.[56] In France, black musicians lived and worked together as part of an expat enclave. In Italy, they were expected to assimilate. They lived among Italians, ate Italian food and joined Italian bands, often serving as the only nonwhite musicians. Although the identities of many of these musicians have been lost with time, some, like Jack Russell (clarinet/alto sax), Johnny Gratton (drummer/dancer), Alphonse Mathaus (drummer/singer) and Herb Flemming (trombone) left their mark on Italian jazz. Reflecting back on the experience thirty years later, Flemming admitted that he had been wary at first about moving to Italy:

When a French impresario asked me in November 1931 if I wanted to join an Italian band performing in Florence, I was really worried because I didn't know if I could adapt to musicians who [I assumed] didn't know Duke Ellington and the other pioneers of jazz. I was very surprised when, upon arriving in Florence, I discovered that the Italian musicians were not only excellent performers, but also willing and eager to collaborate.[57]

Flemming eventually made his way to Rome, where he became a featured performer with the Sesto Carlini Orchestra. As Flemming explained, Carlini "wasn't just a bandleader, he was a friend to his musicians." Under Carlini's gentle guidance, the band excelled. "He always had a smile on his lips, and with his profound musical knowledge he was always ready to offer assistance instead of ridicule." Like most Italian jazzmen, Carlini was con-servatory trained and had started his career playing in symphony orches-tras. "His technical prowess was no doubt due to this classical training," said Flemming. "His fingers seemed to fly whenever he performed a sax or clari-net solo." The other members of the band were equally gifted: "I never heard those imperfections that one so often hears among section musicians when they have to play a particularly fast and difficult section," said Flemming. But Carlini demanded more from his players than flawless technique: "He once told me: 'The more versatile my musicians are, the higher the prestige for myself and my orchestra.' "[58] Consequently, Flemming was encouraged to broaden his musical repertoire:

I remember the first time we played at the Teatro Capranica ... It was my first public appearance, and just before the end of the first set I was supposed to improvise on a theme from [Mascagni's] *Cavalleria rusticana*. I was very nervous. Carlini, seeing how upset I was, said to me: "Flemming, remember your experi-ence with Jim Europe's band. Start calmly, and you will see that everything will go smoothly."[59]

As Italy's reputation for jazz improved, African American musicians began adding the country to their European tours. Louis Armstrong visited briefly in 1935 – a topic to be discussed in more detail shortly – and there were countless others before him, including Sidney Bechet.[60] Undoubtedly, the most influential black performers to spend considerable time in Italy during the 1920s and 30s were Sam Wooding and Harry Fleming.[61] Although their lengthy tours overseas made them minor figures in the United States, in Italy Wooding and Fleming were received as international celebrities.[62] As Wooding later explained:

We found it hard to believe, but the Europeans treated us with as much respect as they did their own symphonic orchestras ... That would never have happened back here in the States. Here they looked on jazz as something that belonged in the gin mills and sporting houses, and if someone had suggested booking a blues singer like Bessie Smith … on the same bill as [the opera singer] Ernestine Schumann-Heink, it would have been regarded as a joke in the poorest of taste.[63]

Harry W. Fleming, a dancer and bandleader born in the West Indies and raised in the United States, enjoyed similar experiences.[64] Fleming visited Italy regularly during his extensive European tours and is credited as being the first to introduce tap dancing to Italian audiences.[65] His fifteen-piece band served as an ad-hoc international federation of jazz musicians: in addition to two African Americans – Roy Butler (saxophone) and Albert Wynn (trombone) – the ensemble included performers from Denmark, France, Spain, England and Italy (Figure 3.2). Many Italians embraced the multiethnic, international quality of touring ensembles like Fleming's. Others were not so kind. One of the most vehement opponents of African American jazz was the Marxist theoretician and politician Antonio Gramsci. Writing from his prison cell in 1927, he bemoaned the arrival of "Negro" jazz culture:

If there is a danger, it lies in the Negro music and dancing that has been imported into Europe. This music has completely won over a whole section of the cultured population of Europe, to the point of real fanaticism. It is inconceivable that the incessant repetition of the Negroes' physical gestures as they dance around their fetishes or that the constant sound of the syncopated rhythm of jazz bands should have no ideological effects.[66]

Criticism came from the right as well. For example, on March 30, 1928 the future vice secretary for the PNF, Carlo Ravisio, published an article in *Il Popolo d'Italia* denouncing the continued fashion for foreign music. Ravisio did not reject jazz specifically. Instead he lamented the growing disinterest in Italian musical instruments (violins, mandolins and guitars) as "American" ones (saxophones and drums) became more popular.

It is heinous and injurious to tradition, and therefore to the race, to pack away in the attic the violins, mandolins and guitars in order to make room for the saxophones and banging drums whose barbaric melodies live only due to ephemeral fashion.[67]

Ravisio was especially concerned by the growing prominence of African American performers like Josephine Baker. "It is stupid. It is ridiculous. It is anti-Fascist to go into raptures over the belly dances of a mulatto woman or to run like fools after every American fad that comes over to us from across the ocean."[68]

In light of these newest trends, Ravisio called on Italians to discontinue their "anti-Fascist" behavior and focus instead on promoting a new form of jazz created specifically by and for Italians. "We must create these things

Figure 3.2 Harry Fleming and his orchestra on stage at the Barberini Cinema-Theater in Rome (1932).
Source: Photographic archive of Adriano Mazzoletti.

ourselves – our ways of life, of art and of beauty – in the same way that we have created our own form of government, our own laws and our incredibly original institutions."[69]

This focus on the creation of a national style was reflected in various reviews of popular music that appeared in the Fascist press. For example, six months after Ravisio's piece, a long review article in *Il Popolo d'Italia* described an array of new recordings on the Italian market, two of which – "Pasta frolla" and "Saluta" – were composed by Italians. After criticizing the weaknesses of several American compositions, the reviewer praised the two fox-trots by Italian composers. Describing them as "two masterpieces of the genre," he explained that although the "thematic material on which they [were] based" came from America, the composers had created dance music that was effectively Italian through a process of appropriation and adaptation. In an effort to clarify why such a transformation was possible, the reviewer reminded readers of the Italian American Nick LaRocca and his reputed role in the origins of jazz:

It is helpful to remember that one of the most recognized and talented jazz musicians – if not the actual creator of the genre – is an Italian who has lived in America for many years and whose talents have made him the most famous and popular American composer of dance music. Therefore, even jazz, is not fully American.[70]

That the origins of jazz could be linked to Italy did not sit well with some Italian composers. Pietro Mascagni, for example, was horrified by the new cultural craze. Time and again he denigrated jazz and all its accouterments. He even went so far as to propose that the music be officially outlawed, not just in Italy, but also in the United States. Mascagni was a force to be reckoned with in Italy's music community, but for young composers like Alfredo Casella, the older man's threats fell flat. In an article for the *Christian Science Monitor* titled "Mascagni and Jazz," Casella dismissed the older composer's opinion as "the expression of one confronted by an art which he cannot understand." Claiming to prefer the rhythmic energy of jazz over Mascagni's neo-romantic operas, Casella told readers in the United States: "Whatever be the respect in which one holds the name of Mascagni, it would certainly be difficult to maintain that he represents the musical thought of new Italy."[71]

Officials at EIAR largely agreed. Opera was important as a symbol of Italy's glorious past, but the nation's future required a more mechanized, modern energy. In an effort to determine what music might best accomplish this, EIAR regularly distributed surveys to radio listeners through *Radiorario* and its later replacement *Radiocorriere*. In the past, many scholars have assumed that the Italian government's takeover of radio broadcasting led to an inevitable rejection of jazz, especially jazz performed by non-Italians. But in truth, just the opposite occurred.

EIAR-Jazz

In response to a listener survey distributed in 1928, EIAR launched a new radio initiative from its Milan station in 1929 called *EIAR-Jazz*. The first broadcast occurred on March 31 – Easter Sunday. This was clearly meant as an affront to Pope Pius XI, who just two months earlier had signed the Lateran Accord with Mussolini. Pius XI came into power the same year as Mussolini, 1922. Although he disliked the Prime Minister's violent, dictatorial methods, he was willing to work with him for the sake of the Church's future. By signing the Lateran Accord, Pius XI agreed to place his public support behind the Fascist regime. In exchange, Mussolini guaranteed political independence for the Vatican State. Coming to a compromise was not easy for the two leaders. The treaty had been three years in the making, and many of the delays were due to concessions Pius XI had asked of Mussolini. For example, Mussolini had his children baptized in 1923, and in 1926, he confirmed his marriage to Rachele in a Catholic ceremony (their first marriage in 1915 had been a civil ceremony). Among the many sticking points for Pius XI had been Mussolini's promotion of popular culture, most notably the "immoral" elements of the jazz age: nightclubs, evocative dances and revealing ladies' fashions. For several years, the Vatican's official newspaper *Osservatore Romano* had run a series of articles condemning the American imports,[72] and as early as 1927, Pius XI had voiced concern about "the discordant cacophony, arrhythmic howls, and wild cries" of jazz. "To listen to the music and see the dances puts one in a profound malaise," he claimed.[73] In all fairness, these concerns about the negative influences of foreign popular culture were not groundless.

Under Mussolini's watch, the jazz age had introduced an increase in drug and alcohol consumption among Italian youth. As firsthand witnesses later explained: It was a reckless era, with "plenty of champagne," and even a little cocaine. "At that time, taking some 'white' was quite normal in high society,"[74] especially among women. "In the evening, at the Salone Margherita and the Apollo [in Rome], the beautiful actresses sniffed the 'snow' with pretty quills, much to the enthusiasm of their fans, who … after the show or the last song, gifted them with cocaine cases made of platinum and diamonds."[75] It was a heady time, and in response to the Pope's concerns,

Mussolini declared the closing of numerous dance halls.[76] But this was merely a ruse.[77] Theaters, cinemas, hotels and restaurants continued to host jazz performances and dances, and with the premiere of *EIAR-Jazz* – on Easter Sunday, no less, the holiest day of the year – even private homes were turned into dance halls on a daily basis.[78] Response to Mussolini's handling of the Vatican was mixed among Italians. Americans, however, generally approved of the Prime Minister's approach. For example, the Director of the American Academy in Rome, Gorham Phillips Stevens, told colleagues at home that he appreciated the way Mussolini had dealt with the Vatican, claiming that his "straightening out one thing after another" had brought "tremendous good" to Italy.[79]

An article in *Radiorario* announcing the premier of *EIAR-Jazz* ensured readers that the new program would feature the music of "professional performers from the most noted jazz bands in Europe and America."[80] Although the various musicians were not identified by name, readers were assured of the musicians' many talents: "In *EIAR-JAZZ* every musician is an expert on his instrument. Many know how to play the trumpet, violin and piano, and four of the band members know how to play five different instruments, and all of them well."[81] The announcement also outlined the primary purpose of the daily broadcasts:

Rhythmic music, which is inadequately called "jazz," has arisen to meet the needs of dance; on the radio it is intended for dancing and not simply listening. Even when the basis for the music is an ordinary song, a classical tune or an opera aria, it is nevertheless transformed into a fox-trot or a waltz in the end.[82]

The inclusion of this explanation was likely in response to a disagreement that had erupted the week before and was described in a *Radiorario* article titled: "Jazz expulsed from … Dance Halls!" As the reporter explained, "an assembly of composers, songwriters and dance teachers" had just voted, "after a laborious and heated discussion, to put forward a resolution to shun jazz." The reason for this rejection was based solely on the music, which in its current state was deemed to be "too loud and disruptive." But as the *Radiorario* reporter explained, the matter was not yet fully resolved: The assembly came to the conclusion that "a very attenuated form of jazz could be tolerated" if "orchestras would expel thunderous instruments like the bass drum and trombones." Describing "these new guidelines for jazz" as "interesting" when considered within the context of tasteful dance music, the reporter suggested that the "expulsed instruments be replaced" with softer instruments like "the Moroccan drum" and "vibraphone."[83]

The officials who implemented *EIAR-Jazz* anticipated some criticism from listeners, and in an effort to quell this backlash in advance, they stressed that "a good deal of hard work" had gone "into the preparation of the jazz programs" and the compilation of the "new library" of jazz music, which contained "the names of great composers, [also] famous in other fields." Noting how "extremely important" it was that "the modern bands succeed," the announcement reminded readers of the recent advancements in jazz and asked them to give the new program a chance:

An orchestrator must have great talent to use effectively all the musical and instrumental material at his disposal. To create jazz today is a delicate art, and as a remarkable musical refinement, it is essential … We are now a long way from the crudity and disorderliness of the early bands, and we are sure that the well-attuned ears of our million listeners will welcome *EIAR-Jazz*, even if for some it might require a little patience.[84]

EIAR-Jazz was a major initiative, with an extensive broadcast schedule. The program aired a minimum of four hours a day, every day, in one-to-two-hour segments with an additional two-hour broadcast on Sunday evenings from 6:00 to 8:00.[85] Although the new format had been created in response to listener surveys, the sudden preponderance of jazz over the airwaves sparked a cultural debate within the Fascist party. For example, Franco Abbiati, a loyal Fascist and well-known music critic for the *Corriere della Sera*, declared jazz "an offense to good taste," "a threat to public health," "the musical Anti-Christ." Abbiati disdained the manner in which a "cultured and genuflecting Italian public" had embraced "the newest Negro-American art." Most offensive to him was the fact that jazz, with its "heart-stopping, syphilitic … phallic rhythms" had replaced the traditional music of Naples, the "sweet song of Piedigrotta."[86]

Not surprisingly, Mascagni, who had recently been appointed to the government's Supervisory Committee for Radio Broadcasting, bewailed the overwhelming presence of jazz as well and its growing dominance over opera:

The publicity given to opera is not at all comparable to that given to *musica leggera* and jazz. The enthusiastic young people who once sacrificed all their energies to promoting it, and the entrepreneurs who in the past supported opera and real music enthusiastically and successfully around the world, have either become wealthy [and retired] or have died. Their successors do not understand real music; they are business people whose only goal is to make a fortune as soon as possible. From this point of view, *musica leggera* and jazz – which aim to satisfy the most vulgar pleasures – are much more lucrative work. Jazz has now taken over the radio. Its terrible voice excites listeners and kills what little love for real music might have still remained. Perhaps jazz will win, and opera will be eliminated. I only hope that public taste will soon recover from this sickness.[87]

It is interesting to note the use of the term "musica leggera" here. This was a recent addition to the Italian language, used to designate the new "light" (i.e. entertaining and/or easy to listen to) music associated with the latest technologies: gramophones, radios and film. Although many Fascists accepted the arrival of this new jazz-related genre, others, among them Mussolini's brother Arnaldo, looked to radio as a mouthpiece for the regime, with little room for "the traps of dilettantism, of futile worldliness, of the spirit of a traditional popularizing culture of dubious taste."[88] Mussolini disagreed. The new media required new genres to lure a new generation of listeners. "Vanished are the days when all of Europe pays close attention to [political] speeches," he claimed. "When political matters are discussed on the wireless, the people listen to a sentence or two and then switch it off."[89] In Mussolini's mind, the only way radio could attract the masses was through entertainment. Consequently, performances of *musica leggera*, including jazz, often bracketed daily newscasts and government updates.

With *EIAR-Jazz*, the debate over popular music pitted those who embraced it as "an erosion of fundamental Italian values and attitudes" that represented a lowering of "moral and aesthetic standards" against those, like Mussolini, who saw its increased presence "as an expression of healthy evolution."[90] Race became a point of contention as tempers flared over *EIAR-Jazz*. Consequently, discussions of popular music became ever more divided along national/racial lines, i.e. Black America versus White Italy.

Black Jazz versus White Jazz in the Italian Press

In response to the establishment of *EIAR-Jazz*, Guido Carlo Visconti, a newly appointed member of the Italian senate, published an article in *Il Giornale d'Italia* titled "Out with the Barbarians!" that began with a declaration of cultural rights and a description of its most recent threat:

We have the right, indeed, I prefer to say a duty, to imprint genuine Italian identity not only on our customs, hobbies and games but also on our art. Yet today, under Fascism, we, who have a musical heritage that is undoubtedly the richest and most varied among those of all civilized peoples (ranging from oratorios to melodrama, from the symphony to the quartet, from lyric opera to dance), we are resigned to acknowledge, unquestioned and unchallenged, the dominance of the Negroes' wild music.[91]

Visconti claimed there was no escape from jazz: "even in the most modest and least cosmopolitan provincial city, you cannot enter a hall, be it public or private, without your eardrums being torn by the clash of the most divisive cacophony." Believing at first that the "tangle of rhythms" and "deafening tumult of noise" was simply "a joke in bad taste," Visconti described his shock upon hearing from EIAR officials that jazz had been embraced as "music made to express the spirit, the passions and the agony of humanity today." Visconti explained to his readers how such a travesty had occurred: "To serve deference to fashion," we "opened our doors to men of inferior races, as though they were the apostles of a new truth, the heralds of a new beauty." And over the course of several years, "as Negroes performed in our theaters," their "white" audiences learned to dance in a manner "parodying the grotesque and sometimes obscene movements of savages and chimpanzees."[92]

Realizing that the "clumsy delirium" brought to Italy by "crowds of black men" was not one of those fads "that occasionally speed past like meteors, without leaving a trace," Visconti demanded a call to action:

We must react against the jazz band, as we have reacted against cocaine, and as one should take action against the use and abuse of all types of alcoholic beverages – whiskey, gin, cocktails – which serve no purpose other than to turn humanity into cretins. But who should take up this crusade: the Church, the Press, the Educational Institutions, the general public? That is not enough; it requires coercive measures that only the government can take.[93]

Visconti called upon Mussolini to establish a "rigid, severe, unrelenting protectionist policy" against musical influences from abroad. "Don't we put import duties on foreign products to protect our industries against invasion and competition? One could do the same … to save the Italian character of our spirit" by levying "heavy taxes against all the managers or owners of Kursalons, night clubs and Music-Halls who refuse to give up the great attraction of the jazz band." But there was no time for delay. "We must act quickly," warned Visconti, "before the hopeless corruption of the jazz band's cacophony" dulls "the musical sensibility of our youth" to the point that they can no longer find the beauty in Bellini's "Casta Diva" or "humor in [Rossini's] *The Barber of Seville*."[94]

Visconti's vitriol against jazz wasn't completely surprising, given his personal stake in Italy's musical culture. Only six years earlier, he had founded "Italica," a nonprofit organization dedicated to the promotion of works by lesser-known Italian composers. Like Mascagni, Visconti considered the arrival of jazz a threat to native Italian culture. And he wasn't the only one. Even some of the Futurists, the first in Italy to praise the importance of black culture to the advancement of modern art, began to note with disdain the rising popularity of African American jazz over their own avant-garde productions. For example, Anton Giulio Bragaglia, one of the first Futurists to open a nightclub in Rome, made a clear distinction between "Negro jazz" and native Italian dance music in his book *Jazz-Band*. Published shortly after the implementation of *EIAR-Jazz*, the book was a compilation of twenty-nine previously published essays concerning what he considered to be the abysmal state of Italy's current popular culture.[95] Although Bragaglia had once embraced African American music and dance as important influences on modernist art, he had come to believe that the predominance of the music, and the growing trend by many Italians to imitate and emulate it, was having a derogatory effect on the nation's performing arts.[96] In *Jazz-Band*, Bragaglia used violently racist remarks to build an argument against the recent craze for all things American. His biggest complaint involved the disastrous effects of Hollywood films, filled with the "animalistic dances" of "colored people" driven by the "epileptic chaos of the syncopated rhythm found in jazz."[97] Indeed, Bragaglia viewed all foreign influences on Italian culture – "Anglo-Saxon snobbery, the devilishness of the American Negro, the usual Parisian mannerisms and their crazy orchestras" – with disdain. Only by "invoking Italian dances," with "their urbane steps of elegance and refinement," could modern performers escape "being bestial in any way or imitating the beasts."[98] Simply put, Bragaglia called on Italians to change their ways:

Our amusements, games and entertainments must aspire to a higher level. And in the music-hall, in the caffè-concerto, in the variety show, in the circuses and in every type of performance, the Negro essence must be rejected in the name of good sense. The typical Black-Follies infect the dance halls; they unknowingly debase themselves in the hysterical epileptic atmosphere that they construct with their savage ways. The time has come to kick out the dogs, especially the dancing dogs, and in particular those [dogs] of black color.[99]

For Bragaglia, jazz was a physical art, indistinguishable from dance. Consequently, he viewed the popularity of African American performers like Josephine Baker and Harry Fleming as an attack on the modernistic revolution being fought by native Italians, most notably the Futurists. Bragaglia was not the only Futurist to change his mind about African American culture. In 1937 Marinetti declared: "In an effort to assist Italian musicians ... let us fight against ... African American melodies and ostinatos, those songs and dances we regarded as original twenty-five years ago, but now realize, in fact, are not."[100] Even the graphic artist Fortunato Depero, who designed an advertisement campaign for Campari in 1930, made a visual distinction between African and Italian musical culture in his poster designs for "Bitter" and regular Campari.[101]

In response to the onslaught of racially charged attacks on jazz, Casella came to the genre's defense once again in two articles published in *Italia Letteraria* in 1929. In the first article, published on April 7, he described the current state of jazz appreciation in Italy:

In the last decade a musical phenomenon of the upmost importance has arisen: *jazz*. And it would be stupid to misunderstand its value and its consequences ...

Those who don't understand anything about *jazz* go on saying that this music is a hellish product, devilish, invented by Beelzebub to ruin humanity. They write that African American music is a barbaric art form designed for no other reason than to excite the tired, worn-out senses of a corrupt and decadent public.

This foolishness is profoundly far from reality. *Jazz* is an artistic product – not a decadence – caused by the coupling between the musical genius of a race that is still virginal and immature (the Negro race) and the open-minded, healthy and optimistic spirit of North America.[102]

Describing jazz as an innovative, improvisatory art, Casella compared it to the Italian tradition of *Commedia dell'arte* and emphasized its importance to the advancement of European culture:

One could argue that jazz is not really a new music, but rather a new way of playing certain instruments ... But the fact still remains that jazz has contributed greatly to bringing rhythm back into European music, and it has oriented the public spirit towards new horizons that are fresher and more serene. And although it might sound crude, we must say that this music is healthier than the decadence of romanticism and the recent pre-war era. I consider the jazz phenomenon as essentially comparable to that of the *Commedia dell'arte*. Because jazz is the same thing: a true and proper art of improvisation on a canvas of predetermined sounds, wherein the music continually revives and transforms itself according to a collaboration between composer and performer that has never existed before in music ... For this, and for many other reasons, jazz deserves regular study, instead of superficial and empty insults ... And I am honored to be one of the first European musicians to have understood the singular importance of this grand phenomenon, even before the Americans themselves.[103]

In his second article, published several months later, Casella confronted, among other things, the issue of race by describing the history of jazz as a series of cultural appropriations:

Jazz as we know it today, I would say, is essentially very American. This art synthesizes with admirable eloquence the sound of that dizzying mixture of blood and races that is the United States. Born in the jungle, this art was transformed in the heart and on the lips of the American Negro before it finally reached the North, where it found its ultimate expression in the work of whites, like Whiteman (Christian) or Berlin and Gershwin (Jewish).[104]

Casella was not convinced that the Europeans' attempts at jazz had been wholly successful. That said, he admitted that "a huge advance in the realm of Italy's *musica leggera* and popular music" in recent years was largely due to the arrival of jazz:

If one thinks about ... the rhythmic and instrumental richness that the *dancing* American has finally introduced through *jazz* during the following period (1914–1929), one gains a fair idea of the good that African American art has brought to music. In fact, I don't hesitate to confirm that I consider *jazz* (the American version, not that of the Europeans, which is an imitation) an incredibly powerful educational tool for the masses.[105]

Casella admitted that he did not know what the future held for jazz in Italy. "Will it remain dance music? Or could its techniques serve as a foundation for symphonic and theatrical art?" But he was sure that Americans would continue to lead the way in its evolution. "I believe that the watchword for the Europeans is to view jazz [not only] as an artistic fact of the highest importance, but also as an internal affair of the United States that the composers of that country will have to attend to themselves."[106]

Mussolini appears to have been influenced by Casella's ideas. During an interview in 1933, he commented on the topic of music and national character: "The language of music is international," he said, "but its essential nature is purely national. Music seems to me the profoundest means of expression for any race of man. This applies to performers as well as composers."[107] On the issue of race, specifically, he claimed:

Of course, there are no pure races left; not even the Jews have kept their blood unmingled ... Race! It is a feeling, not a reality; ninety-five percent, at least, is feeling. Nothing will ever make me believe that biologically pure races can be shown to exist today ... No such doctrine will ever find wide acceptance here in Italy ... National pride has no need of the delirium of race.[108]

Strange words coming from the man who just five years later would implement Italy's race laws. One cannot help but wonder if Mussolini actually meant what he said or was simply telling his interviewer, Emil Ludwig, what he wanted to hear. Ludwig (born Emil Cohn) was a German author of Jewish descent who made no secret of his disdain for Adolf Hitler, the recently elected Chancellor of Germany, who had just enacted a series of anti-Jewish laws. When Ludwig asked Mussolini what he thought about anti-Semitism, the dictator boldly claimed: "Anti-Semitism does not exist in Italy," because "Italians of Jewish birth have shown themselves to be good citizens. They fought bravely in the war," and today "many of them occupy leading positions in the universities, in the army, and in the banks."[109]

Mussolini continuously touted his disdain for anti-Semitism to the foreign press, especially as his collaborations with Hitler strengthened. For example, on June 25, 1936 he declared to the *New York Times*: "The Jews of Italy have had, presently have, and will continue to have the same treatment as any other Italian citizen, and ... there is no place in my mind for any form of racial or religious discrimination."[110] Sadly, this inclusive, antiracist attitude would soon disappear.

In his interview with Ludwig, Mussolini embraced the idea of promoting a "new" Italy via popular music, which he compared to other "elements of spectacle" (namely, women, the Fascist salute and political emblems) that facilitated his ability to capture the attention of the masses:

Music and women allure the crowd and make it more pliable. The Roman greeting, songs and formulas, anniversary commemorations, and the like – all are essential to fan the flames of the enthusiasm that keeps a movement in being. It was the same in ancient Rome.[111]

On the topic of spectacle, Ludwig noted that he was "surprised" that Mussolini had "not made more use of the cinema for propaganda purposes." The dictator agreed that film was important. "Soon we shall have more money to spare for the cinemas," he said. "Today the film is the strongest available weapon."[112]

Jazz in Film

Numerous scholars have noted Mussolini's love of American cinema. One issue that has not been widely discussed, however, was the role he played in film history. Throughout the 1920s, American film companies invested heavily in various sound technologies for cinema. By 1927, two companies – Warner Bros. and Fox – found themselves competing in a neck-and-neck race to be the first to release a commercial film with synchronized sound. While Warner Bros. had invested heavily in a recording-on-disc method developed by Western Electric and trade-named "Vitaphone," the Fox Film Corporation had purchased patents for a sound-on-film technology, called "Movietone," which eventually became the industry standard.[113] Most film histories list *The Jazz Singer*, released by Warner Bros. on October 6, 1927, as the first feature film with recorded sound. And technically, it was. But two weeks previous to its release (on September 23, 1927), Fox premiered the first talking newsreels as an accompaniment to its Movietone feature *Sunrise*, directed by F. W. Murnau. Although *Sunrise* only offered synchronized music, the newsreels offered music and dialogue by featuring a performance of the Vatican Choir in Rome and a "message of friendship" from the "Man of the Hour, His Excellency Benito Mussolini, Premier of Italy."[114]

As a reviewer for *Variety* noted, the initial popularity of the *Sunrise* screenings was largely due to the "talking" short, which gave "all the barbers in five boroughs" the opportunity "to hear Ben Mussolini speak his piece."[115] Speaking in broken English, Mussolini made a point of praising American ingenuity and highlighting the invaluable contributions made by Italian immigrants to American society:

I am very glad to be able to express my friendly feelings towards the American nation. [The] Friendship – with which Italy looks at the millions of citizens, who from Alaska to Florida, from the Pacific to the Atlantic, live in the United States – is very deeply rooted in our hearts. This feeling, created by mutual interest, [has] also contributed in [the] preparation of an even brighter era in the lives of both nations. I greet the wonderful energy of the American people, and I see and recognize among you, ... my fellow citizens, who are working to make America great. I salute the great American people. I salute the Italians of America, who unite in the single love of two nations.[116]

Although the idea of an all-talking newsreel was slow to take hold in the United States, the new technology captivated Mussolini. "Let me speak through [the newsreel] in twenty cities in Italy once a week," he reportedly said, "and I need no other power."[117] Mussolini created the Istituto Luce (L'Unione Cinematografica Educativa), a state-run agency in Rome charged with the creation and distribution of documentary newsreels, for just this purpose.

Throughout the 1930s, jazz and its inherent links to new technology played a vital role in Mussolini's attempts to attract and lead the nation's youth. Although radios and gramophones brought jazz into the homes and businesses of those who could afford the devices, film, more than any other medium, introduced jazz to the masses. In addition to Italian newsreels, some of which offered brief glimpses of life in America, Italians were treated to an array of full-length films during the 1920s and 30s, the majority of which were produced in Hollywood. Movie attendance was the most popular form of mass entertainment in Fascist Italy. According to a survey conducted by the Società Italiana Autori e Editori (SIAE) in 1936, the cinema dominated all forms of entertainment, with ticket sales exceeding 65 percent of total entertainment expenditures paid.[118]

Film brought a face to jazz – and in many American films, this face was black. Indeed, it was the advent of talking films that solidified in the minds of many Italians the idea that American jazz was originally an African American phenomenon appropriated and commercialized by white musicians. Such a message is clearly expressed in *The Jazz Singer* (*Il cantante di jazz*), which caused a sensation when it was finally released in Italy in 1928. The film tells the story of Jakie Rabinowitz (Al Jolson), a young Jewish man torn between his desire for a life on the stage and loyalty to his parents, who expect him to follow in his father's footsteps and become a cantor. When Jakie refuses the traditional path and chooses vaudeville, his father kicks him out of the house, calling him nothing but a "jazz singer." The climax of the film comes towards the end, when Jakie, who now sings under the name Jack Robbins, returns to New York for his Broadway debut. As he sits in his dressing room, applying black greasepaint to his face, he is visited by his mother, who begs him to visit his dying father and sing in the temple on Yom Kippur. Jakie refuses at first, but later relents and chooses family over opening night. But all is not lost. The final scene shows Jack Robbins in blackface singing "Mammy" on a Broadway stage as his mother sits proudly in the audience. This scene reveals two things simultaneously: that singing jazz is an act of cultural appropriation (Jack Robbin's use of blackface makeup and African American dialect), but that such cultural appropriation does not require the rejection of one's own cultural heritage (Jakie's obvious reconciliation with his family and faith).

The Jazz Singer was not the only film to promote the ideas of cultural appropriation and assimilation. In 1930, Paul Whiteman and His Orchestra were featured in the full-length musical revue, *King of Jazz*. This film has no storyline or plot. Organized along the lines of a large-scale variety show, it contains a series of musical numbers, the most notable being a rendition of

George Gershwin's *Rhapsody in Blue* performed by an expansive jazz orchestra and a throng of dancers. The general conceit of the film is that it offers a musical rendition of the various "melodies and anecdotes" preserved in "Paul Whiteman's scrapbook." The film's opening number is an animated cartoon that purports to reveal how Whiteman came to be crowned the "King of Jazz." As a narrator explains: "Once upon a time, Paul, tiring of life in the city ... went big game hunting ... in darkest Africa." The cartoon reveals Whiteman's African adventure, where he tussles with a lion that he eventually manages to tame by singing a chorus of the Negro spiritual "My Lord Delivered Daniel." Whiteman then trades in his rifle for a jazz fiddle, and swings to the accompaniment of a medley of dancing animals (ostrich, snake, gorilla, rabbit, elephant) before a monkey throws a coconut that leaves a lump the shape of a crown on Whiteman's head, thus anointing him the "King of Jazz."

Later in the film, Whiteman confirms the theme of cultural appropriation implied in the cartoon when he introduces Gershwin's *Rhapsody in Blue*: "The most primitive and the most modern musical elements are combined in this rhapsody, for jazz was born in the African jungle, to the beating of the voodoo drums." A pseudo-African/Caribbean figure (in full-body black paint) appears at this point, dancing on a giant drum.[119] As the beat dies away, the ascending wail of a Klezmer clarinet marks the beginning of Gershwin's composition. As this choreographed performance of *Rhapsody in Blue* attempts to show, the roots of jazz may trace back to Africa, but in the context of contemporary American music, jazz is a fully commercialized, lily-white spectacle of the Broadway stage.

The final scene of *King of Jazz*, titled "The Melting Pot of Music," presents the European immigrants' contributions to American jazz. As the narrator explains at the beginning of the scene, "America is a melting pot of music, wherein the melodies of all nations are fused into one great, new rhythm – Jazz!" This is followed by a medley of folksongs and dances from England, Italy, Scotland, Germany, Ireland, Spain, Russia and France. There is no reference to African American influence, except for the hint of a gospel tune at the very end.

In the United States, *King of Jazz* did not do well at the box office, even though it received an Academy Award for Best Art Direction. In Italy, however, the film drew record crowds when it was released under the title *Il re del jazz*. Italian audiences were especially excited by the film's inclusion of featured performances by well-known Italian American musicians: most notably Joe Venuti, Eddie Lang (born Salvatore Massaro) and Mike Pingitore.

For many, *Il re del jazz* – with its mix of big band swing numbers, evocative dances, comedy routines and cinematic special effects – served as a visual example of what modern *European* jazz might be. As one Italian journalist noted, under Mussolini's watch, films like *Il re del jazz* offered new models for the nation's youth:

The situations, gestures, physiognomies and environments they see, like the words they hear, enter into their memories as real, lived experience; they stir up fantasies, stimulate dreams, and can even form characters. Many youth today possess a temperament that might be best defined as cinematographic.[120]

American films also strengthened racist stereotypes among Italian audiences. During the 1920s and 30s, a growing number of African American actors appeared in American films, although rarely in a flattering light. In the silent era they generally appeared as jesters or fools, "high-stepping and high-falutin' and crazy as all get-out."[121] In the 1930s, almost every American film imported to Italy, from light-hearted comedies like *It Happened One Night* (1934) and Shirley Temple's *The Last Rebel* (1935) to spectacles like *Gone with the Wind* (1939), presented African Americans as domestic servants.[122] And when they weren't cleaning, cooking or working in the livery stables, African Americans were singing the blues or playing jazz. Italian film critic Romolo Marcellini confirmed these stereotypical perceptions in 1936, when he described the residents of Harlem as shown in American films:

The whole world is very familiar with Negroes: they have big lips, curly hair, flat noses. The largest block of Negroes exists in the nightclubs and in the neighborhood of Harlem; the Cotton Club has the greatest singers and dancers of the Negro people. The elevator operators of New York seem to be the liveliest Negroes in the world. Records convey the songs and voices of the Negroes. The cinema presents us with the most unsettling rumbas of black-mulatto girls, the most pleasant Negro waiters on trains [in] white jackets, [with] eyes like white porcelain.[123]

As Marcellini's observations reveal, by the time the swing era reached its zenith in the mid-1930s, the American films shown in Italy featured performances by famous African American musicians. Often extraneous to the central plot, these performances served no other purpose than to create a sense of atmosphere in a nightclub or at a theater. Primary examples include Cab Calloway's performance of the song "Reefer Man" in *International House* (1933), the stage show performances of Duke Ellington and His Orchestra in *Belle of the Nineties* and *Murder at the Vanities* (1934) and Louis Armstrong and his band's appearance in a swanky café scene in *Pennies from Heaven* (1936).[124] Film gave American performers, both black and white, a musical voice, and it was this voice, more than anything else, that captivated Italian audiences. Consequently, with the release of each new film came an increasing demand from audience members to hear their favorite tunes again, either on the radio or on gramophone discs. Record companies took advantage of this growing audience, and throughout the first half of the 1930s, American recordings, by both black and white performers, flooded the Italian market.

The Recording Industry

As he did with radio, Mussolini took an interest in the recording industry when foreign influences began to dominate the Italian market. Throughout the 1920s, gramophones were relatively expensive, and the production of discs was limited.[125] Although several Italian companies had been founded in the early years of the twentieth century – Fonodisco Italiano Trevisan (renamed Fonit in 1926), Fonotecnica and Fonotipia[126] – the Italian record industry was primarily in foreign hands during the 1920s and early 1930s.[127] But all this changed in 1933 when Mussolini established Cetra, a state-run recording and distribution company.[128] Due to the growing demand among Italian radio listeners for additional music programming, EIAR turned to recorded music in the 1930s as a viable source. But playing recordings produced by commercial record companies proved expensive for EIAR. As an article in *Radiocorriere* explained in 1932, EIAR's broadcast of "up to two hours of recorded music" each day required the payment of licensing fees to an array of record labels, most of them foreign.[129] Thus Cetra was founded to serve as a partial corrective of this economic imbalance. To begin, Cetra took over as the primary Italian distributor for most foreign record labels. In the case of jazz, this meant that well-known labels like La Voce del Padrone (the Italian branch of My Master's Voice), Columbia, Odeon and Parlophon could only sell records in Italy under contract with Cetra. Italian companies continued independently, and in the case of Fonit, this meant the continuance of its distribution of recordings on the UK's Polydor label and the right to reissue American recordings originally released by Decca. This new distribution model gave the Italian government and Italian companies control over the foreign music that entered the country as well as a cut of the profits. Cetra's greatest advantage, however, was its connection to Italian radio. Cetra recordings were produced in EIAR's Turin and Rome broadcasting studios, which were outfitted with the machines needed for the incision and reproduction of discs. This arrangement meant that a performance broadcast live on the air could be recorded simultaneously and later sold for a profit to listeners interested in hearing the performance again. Although unique in Europe, this setup wasn't wholly original. A similar system had been set up in the United States in 1929 when RCA acquired the recording company Victor for the same purpose.[130]

The increased broadcast of gramophone discs on Italian radio inevitably led to the establishment of specialty periodicals, like *Il disco*, aimed at the growing market of record collectors. One of the most famous reviewers of jazz recordings during this period was Vittorio Mussolini, whose interest in the music was largely fueled by the innovative work of Duke Ellington and Louis Armstrong. In an article published in 1934 and titled "Cinque dischi hot" (Five Hot Discs), Vittorio Mussolini became one of the first to welcome officially the arrival of "Hot" jazz on the Italian market:

Those who enjoy this species of jazz music will be glad to know that these five new discs contain all the elements that make the "hot" disc interesting: the rhythm, the perfect tightness of tempo, the singing – these elements are never abandoned on these recordings by the most famous orchestras.[131]

As Vittorio Mussolini's article makes clear, some of the recordings under review had been released in anticipation of new films arriving from Hollywood:

Duke Ellington and his famous Orchestra return publicly with a magnificent recording of "Ebony Rhapsody," a fox[trot] that is part of the Paramount film *Murder of Vanities* [sic] and that is a transcription of the famous Hungarian Rhapsody No. 2 by Liszt. This might seem an absurdity, but those who have listened to this disc have a good impression of it, because [the Rhapsody] is so well orchestrated and arranged that the tempo and music are not subjected to significant changes. Of course, it is an arduous transcription, but the ingenuity of these Negroes deserves forgiveness.[132]

Clearly, Vittorio Mussolini had not yet seen the film wherein the Ellington Orchestra's exhilarating performance of "Ebony Rhapsody" is presented as a metaphorical "rape" of European culture. The performance is part of a stage act titled "Rape of the Rhapsody." It begins with an all-white orchestra performing Liszt's Hungarian Rhapsody No. 2. As they are playing, Ellington and his musicians deftly insert themselves within the ensemble, adding jazz licks between phrases until the white conductor and his musicians are driven away in frustration. Liszt's music is then transformed into the "Ebony Rhapsody," which brings great pleasure to the dozens of young women, both black and white, who appear on stage and dance with great abandon. The scene ends abruptly when the original white conductor returns with a machine gun and enacts his "revenge" for Ellington's musical "rape" by mowing down everyone on stage with a barrage of bullets. No doubt, it was scenes such as these from American films that contributed to racial prejudices against jazz in Italy.

But back to the review: if Vittorio Mussolini's interest in Ellington was the result of respect for the bandleader, then his interest in Louis Armstrong was nothing less than idolization:

> Which brings us to the most characteristic of hot orchestras, that of Louis Armstrong's Negroes. For them, the "hot" [style] is a natural thing, and they had the rhythm in their ears as soon as they were born. Thus, if one wanted to define the "hot" style, one could say that it is the fox[trot] arranged by Armstrong, without fear of making mistakes. Louis plays the trumpet in a perfect manner. He alone has the capacity to achieve on it the specific timbres of the clarinet or violin. He sings in a funny accent that leads instinctively to laughter and is no less effective in "Georgia on My Mind" or "Lazy River."[133]

Louis Armstrong in Italy

Several months after this review appeared, Armstrong visited Italy for the first time and presented two concerts, on January 15 and 16, at the Teatro Chiarella in Turin. The concerts sold out almost instantly and were warmly received by those in attendance. As a local reporter noted after the first concert: "Armstrong is great, and only those with an ignorant, preconceived aversion to his art could impede its diffusion" by refusing to participate as a member of its "most diverse public."[134]

According to the reporter, the draw of Armstrong's music was its deep, emotional expressiveness, which was the result of his sufferings as an African American who came of age during the World War:

> Armstrong is black and is already thirty-four years old: thus by reason of blood he knows and suffers the pain and repressed aspiration of his race; due to the environment in which he lived and his age, he took part in all the anxieties and torments that afflict the soul of those who opened their eyes to the world when the conflagration of war enveloped it, and of those who tackled their earliest virile experiences while the reverberations of the enormous funeral pyre made humanity suffer.[135]

But it wasn't just the war that influenced Armstrong's music. As the reporter explained, his mentors and formative experiences proved equally influential:

Armstrong was born in New Orleans and had King Oliver and Fletcher Henderson as teachers. Thus, while still a babe at his mother's breast, he imbibed through his senses the rhythm and the drama of Negro music; he learned everything that is profound, genius, orgiastic, sad, sweet, ancient, anti-traditional, fatalistic and combative about "jazz" from the people who served as its fathers and earliest disseminators. No one more than Armstrong can thus love, feel and render this music. Today he is its most complete and celebrated exponent and propagandist.[136]

Turin embraced Armstrong for his exhilarating music and everything that it represented. As the reporter noted towards the end of his article, Armstrong was more than a famous entertainer. Through his music, he offered audiences a vision of the universal "Negro."

Louis Armstrong's trumpet and voice are the pain and the voice, the ardor and the sad fate, the intimate satisfactions and the dark injustices of the poor and naive Negro and the evolved and cunning Negro. Everything merges in the infinite crucible of Armstrong's art and sensitivity, and his rude, ruthlessly honest, communicative musical appearance emerges. Last night, Louis Armstrong proved this to the people of Turin. In Turin, he was accompanied by the triumph of his art.[137]

Armstrong returned to the United States directly after his second concert, and on the way home, he wrote a letter of thanks to Alfredo Antonino, the avid record collector and fan who had worked hard to make his visit a success.

Steamer Champlain, Jan. 24th 1935

Dear pal Alfredo,

I imagine this will be a big surprise to you when you receive this letter written by me out here in the middle of this Atlantic Ocean. Yes – this means that I have at last decided to return home in dear ol' Chicago Illinois, USA.

Canetti (my manager) and I had a little disagreement (quarrel), and since we couldn't patch things up I thought it best to return to America.[138] As I have stayed over in Europe long enough anyway. So I'll say that Torino Italy was the last place that I played my trumpet, and had my biggest success in All Europe. And I'm tellin' you Pal, I am a real happy man to think about it. And I must thank you again for making it possible.

I may be able to do something real nice for you some day, you never can tell, maybe you'll come to America some time. Eh? I hope so. Just look me up if you do. And you must say hello to all the "Hot" Fans in Torino.

My darling wife Alpha sends best regards to you and all the fans.[139] She's thrilled highly over my success in good ol' Torino – "yea, man."

Pal, you must answer this letter right away, as I'll be home by the time you get this letter. Again, thanks a million Zillion times for making it possible for my success in Torino. Good bye, "Gate." [Armstrong's nickname for Antonino]

I am, SWINGINGLY yours, Louis "Satchmo" Armstrong[140]

This letter reveals much about how comfortable Armstrong felt in Italy among his newly found friends and fans. That said, if Armstrong had arrived just a few months later, he likely would not have enjoyed such a warm reception.

Italy's Invasion of Ethiopia

Throughout the summer of 1935, race relations in Italy became strained as Mussolini embarked on a quest for expanded power that involved the seizure of Ethiopia (then known as Abyssinia), one of the few independent states in a European-dominated Africa. Mussolini had been threatening an invasion of Ethiopia for nearly a year. He believed that if Italy was going to claim its place as an equal among the great European nations, it needed to stake a claim in Africa, as France and Great Britain had done a generation before. Rejecting arbitration offers made by the League of Nations, Mussolini's troops invaded Ethiopia on October 3, 1935 with 2,300 machine guns, 230 cannons, 156 tanks and 126 planes. Among the aggressors were Mussolini's sons, Vittorio and Bruno, who were hailed by Italians as heroes for the incendiary bombs they dropped on civilian homes and hospitals. This was the beginning of Mussolini's colonial war, and the end of Italy's membership in a united Europe. Within days of the invasion, the League of Nations imposed sanctions on Italy that applied to all Italian imports and any exports that could prove beneficial to the war effort.[141] In response, Mussolini launched a series of bans, or at least limitations, on foreign imports, especially those coming from Great Britain, Italy's loudest critic at the time.

As to Italy's relationship with the United States: prior to 1935 Mussolini had enjoyed a relatively positive rapport with American politicians and businessmen. To them, he stood as an important ally – the man who had restored Italy's economic fortunes and suppressed social agitation and the threat of Communism. Although this state of affairs was threatened with Italy's invasion of Ethiopia, it was not destroyed. The US government remained neutral during the conflict, even though many American citizens did not. Not surprisingly, the loudest debates over the conflict came from the African American and Italian American communities. Italy's aggression against Ethiopia sparked numerous demonstrations and fund-raising activities on both sides. For example, the National Association for the Advancement of Colored People (NAACP) informed the public about the Ethiopian conflict through a series of articles and commentaries published in *Crisis*, the organization's official magazine. In addition, the NAACP Board petitioned the League of Nations (of which the United States was not a member) to protect Ethiopia's national status, and it lobbied the US Congress to abandon the neutrality legislation that they had adopted for economic reasons.[142]

Italian Americans became equally engaged in the debate, but almost universally in support of Mussolini. Even before the war began, at least fourteen Italian American societies petitioned President Roosevelt to maintain "strict neutrality" if and when the invasion took place. Reminding the president that Italian Americans constituted a "considerable portion of the citizens of the United States," they highlighted the "traditional affinity of interests" that linked Italy and America. Once the war was under way, the *Voice of Italy* published an editorial criticizing the *New York Times* for the "unfair attitude" it displayed in favoring the arguments presented by the "American Friends of Ethiopia" over those of the "American League for Italy."[143] Both armies committed atrocities during the conflict, but Mussolini's implementation of chemical weapons in December 1935 instigated a fresh wave of anti-Italian sentiment in the United States, even though, officially, the government refused to take sides.[144]

One cannot help but wonder if this renewed hostility against Italian Americans in late 1935 instigated to some extent Nick LaRocca's infamous racist rants against African American musicians the following year. In a torrent of op-ed articles, interviews and letters, LaRocca raged against anyone and everyone who tried to discredit the historic importance of Italian American musicians, like himself, and the ODJB. In an article published in 1936 in *Metronome*, for example, LaRocca described New Orleans Dixieland as "strictly a white man's music" with no link to African American culture:

Many writers have attributed this rhythm that we introduced as something coming from the African jungles, and crediting the Negro race with it. My contention is that the Negroes learned to play this rhythm and music from the whites, and I'm sure that you could all go over to Africa and never hear anything remotely resembling our music, unless it were a phonograph recording of some American or foreign band playing American music.[145]

LaRocca's racist comments earned him little sympathy at the time, and attitudes such as this only heightened the vociferous criticism penned by members of the NAACP and followers of Martin Garvey's Back to Africa movement.[146] But one prominent black musician, Josephine Baker, shocked American fans when she publically voiced support for Mussolini. Referring to Emperor Haile Selassie by the Ethiopian term "Negus" (King), she explained why she would continue to stand by Il Duce:

The Negus is really an enemy of the colored race, for he maintains slavery, which Mussolini is determined to stamp out. If need be, I am willing to recruit a colored army to help Italy. I am going to tell all the colored persons of the world that if they line up against Mussolini they will not aid their race. On the contrary, they will be adding to the slave merchants that Il Duce is determined to crush. I am willing to travel around the world to convince my brothers that Mussolini is their friend.[147]

Italian songwriters also voiced their support for Mussolini. For example, Rodolfo de Angelis released "O Duce d'Italia" (O Duce of Italy) on Columbia records in 1935.[148] This was followed in 1936 by "Va fuori d'Italia prodotto straniero" (Get out of Italy, Foreign Product)[149] and "Addio Canzoni Americane" (Goodbye American Songs), which appeared on the Italian label, Grammofono.[150]

Germany offered financial support to Italy during the Ethiopian war, but its cultural policies did not affect Italian practices right away. For example, on October 13, 1935, Italians read in their morning papers that "[t]he Commissioner of the Reich's Radio Service" had "prohibited the transmission of jazz, stating that Jewish intellectuals and Bolsheviks had imported this type of music into Germany."[151] In Italy, jazz continued to be broadcast regularly. As a genre, it was never banned from Italian airwaves, and in the mid-1930s it was jazz, more than any other genre, that dominated EIAR broadcasts (Figure 3.3). That said, with the onset of the Ethiopian conflict, some changes did occur. For example, on August 8, 1935, EIAR sent a directive to all affiliated stations "absolutely abolishing" from all radio programming and transmissions: "music in a Negro character (popular Negro songs or imitation thereof, choral and solo, typical orchestras, etc.)" and "dance music with choruses sung in English." In addition, foreign musicians who held official positions with EIAR and Cetra, like the English bandleader Claude Bampton, were promptly fired.[152]

Mussolini's invasion of Ethiopia changed Italy's economic relationships with other European countries and the United States, but it did not lead to a complete elimination of American music. As the pages of *Radiocorriere* confirm, American jazz continued to play on the radio, and compositions

LA PERCENTUALE DEI VARI GENERI DI TRASMISSIONE
NEL PRIMO SEMESTRE DELL'ANNO 1934

(LA PERCENTUALE È RAPPRESENTATA DAI MICROFONI)

Figure 3.3 The Percentage of Various Kinds of Broadcasts during the First Half of 1934 (the percentage is represented by the size of the microphone) (1935).
Source: *Annuario dell'anno XIII: dieci anni di radio in Italia* (Turin: Società editrice torinese, 1935). Archive of Anna Celenza.

by American composers, both black and white, continued to be performed by Italian ensembles. If Mussolini felt any frustrations over music at all during the Ethiopian war, it was with Southern Italy's continued refusal to embrace the regime's modern identity. Consequently, he banned journalists from publishing photographs of Italian soldiers playing the mandolin and quipped that he should launch a "March on Naples" in an effort to "sweep away all the guitars, mandolins, fiddles and folksingers."[153]

Throughout the conflict in Ethiopia, Italy's Fascist regime continued to promote jazz as an important symbol. For example, in December 1935, as part of the EIAR Annual Report distributed to radio listeners, government officials emphatically declared the importance of jazz and confirmed plans to continue its transmission over national Italian radio:

Dance music, *jazz* music? The Italian Radio has never abused *jazz* music. It has followed the fashion wisely and with restraint, taking into account that if among its listeners there are those who would like nothing else, there are many others who are bothered by it, not simply because it might be barbaric, but because many of the emotions that arise from it are lost when the visual element is missing. Without joining the ranks of those who take pleasure in searching for grotesque expressions in art and applauding the new simply because it's new; without caring if one is encountering "parody" or originality, we confess that we like *jazz*. Because it seems to us that there is no music that more effectively responds to contemporary life; a well-marked rhythm; a form of servitude that gives the illusion of perfect independence. It's music that appeals to the youth. And we are always with the youth.[154]

The war with Ethiopia emphasized the importance of Italy's youth – most notably the young men who took up arms in support of Mussolini's expansionist agenda. That said, the war also strengthened a racist sensibility among many Fascist officials who called for greater differentiation between the "uncivilized" vanquished Africans of the new colony and their "civilized" Italian conquerors. Miscegenation became a popular fear in the Italian press, which in turn led to official efforts to enforce segregation laws in the conquered territory.[155] The topic of segregation grew more prevalent in musical discussions, too. Although jazz continued to flourish in Italy,[156] many advocates of the music began to make clear distinctions between the early jazz of black Americans and what they defined as a more recent form of the genre cultivated by white Europeans. This distinction is perhaps most clearly seen in two books published shortly after the war: Augusto Caraceni's *Il Jazz: dalle origini ad oggi* (Jazz: From Its Origins until Today) and *Introduzione alla vera Musica di Jazz* (Introduction to True Jazz Music) by Ezio Levi and Gian Carlo Testoni.

Caraceni's book appeared first, in 1937. Approaching the various parameters of jazz in a systematic manner, he presented a history of the genre, from its "distant origins" (i.e. plantation songs, spirituals and the blues) in African American communities to its commercialization in the 1920s and current state in 1930s America and Europe. The effect of race on the development of jazz served as a recurring topic for Caraceni, and at various points he emphasized what he saw as the differences between African Americans and Europeans. For example, at the beginning of his study, Caraceni reminded readers of the African American contribution to the origins of jazz:

As each race carries within it an indestructible tradition, so the Negro has contributed to the modern sensibility an ingenious and spontaneous spirit and the breath of a style different from our own, a force still virginal and uncorrupted by influences extraneous to its nature. In fact, he hears and sees very differently from the way the white man hears and sees. Recently, [when] put in contact with civilization, the Negro infused his mysticism and barbaric ardor into the field of music, creating an unlimited array of new experiences.[157]

Describing "Negro spirituals" as the "music that gave birth to jazz," Caraceni explained how this music "was monopolized and harmonized by Jews" and thus turned into a popular musical form that "earned millions" and "served as American propaganda."[158] In the hands of Italians, jazz changed again, he claimed, and to prove his point Caraceni included a chapter highlighting the recent advancements of European jazz.[159] In many ways, *Il Jazz: dalle origini ad oggi* reflects the state of race relations in Italy after the invasion of Ethiopia. Caraceni approaches the topic of jazz with intellectual curiosity, simultaneously praising the music while advocating caution in the consumption of this "foreign" art. He makes a clear distinction between the "Hot" jazz derived from African American culture and the more commercialized "straight" form created later by Jewish composers. Although a few Italians are mentioned in connection to contemporary jazz, Caraceni nonetheless considers jazz a wholly foreign music. This is most clearly displayed in the book's cover, which shows a caricature of an African American in profile with black skin, a wide flat nose and bulging red lips playing a diminutive saxophone.

In their *Introduzione alla vera Musica di Jazz*, which was published in February 1938, Levi and Testoni tried to mitigate some of the prejudices found in Caraceni's book. They even went so far as to quote the African American bandleader, Don Redman, who refused to see race as a characteristic of good jazz: "Frankly, I do not believe that jazz is applicable to one race more than another. For my arrangements and my hot solos, give me a motive that is a good motive, whether it's written by a Jew, an Italian or an Irishman."[160]

Introduzione alla vera Musica di Jazz is considered by many to be the most important book on jazz published in Italy before World War II. Like Vittorio Mussolini, Levi and Testoni enlivened the pages of *Il Disco* with their assessments of African American jazz. Even more importantly, in 1935 they founded Milan's *Circolo del Jazz Hot*, the first music association in Italy committed to the promotion of "Hot" jazz. Unlike Caraceni's book, which presented the evolution of jazz as a progression from black to white, *Introduzione alla vera Musica di Jazz* attempted to remove the topic of race altogether by offering an ahistorical assessment of the aesthetic and cultural benefits to be found in "Hot" jazz. As Levi and Testoni explained to readers, the goal of their book was not to incite debate, but rather to lay a path for the continued growth and development of Italian jazz:

To encourage a national production of jazz recordings (and above all of better jazz, i.e. "Hot") does not seem to us the work of snobs or xenophiles. Nor does it mean competition with the production of domestic songs and dance music; each has its own place, its own exact function, and its own consumers. In every way, it is clear to see how compensating the need for good jazz music (a need that no one can now deny) with our own artists and compositions would benefit both our national art and our national economy.[161]

For anyone who might doubt the verity of the authors' patriotism, the book's dedication made their loyalty clear: "To Vittorio Mussolini, with great sympathy, for having been among the first in Italy to comprehend and appreciate the true music of jazz." And Vittorio wasn't the only member of the Mussolini family to confirm an affinity for this music. When Il Duce was asked in 1937 which music he most preferred listening to in his spare time, he responded without hesitation: "Do not be surprised when I tell you that I have no antipathy towards jazz as dance music, and that I find it amusing."[162]

Ellington and Armstrong could still be heard on the radio in 1937. But that was soon to change. As Italy became more dependent on the financial support offered by Germany, Mussolini felt pressured to align his cultural policies ever closer to those of Hitler. In 1938, a point of no return was reached when Mussolini, much to the surprise of many Italians, formally implemented the nation's race laws. As we shall see in the following chapter, these laws not only limited the influence of American culture, they also promoted a distinct style of Italian jazz that eventually influenced the "American" sound of singers like Frank Sinatra.

4 | Jazz Italian Style

On July 14, 1938 the *Manifesto degli Scienziati Razzisti* (Manifesto of Racial Scientists) was published in the *Giornale d'Italia*. Written by a group of university professors and prominent Fascist officials, the manifesto described the ten "scientific" principles of Italy's new race laws. To summarize: it claimed that numerous human races exist, that some races are more advanced than others, and that conceptions concerning race were based on biological characteristics. It denied the assertion that various races had inhabited the Italian peninsula in the historic past, claiming instead the existence of a pure Italian race that was Aryan in origin and excluded Jews. Asserting that the physical and spiritual characteristics of Italians should remain uncorrupted, the manifesto called for a division of races. Simply put, it emphatically stated that the time had come for Italians to "embrace racism."[1]

The manifesto was commissioned by the Ministero della Cultura Popolare (Ministry of Popular Culture, commonly abbreviated to MinCulPop). Established by Mussolini in 1937 as a means of centralizing the regulation of various facets of popular culture (literature, film, music, radio, theater, tourism, etc.), MinCulPop's primary objectives were to promote Italian identity and organize Fascist propaganda. As a means of spreading the new initiative across as broad a spectrum of Italy's populace as possible, the illustrated magazine *La Difesa della Razza* (The Defense of the Race) was put into production. Published biweekly and circulated broadly among the general public, *La Difesa della Razza* was even distributed in schools in order to "propagate a more precise consciousness of the problems of race" and facilitate "Italian racism" among the nation's youth.[2]

Italy's sudden implementation of formalized racism caught many off guard. Frank Snowden, Jr., an African American scholar living in Italy at the time, noted his shock upon seeing the first issue of *La Difesa della Razza* and realizing that "the Negroes of America … were to be included in the Italian racism that was in the process of development."[3] Similarly, Albert Viton, the Rome correspondent for *The Nation*, published an article shortly after the laws went into effect that attempted to assess attitudes among the

115

general population. According to Viton, many Italians disliked their government's new racist stance, describing the legislation as proof that Mussolini had finally "lost his mind."[4] But the new laws didn't surprise everyone. The specter of government-supported discrimination had been hovering over the music industry ever since Mussolini's invasion of Ethiopia, and in the months leading up to the Race Manifesto the rhetoric in the Fascist press had increased exponentially.[5] In February 1938, for example, an article in *Il Popolo d'Italia* raised fears about the "Jewish problem" as it related to jazz:

We all know that Judaism simultaneously seeks to accumulate money and brutalize humanity in order to make the illusory quality of the "chosen people" shine brightly, and modern jazz is one of the strongest and safest Jewish weapons. With four musical notes, a lot of exasperating monotony and a strong dose of sensual bestiality, the Jews from overseas have managed to destroy the artistic sense of many people and to accumulate millions.[6]

Noting the continued popularity of recordings by Jewish American musicians in Italy, the author called for immediate action:

The time has now come for the Italian populace to widen its sacrosanct racial campaign into this field [*musica leggera*], too. And it is necessary that the initiative start with radio programs. This issue is much more important than any contract with the record companies, and it should not be stopped because of the stupid mentality of some third-rate "Maestro."[7]

The "Maestro" referenced here was no doubt Pippo Barzizza, who had taken over as Director of the Orchestra Cetra in 1936 when the Englishman Claude Bampton was fired. A prominent proponent of American jazz, Barzizza was responsible for countless "Italian" renditions of popular American tunes like "Lasciati andare" (Let Yourself Go) by Irving Berlin and Duke Ellington's "Serenità" (In the Mood). And in November 1937, a reporter for Turin's daily paper, *La Stampa*, specifically blamed Barzizza's Orchestra Cetra for "the incessant influx of jazz" on Italian radio.[8] Not surprisingly, Barzizza's performances of American tunes only exacerbated his critics' attacks against foreign music. In an article published in June 1938 titled "Nationalism in Music," Senator Visconti once again declared his discontent over the continued importation of jazz. For him, the most egregious destruction of native Italian culture was being carried out by African Americans:

These Negroes join us as conquerors and rulers. Their music – if indeed you want to call it music, made up as it is of loud noises and asthmatic rhythms – has been imposed on us. And currently it seems that next to jazz, all other music – our music, the music of civilized peoples, of white people – cannot possibly survive.[9]

One might imagine that with this uptick in criticism, the death of jazz came quickly in Italy after the race laws went into effect. But such was not the case. Whereas Hitler's Germany had been efficient and systematic in its implementation of racist legislation, Mussolini's government proved less meticulous.[10] In the realm of popular music, exceptions were made on a case-by-case basis, and economic concerns in the radio and recording industries often outweighed the need to enforce the laws rigidly.

That said, the facets of everyday life changed dramatically for countless musicians.[11] To give just three examples: Harry Fleming discontinued his tours through Italy in 1938,[12] the string bass player in Barzizza's Cetra Orchestra, Giuseppe Funaro, was dismissed because of his Jewish heritage and Ezio Levi, the cofounder of Milan's *Circolo del Jazz Hot* and coauthor of *Introduzione alla vera Musica di Jazz*, immigrated to the United States due to racial persecution. Levi had recently been hired by Vittorio Mussolini to serve as the in-house composer for a new film company he had set up with American producer Hal Roach called RAM (Roach and Mussolini) Productions.[13] The company's purpose was to produce high-quality musical films in Italy. But as Levi later explained, the arrival of Italy's race laws terminated his work with RAM:

Vittorio knew I was a musician. One day, he called me from Rome and said: "Ezio, did you know that I now have a film production company? I am currently making a modern film, a really beautiful one. I would like it if you would compose the music." I responded, "It would be a pleasure." Then he called a second time: "Ezio, instead of working ... it's summer ... Go get a passport and take a long vacation abroad." I fell into despair, because I thought that he no longer wanted to work with me. Then I read the "Race Manifesto" the next day in the *Corriere della Sera*, and I began to make a thousand conjectures. He had said nothing else. He had not told me more. My father understood everything: "Look Ezio, these people are crazy: they have said that the Italians are Italians, but the Jews are not." So I went to Paris, because I had to get a visa for America. It was easier to apply for it in Paris, more tranquil than in Italy, the country I was escaping. And it took me six or seven months, I think, because with all the refugees from Germany, the quotas for America were full.[14]

Unfortunately for Levi, the United States proved to be even less welcoming than Italy. Levi arrived in New York on April 6, 1939. Traveling from Cherbourg, France, on the Queen Mary, his entry was comfortable, to say the least. But upon reaching Ellis Island, he was detained for several days. As he later explained, his efforts to find work in the music industry were blocked by Domenico Savino, the successful songwriter who, as a child, had immigrated to the United States from Sicily.

[Savino was] a middle-aged gentleman, very rich and also very presumptuous, married to an authoritarian woman who was also his manager. She was the one who introduced me to her husband when I tried to insert myself into the American musical world, but I soon discovered how difficult it was to enter that little mafia of *musica leggera*.[15]

Eventually, Levi got what he thought would be his big break: an interview with Irving Mills. In addition to being one of the most powerful music producers and publishers, Mills had served as Duke Ellington's first manager and promoter. But once again, Levi was given the cold shoulder:

This "contact man" of mine got me an appointment with Irving Mills, who was perhaps the biggest publisher in the United States. He was also Jewish. I was in heaven. He received me and was very polite. At a certain point he began to talk to me in an incomprehensible language. He could see that I didn't understand and, quite annoyed, asked me: "You are a Jew, aren't you?" "Of course," I replied. "Then why don't you answer?" I told him that I did not understand Yiddish. You see, he was a Russian Ashkenazi Jew. I was a western Sephardic Jew. He became so angry that he rudely chased me away. Thus ended my only true and important contact with American show business.[16]

Levi was deemed "the wrong kind of Jew" in New York. And his previous connections with Vittorio Mussolini did him no favors. According to the US census, Levi was unemployed and living in a boarding house in Morningside Heights in 1940. By 1941, he had given up on the idea of establishing a livelihood in New York and had immigrated to Lima, Peru, where he pieced together an income writing music for the expat Italian community there.

Italy's race laws ended Levi's contributions to Italy's jazz scene and cut short Vittorio Mussolini's new venture with Hal Roach, but they did not completely muddle agreements between Italian and foreign record labels. Fonit continued to exchange recordings with its American partner Decca, and Cetra still served as the primary distributor for Parlophon, Columbia, Brunswick and Victor. Although Italian radio limited its transmissions of music performed by African American and Jewish musicians, it did not eliminate them completely. *Radiocorriere* continued to advertise recordings by composers like Duke Ellington, Louis Armstrong and Irving Berlin, and as a quarterly report published in 1939 explained, EIAR broadcasts continued to feature performances of Italian bands playing music by foreign composers:

During the two-month period September–October (just to give a few figures), the house orchestras of EIAR stations performed 3386 "pieces" of *musica leggera* composed by Italian authors, in comparison to 528 "pieces" by foreign composers.

During the same period 4376 discs with popular songs, dance music, etc. by our authors were played in comparison to 918 by foreign authors.[17]

In response to these statistics, Santi Savarino, the editor of *La Stampa* and no fan of jazz, replied despondently:

An average of 153 pieces of *musica leggera* a day! In our opinion that is too many ... And let's be clear about all the misuses of gezz, or giazz if you want (But why don't we just decide to call it something Italian like "musica ritmica" since it concerns music within which rhythm prevails?), because the time has come to clarify some misunderstandings that one could embrace unintentionally. One says: Italian music. But nowadays, "Italian music" cannot and should not be understood to mean music by an Italian composer, or by an Italian writer of words (please, do not call him a poet), or by an Italian publisher ...[18]

Indeed, as Savarino noted, the definition of Italian music began to expand under the implementation of the race laws. If the performers were Italian, then the music was too; if the music was deemed to have been sufficiently "Italianized," its origins no longer mattered so much. Consequently, jazz, in all its rhythmic glory, continued to dominate the primetime broadcasts on EIAR, despite the protests of some critics. And like so many other things, jazz found its own distinctive style and became "Italian" under Mussolini's new racist regime.

This is why Cetra and Fonit faced little to no resistance in 1939 when they continued to release recordings of Italian bands playing tunes by composers like W. C. Handy, Duke Ellington, Irving Berlin and George Gershwin.[19] As Luigi Colacicchi, a pioneer of Italian ethnomusicology, noted in 1939, the "original styles" of American jazz, which had been so popular during the mid-1930s, were now in the process of transforming into a distinctly Italian style, thanks to the performances of native musicians:

In Italy, where the authentic styles of jazz are naturally in short supply due to the nature of our own musicality, EIAR's Cetra Orchestra has nevertheless established itself in recent years by performing hot and straight jazz. But now that the furor over hot jazz, which reached its apogee around 1930–35, has passed, this type of music seems to be in decline. Hot jazz and straight jazz are conforming into a single style of jazz that tends to be quite melodic: a style that also represents a return to *musica leggera*, to the simple values that are essential in music.[20]

As Colacicchi noted, a clear, lyrical line was one of the most important elements in the development of the new Italian sound. And this desire for lyricism was firmly tied to the voice and its importance in Italian music history. For centuries, Italians had generally viewed the musicality of their culture as being expressed primarily with the voice, through song. Be it Gregorian chant, opera or regional folk songs, vocal music, more than any other genre, was embraced as a historically significant characteristic of Italian culture. Needless to say, as the Italians began to make jazz their own, it was the lyrical, vocal form, more than anything else, that began to dominate the airwaves in Mussolini's Italy.

Equally distinctive to the Italian sound was the regular use of strings alongside the typical woodwind and brass instruments and the addition of an accordion and guitar to the rhythm section. Like many US radio and recording companies, Italy's EIAR and Cetra sponsored their own jazz orchestras with noted bandleaders, like Cinico Angelini and Pippo Barzizza. But the funding for these ensembles differed from American models; in Italy the government heavily subsidized the popular music industry, and this included the production and distribution of jazz.[21] It is a terrible irony that the implementation of Mussolini's race laws, heinous and iniquitous as they were, facilitated the development of a distinctly Italian jazz style. And key to the music's continued success was a carefully constructed ecosystem that encouraged a mix of government regulation and commercial profit.

Mussolini's ecosystem of jazz didn't come into existence overnight. Rather, it was the result of a gradual process that began in the late 1920s and reached full development just after the race laws went into effect. For the sake of clarity, allow me to outline the ecosystem's basic principles. To begin, Italy's popular music industry was collectively managed by public and private record labels, bandleaders/radio music directors and state officials (MinCulPop) according to the policies of Fascist corporatism. The term corporatism (*corporativismo* in Italian) is based on the Latin root word "*corpus*," meaning body. And this was the general idea behind the governing of assorted sectors of the Italian economy: the various elements of each industry should function as an organic whole. It was this mindset that enabled foreign companies such as Decca, Columbia, Victor and Parlophon to establish business agreements with private Italian companies like Fonit and state-run entities like EIAR and Cetra. It also encouraged friendly rivalries among musicians under contract with competing labels and between Italy's private sector (as represented by Fonit) and its public sector (as represented EIAR and Cetra). Since MinCulPop had the final word on the distribution of all music in Italy, via sheet music, disc and radio, the capitalist concerns of business never outweighed the desires of the regime. Simply put, Mussolini was able to realize his general goal of maintaining a careful balance in the music industry by funneling the economic power of the private business sector into his own ideological vision of popular music. Under corporatism, Jazz was absorbed into the general category of *musica leggera*, and as such it was identified under an array of different genre names (jazz, jazz band, *giazz, gezz, canzone ritmica, canzone jazzata, musica da ballo, musica sincopata*, etc.) that went in and out of fashion according to changing political alliances.

MinCulPop's newly enforced oversight of the music industry did not thwart artistic innovation or eliminate competition in the field of Italian popular music. Rather, it encouraged competition as a means of developing a thriving creative class. In the realm of jazz, the development of this competitive environment involved generating a sense of rivalry between bandleaders, ensembles, soloists and record labels. Added to this were the two voice competitions initiated by EIAR in 1938 and 1939 that attracted thousands of competitors from across the nation. Under Mussolini's watch, Italy's Fascist government fashioned a state-supported popular music industry that promoted a new style of Italian jazz and in doing so launched the careers of its biggest stars.

The Bandleaders of Italian Jazz

The most popular bandleaders in Italy after the implementation of the race laws were Cinico Angelini, who led the Orchestra da Ballo dell'EIAR (the EIAR Dance Orchestra), and Pippo Barzizza, who directed the Orchestra Cetra. These "rivals" were often described in the press as representing two contrasting sides of Italian *musica leggera*: the first aimed at an audience drawn to a symphonic approach found in traditional Italian music, the second a younger audience fascinated by the fast-paced swing coming out of the United States. But, in truth, the two bands were more similar than different. They drew on much of the same repertoire and even used many of the same instrumentalists and singers. The Angelini/Barzizza rivalry, as it was so often called, was not so much a musical reality as it was a carefully crafted publicity scheme. While the bands' fans, commonly referred to as the "Angelinisti" and "Barzizzisti," debated the virtues of each ensemble, the bandleaders themselves worked as a team behind the scenes, steering the popular programming of EIAR and Cetra and promoting the advancement of Italian jazz.

Angelini and Barzizza were not, however, the only curators of jazz in Fascist Italy. All of the major labels sponsored their own bands, each with its own distinctive leader. Among the most popular were Piero Rizza (Odeon), Alfredo Spezialetti (Columbia), Alberto Semprini and Gorni Kramer

(Fonit). Of these, Kramer was by far the most influential. A virtuosic accordion player with a keen sense of comedic timing, he and his band pushed the stylistic boundaries enforced by MinCulPop and often used parody as a means of presenting performances of the "Hot" jazz commonly associated with African American culture.

To understand more fully the importance of Italy's bandleaders in the shaping of Italian jazz, it is helpful to step back a couple of decades and trace the development of each man's career. Not surprisingly, the tastes and talents of these men deeply influenced the development of jazz during the Fascist era. Formally trained in Italian conservatories, yet drawn to the commercialized dance music that arrived from America during their formative years, Italy's bandleaders made a place for themselves in the space where these musical spheres overlapped, and from 1938 until the end of World War II, they served as the guiding forces behind Italian jazz.

Cinico Angelini (born Angelo Cinico in 1901) spent his childhood in Crescentino, a small village of about 6,500 inhabitants in the northern region of Piedmont (Figure 4.1). As a teenager, he moved to nearby Turin, where he earned a diploma in violin at the city's music institute, now known as the State Conservatory Giuseppe Verdi. Like many other young musicians of his generation, however, Angelini soon abandoned classical music to pursue a career in jazz. A good sight reader and agile improviser, he moved to Genoa to work for Armando Di Piramo, who managed a handful of ensembles during the 1920s.

Di Piramo's business acumen and infallible ability to identify new talent contributed greatly to his success as a music entrepreneur. He served as an influential mentor for countless up-and-coming musicians, one of the most notable being Angelini. In Di Piramo's dance band, Angelini experimented on a variety of instruments: banjo, drums, tenor saxophone and trombone. He also developed his skills as a conductor. So much so that in 1923 he left Di Piramo's organization and successfully established an ensemble of his own, the Jazz Band Perroquet in Turin. As Angelini himself later explained, "the orchestra became the favorite of Prince Umberto of Savoy, who often requested it to play at the dances given at the Royal Palace."[22] Despite their success, the Jazz Band Perroquet disbanded in 1925 when Angelini and several other members left for a long tour of South and Central America. There they familiarized themselves with contemporary Latin American dance music, most notably the tango and rumba. In 1929, Angelini returned to Italy and within a year formed a new ten-piece dance band, Perroquet Royal Jazz, which debuted at the Sala Gay in Turin in 1930 and was featured live for several years on EIAR broadcasts. In Milan, he put together a

Figure 4.1 Publicity photo-postcard of conductor Cinico Angelini, ca. 1938.
Source: Photographic archive of Anna Celenza.

second ensemble, the Angelini Orchestra, before being appointed Director of the Orchestra da Ballo dell'EIAR in 1938. An important aspect of all these bands was Angelini's insistence on the inclusion of a "house singer."

From the beginning of Italian radio, singers played a primary role. The first diva of Italian radio, Luisa Tettrazini, came from the world of lyric opera and was featured in the inaugural issue of *Radiorario* in 1924. But with the rise of jazz in the following years, the singers of *musica leggera* quickly took center stage. Angelini, perhaps more than any other conductor, greatly facilitated the ascent of these popular singers. He was the first bandleader to comprehend fully the importance of the voice to the development of Italian jazz. From the early 1930s on, he regularly incorporated singers into the musical structure of his orchestrations and in doing so proved to be especially judicious when selecting repertoire that might appeal to as broad an audience as possible.

Angelini did not compose any of the songs or arrangements his bands performed. He left that work for others to do. As he noted in an interview years later, one of his earliest sources for new repertoire was the jazz pianist Edgardo Greppi:

> At Greppi's house there were meetings to learn the new pieces that the pianist had transcribed from discs, and participating in these meetings were the Turin musicians most interested in the new music: the trumpeter Mattea, the trombonist Francesco Carbone, the saxophonists La Manna and Monassero and the drummer Patrone.[23]

Angelini worked for a good decade as a performer, but he never became a virtuoso. In the realm of popular music, his greatest success came from his talent as a bandleader at EIAR. When Angelini was hired to conduct the Orchestra da Ballo dell'EIAR in 1938 – the year Mussolini's race laws went into effect – he embraced his new role as musical facilitator. Angelini worked hard to promote the Italian musicians whose talents he respected, most notably his singers, and to build the audience base of Italian radio. As a conductor at EIAR, he had at his disposal Italy's finest jazz musicians and composers. His core ensemble consisted of sixteen instrumentalists, including Giovanni D'Ovidio (trumpet), Potito Simone (trombone), Domenico Ferraro (saxophone) and Michele Ortuso (guitar). On a few occasions, for example, at political events or at performances that were symbolically important for the regime, Angelini expanded the Orchestra da Ballo dell'Eiar into a "super" ensemble, with upwards of twenty-two musicians borrowed from other EIAR ensembles. But even at events such as these, Angelini never took the spotlight off the music itself. An agile and effective conductor, he knew how to keep his musicians engaged and productive and his audiences entertained. Throughout the political turbulence of the 1930s and 40s, he served as a consistent leader at EIAR and a symbolic musical icon for the Fascist regime.

Angelini's "rival" on Italian airwaves was Pippo Barzizza, conductor of the Orchestra Cetra (Figure 4.2). Barzizza was born into a relatively well-to-do Genoese family in 1902, and like many children of the upper class, he began taking music lessons at a relatively early age. At age six he passed the entrance exam for the prestigious Camillo Sivori Music Institute, where he enrolled as a violin student. According to Barzizza, it was his uncle,

Figure 4.2 Publicity photo of Pippo Barzizza surrounded by the instruments of his orchestra, ca. 1939.
Source: Barzizza family archive.

Giovanni Lorenzo Barzizza, who served as his mentor during these early years. The elder Barzizza was a trained musicologist with strong ties to Genoese aristocracy. As the administrator of the estate of a local nobleman, the Marchese Pallavicini, he had easy access to the city's theaters and concert halls, which he visited regularly with his young nephew in tow. Years later, Barzizza reminisced about the times he went to the Teatro Carlo Felice to watch many a famous opera "from a very comfortable box seat."[24] With a piano score in hand, he followed along with the conductor, making sure the singers and instrumentalists never missed a cue. These early experiences ingrained in Barzizza a fascination for orchestration and a deep admiration for Italian lyric opera, characteristics that served him well in later years as an innovator in Italian jazz.

Barzizza excelled in his music studies. In addition to the violin, which he continued to study formally throughout his teen years, he taught himself piano and spent countless hours transcribing opera tunes he listened to over his father's cylinder phonograph. "My father bought me a great German piano ... Luckily, my mother really loved music, and she appreciated listening to the daily progress I made at the keyboard."[25] Throughout his youth, Barzizza trained to become a classical musician. In addition to his violin lessons with a local virtuoso named Professor Biasoli, and his piano practice at home, he studied music theory, composition and orchestration with Renzo Angeleri, "an excellent teacher" and "very handsome man," whose "youthful excesses had caused him to go blind," explained Barzizza.

Maestro Angeleri had an iron memory, and knew, from A to Z, all the operas of the best known composers (Verdi, Puccini, Mascagni, etc.) The lessons were free – free, so to speak, because my mother invited him to lunch every day, to spare him the trouble of returning home ... One day I learned from my parents that he had died. It was a great sorrow to me. I never got to tell him personally how grateful I was for his diligent and valuable instruction.[26]

As Barzizza's studies in composition progressed, his interest in classical violin began to wane. He took up an array of instruments – banjo, accordion and saxophone – spurred on by the music he heard on the "marvelous gramophone discs" that "friends and colleagues brought back for him from their transatlantic trips to New York."[27] Barzizza transcribed every recording he could get his hands on – line by line and section by section – and in doing so perfected his orchestration skills. By 1920, he was performing as part of a sextet (violin, cello, bass, drums, piano and banjo) in high-end cafés. He also got a job as a piano player at a local cinema, supplying improvised music accompaniment to silent films imported from the United States.

Barzizza's first big break in jazz came in 1922, when Armando Di Piramo offered him a permanent position in his band. "With Di Piramo we played dance music," explained Barzizza, "and there I began to experiment on various instruments."[28] Barzizza usually played saxophone and violin for Di Piramo, but within a few years, his competency had expanded to a total of nine instruments: violin, piano, accordion, banjo and all five sizes of the saxophone, from soprano to bass. Although Barzizza was forced to leave the band in 1923 to fulfill a year of mandatory military service, by 1924 he was back with Di Piramo, now in Milan, where the orchestra had secured a residency at the Caffè Cova, an elegant venue near the Teatro alla Scala. Di Piramo introduced Barzizza to a wide range of musicians, both Italian and foreign. For example, it was thanks to Di Piramo that Barzizza befriended the saxophonist Sid Phillips, who played with a popular British group, the Riviera Five.[29] According to Barzizza, "it was a fortunate encounter: I taught Sid the basic rudiments of arranging and harmony, and he gave me saxophone lessons."[30]

Barzizza's first experiences in the recording studio were with Di Piramo's Orchestra, and the bandleader facilitated his entry into music publishing too. Although Barzizza only spent two years with Di Piramo, the lessons he learned proved invaluable. In 1925, when the twenty-three-year-old Barzizza set out on his own, he knew what it would take to succeed as a bandleader. Determined to make his mark in Italy's new burgeoning jazz industry, he established the Blue Star Orchestra, one of the first truly distinctive Italian swing bands.

The Blue Star Orchestra fluctuated between six and seven musicians, all multi-instrumentalists who performed on a total of thirty-six instruments, including French horn and mellophone. As Barzizza later explained, he got the idea for his ensemble from listening to Paul Whiteman recordings:

I had always had the idea in my head to form an ensemble capable of realizing all the effects that I heard on the recordings by Paul Whiteman. In early 1925 I met a Calabrese musician, the trumpeter and pianist Giovanni Miglio. With him, and a few others who played a variety of instruments, I formed the Blue Star Orchestra.[31]

Those who had the opportunity to witness a Blue Star performance no doubt found the complex choreography required for the ensemble's constantly shifting instrumentation as mesmerizing as the music itself. Barzizza took complete control of the ensemble, from auditioning new band members and booking the performances to composing the arrangements they played. Even the most cursory study of the parts he prepared reveals his comprehensive control of the final musical product. In addition to including instructions in each man's part describing when he should switch from one instrument to the next, Barzizza notated many of the "improvised" solos performed by each band member. In the early years, these solos were often direct transcriptions of those preserved on recordings by foreign performers such as Frankie Trumbauer, Joe Venuti, Louis Armstrong and Bix Beiderbecke. Later, the solos took on a distinctive character, more lyrical in nature and with motivic references drawn from Italian musical sources.

As a conductor, Barzizza energized performances with a choreographic approach to keeping the beat that was all his own. His looks were disarming in a professorial way. Small and agile, he resembled a tightly wound spring, ready to pounce at the next downbeat. Bald, with round wire-rimmed glasses and a quick smile, he looked more like a scholar than a jazzman. But on the dance floor, there were few bandleaders who could compete with his complex harmonies and rhythmic drive. As Maria Sirotti, a cashier at the Grand'Italia, remembered, Barzizza and his Blue Star Orchestra made quite an impression during live performances:

The orchestra appeared on stage at the Grand'Italia wearing double-breasted blue jackets and white trousers, with stiff collars and a handkerchief in the pocket. They were all very elegant. I particularly remember [the trumpet player] Luigi Urbani, a beautiful boy. In short, [the Blue Star Orchestra was] a great success, and people flocked to hear them. They played at 5:00 for tea and then in the evening from 8:30 until 10:00. They alternated sets with a string ensemble that performed classical works. [The Blue Star Orchestra] did not play music for dancing. Theirs was a real jazz concert. Those who wanted to dance had to go down to Chez Vous, where other orchestras played from 10:30 onwards.[32]

One of Barzizza's greatest talents was his ability to transcribe complex arrangements from imported recordings and create new instrumentations more fitting to the Italian style. In many ways, the Blue Star Orchestra served as his instrument. Paying close attention to the talent and technique of each performer, he created distinctive orchestrations that garnered the admiration of performers and listeners alike. Paul Whiteman functioned as a role model for Barzizza, both as a conductor and as a businessman. Like Whiteman, Barzizza's commanding confidence and keen sense of numbers, both musical and financial, served him well. These qualities, perhaps more than any other, were the keys to his early success.

The Blue Star Orchestra made its premier in Milan, playing at the Sempioncino. They then moved on to the city's most prestigious venues: Caffè Cova and the Olimpia. Within just a few years, they had expanded their reach, playing the major cities of northern Italy before venturing abroad to Paris, Geneva, Cannes, St. Moritz and even Constantinople. Such broad foreign exposure turned the Blue Star Orchestra into one of Italy's most prestigious ensembles, as band member Potito Simone later explained:

First, in the summer of '28, we played at the St. Raphaël Casino, where the orchestra gave a concert to benefit the children of Italians abroad. Then we were booked in Cannes, and finally in San Remo. Our fame, however, had also reached Paris, and the owner of Ciro's came to San Remo to hire us. We played the winter season in Paris, where we were each paid the hefty sum of two hundred francs a night.[33]

In addition to the generous stipends, Barzizza and his band enjoyed interacting with American musicians during their engagements in France. Simone explains:

For a few days in Paris, we played at the same time as Noble Sissle's Orchestra, which included [the trumpeter] Arthur Briggs (who spoke a little Italian), a spectacular trombonist, and a tuba player with a velvety voice who played ... with a cigar in his mouth! We learned more in those days than in many months of activity in Italy.[34]

During these tours with his orchestra, Barzizza earned a good deal of money and established valuable contacts, both of which served him well in later years.

In 1931, Barzizza began an intense five-year period of recording. Under Di Piramo, he had recorded with the French label Pathé. Now he reached out to a wider spectrum of recording companies with strong roots in the Italian and American markets, namely, Fonit, Columbia, La Voce del Padrone, Odeon and Brunswick. One recording clearly marketed to both Italian and American audiences was the Blue Star Orchestra's 1933 recording of "Tempi Moderni" (Modern Times), a tune composed by the Italian American composer Dan Caslar.[35] Most of the recordings, however, featured compositions and arrangements written by Barzizza himself. Viewed as an up-and-coming star in the burgeoning field of *musica leggera*, Barzizza was dubbed "Il Re del Jazz Italiano" (The King of Italian Jazz) by his publisher in 1934. Two years later – after many more recordings and countless publications – Barzizza was tapped by EIAR to serve as the new conductor of the Cetra Orchestra. At first, Barzizza was inclined to turn down the offer. The proposed salary was not generous, and the contract stipulated that he contribute regularly to live radio broadcasts and recording sessions without extra compensation. Still, it was a secure government position, and as Barzizza soon discovered, he was able to earn extra money through royalty payments, both as a composer and as a performer. "In the end," Barzizza later admitted, "I earned quite a lot."[36] Most importantly, the EIAR position offered him the opportunity to work with some of the best jazz musicians in Italy. His Blue Star Orchestra had disbanded in 1933, and he missed composing music for a set group of performers. So he accepted the offer and moved to Turin with his wife Tatina, daughter Isa and infant son Renzo. As his children explained many years later, going to work for EIAR opened up a new world of opportunities for Barzizza:

Pippo finally had his big band: the Orchestra Cetra ... At age 36, he had reached the height of his artistic maturity ... He conducted; he called solos; he had fun; it was all so entertaining ... In short, he put on a show. In concert, he was elegant in his white tuxedo. In the recording studio, he appeared in shirtsleeves. During broadcasts to the audience that loved him – the teenagers, the students, the intellectuals, the most sophisticated of audiences – Pippo was in a state of grace. [37]

Working at EIAR also expanded his achievements in the realm of composition:

He composed memorable songs like "Domani" and "Sera," pages of beautiful music that was ahead of its time harmonically and was expressed with the most sophisticated orchestrations. In this way, he established himself as the best orchestrator of that long, fascinating period. Memorable years, filled with great successes and popularity.[38]

Under Barzizza's leadership, the Cetra Orchestra grew from sixteen members in 1936 to twenty-eight in 1940, and this expansion of the instrumentation transformed the ensemble from a woodwind dominated swing band based on American examples to a more Italianate model featuring a wider array of instruments – including strings, accordion and guitar – played by conservatory-trained multi-instrumentalists. Although Barzizza followed Angelini in his integration of singers into the jazz ensemble, his first priority remained with the orchestra and the development of their skills as soloists. Among the most noted instrumentalists in his ensemble were the brothers Beppe and Luigi Mojetta, both trombonists; the saxophonists Marcello Cianfanelli and Sergio Quercioli; pianist Ezio Gheri; and the excellent trumpet player Gaetano Gimelli.

In addition to Barzizza and Angelini there were other prominent bandleaders, many of whom functioned independently of the government's radio and recording companies. These musicians found their homes with the various recording companies that continued to produce discs in Italy. For example, Piero Rizza was the in-house conductor of Odeon, Alfredo Spezialetti for Columbia Italia, and Alberto Semprini for Fonit. Of all of these, however, none compared in fame or talent to Gorni Kramer, who recorded for Fonit as both a big band director and independent performer (Figure 4.3). Kramer, perhaps more than any other instrumentalist, created the distinctive sound of mid-century Italian jazz.

Born in the small town of Rivarolo Mantovano on July 22, 1913, Gorni Kramer (baptized Francesco Kramer Gorni) was Italy's first accordion player of jazz. His father, Francesco Gorni, was a professional folk musician and a huge fan of cycling. His mother, Teresa Marchiò, had lived in the United States for several years before Kramer was born. The couple named their son after the American cyclist Frank Louis Kramer, who had won his twelfth consecutive national championship the summer Kramer was born. As a child, Kramer learned to play the accordion from his father, and he soon became a regular performer at local festivals.

At age six they put an accordion in my hands. I started to study, and two years later I was already able to play the works of Rossini. For two years, they had me play the melody only in the bass: "To improve my technique," they said.[39]

Guido Deiro likely served as an influence on Kramer during these early years. Kramer's father appears to have been the one who introduced him to the recordings, which were distributed in both the United States and Italy by Columbia.[40] Such an assumption is confirmed by the repertoire Kramer's father taught him during his formative years. Like Deiro, Kramer's father

Figure 4.3 Publicity photo-postcard of Gorni Kramer inscribed to Umberto Principe, ca. 1940.
Source: Photographic archive of Anna Celenza.

presented himself as something of a heartthrob. And as a teenager, Kramer idolized his father, not simply as a musician, but as a man about town.

> They used to call my father Gallo [Rooster], because he was a handsome man. And when he went with his orchestra to the neighboring cities – Mantova, Cremona, Parma, Reggio – everyone went crazy. When Gallo arrived, the party began. And since he was handsome and dashing, rumor had it that he had a lover in each locale. That's why they called him Gallo![41]

Father and son made several recordings together for Odeon, playing a variety of dance tunes: tangos, polkas, waltzes, mazurkas and a few fox-trots.

As Kramer later explained, this was when he began to experiment with improvisation: "I improvised over polkas and mazurkas because I grew bored always playing the same piece."[42] It wasn't long before Kramer's father recognized that his son's musical talent exceeded the challenge of performing in local bands, and in 1930, Kramer's training took a more serious turn. He moved to Parma (about twenty-four miles south of Rivarolo Mantovano) and enrolled as a string bass student at the Royal Conservatory. "I remained there through graduation because it pleased me greatly," explained Kramer. "I sensed that playing the bass was important. It was the base of the orchestra, [like] the foundation of a house."[43]

Throughout his teenage years, Kramer played double bass in the conservatory orchestra and accordion in local dance bands. Although his classical training served him throughout his career, it was Kramer's experimentation on the accordion, the instrument he often said he felt drawn to most, that helped him establish his reputation as one of Italy's most innovative performers:

I had begun to play my instrument as though it was a trumpet or clarinet. I played the melody with single notes. Then, little by little, I began to figure out the correct chords, and it occurred to me that my accordion could be used like a complete orchestra: with the left hand I harmonized, thinking like the wind section, and with the right I made the melody. In this way was born the style that then made my instrument distinctive.[44]

As Kramer later explained, much of the inspiration during these early years came from listening to gramophone discs from the United States.

During the 1920s, there arrived in Rivarolo Mantovano many people who were returning from the United States, where they had immigrated to fifteen or twenty years earlier, and they brought with them many recordings of dance music. Paul Whiteman and other orchestras, and also lots of jazz: Trumbauer, Joe Venuti. I was struck. Later, when I was sixteen or seventeen years old, around 1929 or '30, I began to become familiar with figures like Ellington and Armstrong.[45]

Even more influential than the gramophone discs was the arrival of a radio in Kramer's childhood home.

I remember that at around 5:30 or 6:00 in the morning, I could tune in to an American broadcast using a shortwave radio. Every Tuesday and Saturday Ellington was broadcast. Simply put, I lived off bread and Ellington [during those years].[46]

The broadcasts Kramer was referencing here were those transmitted live from the Cotton Club in Harlem by WHN. Via these broadcasts Kramer was not only exposed to Ellington's various dance tunes, but also the overtures, transitions, accompaniments and the offensively called "jungle" effects that made up the Deep South themed variety shows. The Cotton Club gave Ellington the freedom to experiment with orchestral colors and arrangements in a way that Kramer would not have encountered in most American and European touring bands. As discussed a bit later in this chapter, the influence of listening to these early Ellington broadcasts could be detected in Kramer's own performances during the late 1930s in a profound, yet disturbing way.

Kramer's big break came in 1932. While playing a gig in the tourist resort Salsomaggiore Terme, he was discovered by Stefano Ferruzzi, who took him to Milan and introduced him to Aldo Poggi, the saxophone player and cofounder of the prestigious Orchestra Pieraldo. Poggi was impressed by Kramer's skills as an improviser, and he offered the young accordion player a spot in his dance band. In an interview years later, Kramer described the highlights of those years:

I went to Milan and began to play at the Taverna Ferrario with Aldo Poggi and Pietro Strazza, in their Orchestra Pieraldo. I remember that we played a matinee from 4:00 to 6:30 for students, who paid only eight lire for entry and a drink. Then I would go to the Fonit record store, located in the Galleria Vittorio Emanuele, to buy the newest discs. One time I heard a recording of the Casa Loma [Orchestra]. It pleased me so much that I went home right away, transcribed the music, and that evening we played it with the orchestra. During that period, I was into everything. If I heard a new harmony by Ellington, I would want to decipher it right away, otherwise I would feel ill. I was a man obsessed.[47]

One of the first tunes Kramer remembered playing with the Orchestra Pieraldo was the Bob Carleton tune "Ja-Da."[48] Kramer played with the Orchestra Pieraldo for three seasons, an experience he later described as "an extraordinary school."[49]

Kramer rose quickly through the ranks of Italy's jazz scene, and towards the end of 1934 he debuted as a bandleader at the Embassy Club in Milan. His ensemble consisted of himself on accordion, Romero Alvaro on piano and violin, guitarist Armando Camera, bassist Ubaldo Beduschi and the drummer Luigi Redaelli, who later became a celebrity under the stage name "Pippo Starnazza."[50] As Kramer later explained, the exposure he and his band received at the Embassy Club was invaluable:

At the Embassy we played six hours of jazz. We began at 10:00 [in the evening] and finished at 4:00 in the morning. One night, we played twenty choruses of "Bugle Call Rag." The Embassy was the number one venue in Milan. The club was frequented by the upper bourgeoisie: people who traveled to and from the United

States, who knew and loved jazz. Simply put, they came to dance, but above all else to listen.[51]

Kramer and his band began recording for Fonit in 1935. Among the various American tunes they recorded was "Anime gemelli" (I Wish I Were Twins), a tune by Frank Loesser that had been recorded the previous year by various bands, including Adrian's Ramblers, a large swing band out of New York led by the Italian American, Adrian Rollini.[52]

Adriano Mazzoletti has described Kramer's Embassy quintet as "the first Italian swing band," and there is a great amount of truth to that statement.[53] In 1936, Kramer added Nino Impallomeni (trumpet) and Aldo Rossi (alto saxophone) to the group, and with this expanded ensemble he produced a series of recordings as the Orchestra del Circolo dell'Ambasciata. A review of these recordings, published in *Il disco* in April 1936, described Kramer as a new entity in *musica leggera*, "the revelation of Italian jazz." Commenting on the appellation two months later, Ezio Levi noted that although he was not a fan of everything Kramer had produced, he nonetheless thought that two of the performer's more recent releases, "Espresso della mattina" and "Crapa Pelada," served as "proof yet again that in Italy one can, and there are those who do, make good and true jazz."[54]

Listening to these two pieces, one can hear quite clearly what made them Italian. In the first, Kramer uses the accordion to capture the dissonant grinding of a train against the tracks in a manner that reminds one of the Futurists' fascination with mechanized noise. Kramer's composition might also have been inspired by Ellington's "Daybreak Express," which was recorded in Chicago on December 4, 1933. The opening and conclusion of Kramer's composition imitate closely Ellington's fully orchestrated piece. But in the middle section, Kramer takes off on his own, devising an energized melody that serves as the basis for a series of improvised solos by the trumpet, violin, accordion, piano and saxophone. Here one is reminded of Michele Menichino's lyrical "Pacific Express," recorded by the piano duo Enrico Bormioli and Alberto Semprini in 1933.

No doubt, one of Kramer's most innovative early works was "Crapa Pelada." Here he transformed a nursery rhyme in Milanese dialect into a virtuosic display of improvisatory scat singing distinct in tone and style from American models. On the recording made in 1936 for Fonit, Kramer sings in a whispery slur that evokes the intoxicating mood of Milanese nightclubs. And the lyrics, which were decipherable only to those who grew up in the North, where the tune was sung regularly, present a nonsense tale of juvenile selfishness:

Crapa Pelada la fà i turtei,
ghe ne dà minga ai sò fradei.
Oh! Oh! Oh! Oh!
I sò fradei fan la fritada.
ghe ne dan minga a Crapa Pelada.
Oh! Oh! Oh! Oh! Oh!

Crapa Pelada made tortellini,
But he didn't give his brothers any.
Oh! Oh! Oh! Oh!
His brothers made an omelet,
but didn't give any to Crapa Pelada.
Oh! Oh! Oh! Oh! Oh!

Crapa Pelada is Milanese dialect for Testa Pelata (Bald Head) in Italian. Shortly after the song was released, anti-Fascist sympathizers began to assert that the song's protagonist was Mussolini, and that the division of tortellini and omelets was a metaphor for the division of the African colonies by the European powers and the Fascists' ignoble victory in Ethiopia. This transformation of the song's meaning serves as an introduction to a curious phenomenon in the history of Italian jazz: the rise of the *canzoni della fronda* (songs of revolt). These songs were not written specifically to protest a political event or persona. Rather, they were songs with ambiguous or nonsense texts that were reinterpreted by anti-Fascists as critiques of Mussolini and his government. Another tune by Kramer, "Pippo non lo sa" (Pippo Doesn't Know), was similarly appropriated as a *canzone della fronda*. Although Kramer claimed the tune was inspired by an encounter with Pippo Barzizza in 1939, some anti-Fascists interpreted it as a veiled critique of the PNF Secretary, Achille Starace.

Kramer recorded an impressive series of discs for Fonit, Odeon and Columbia during the 1930s and 40s with an array of ensembles, from large swing bands accompanying the star singers of the day to small combos. In 1941, Kramer received high praise from Vittorio Mussolini in a review describing the recent release of several jazz tunes featuring Kramer on accordion and Semprini on piano:

Semprini's piano and Kramer's accordion come together in a happy marriage to interpret the most beautiful and famous themes from recent films.[55] Here is a slow-paced record where the piano releases a cascade of pearly notes and indulges in fantastical arabesques, while the accordion plays the melody with effects resembling first a saxophone and then a violin. On the B side one finds rhythmic motives that transport us into an atmosphere full of the spicy aromas of a Harlem neighborhood. Kramer has truly created a new manner of playing the accordion and of obtaining unprecedented and unexpected effects that are extremely interesting.[56]

In addition to developing a style of jazz recognized as distinctly Italian, Kramer performed a number of works that appeared to evoke many of the characteristics associated with the poorly named "jungle" style of African American jazz made famous by the Duke Ellington Orchestra during their Cotton Club performances. Photos from the 1930s reveal that Kramer and his bandmates did not shy away from performing in blackface, and as racism grew more prominent in Italy, Kramer's relationship to African American jazz grew more complex. Although Kramer had held performers like Ellington and Armstrong in high regard since his formative years, he did not resist using some of the racist stereotypes promoted by publications such as *La Difesa della Razza*. This is most clearly displayed in his creation of a jazz trio right after the race laws went into effect called the Three Niggers of Broadway. This trio, made up of Kramer on accordion, Cosimo Di Ceglie on guitar and Enzo Caragioli on piano, recorded a series of American tunes for Odeon in September and November 1938 that are best described as sonic blackface.[57] The ensemble's offensive name was apparently considered humorous at the time – a satirical take on the African American jazz that had recently come under scrutiny due to Italy's new policies. In fact, the continued effects of the race laws are reflected in the evolution of the trio's name. When Kramer and his musicians returned to the recording studio in April 1939, the MinCulPop ban on English-language names and titles forced them to change their name to I Tre Negri (The Three Negroes),[58] a name that later morphed into Tre Italiani in America (Three Italians in America) in December 1940. This final change in the band's name reflected the new Fascist directive of mocking all things American. Just six months before, Italy had entered World War II on the side of the Germans and broken its ties with the United States.

Despite the various iterations of the band's name, its "American" style of playing remained unchanged. Kramer never abandoned his desire to perform "American" jazz, but as an astute observer of cultural shifts in Italy's music market he learned how to repackage his public performances of the music in a way that adhered to the demands of Italy's race laws and MinCulPop regulations. Listening to these recordings now, there is nothing distasteful in the music itself. Rather it is the manner in which it was presented – the offensive name(s) of the ensemble and the blackface performances – that cause one to cringe. Equally upsetting is the manner in which this music was received. The "American" jazz that Kramer and his trio performed was warmly embraced by audiences and MinCulPop officials alike, not because it was acknowledged as worthy of praise, but rather because it was perceived as being nothing more than a bit of racist fun at the expense of a political enemy. Greeted as satire, the music produced by I Tre Negri posed no threat to the development of Italian jazz.

Kramer straddled the boundaries between black and white, American and Italian jazz during the Fascist era. As an instrumentalist, he presented "African American" tunes in a satrical style informed by Mussolini's new race laws. As a singer and composer, he created distinctively Italian works that conformed to MinCulPop directives and promoted the ideals of modern Italian culture that dominated the urban centers north of Rome. With songs like "Crapa Pelada" and "Pippo non lo sa," he joined the ranks of Italian songwriters, like Giovanni D'Anzi and Carlo Prati, who developed a distinctive genre of Italian jazz centered on the lyrical qualities of the human voice. Italian jazz, more than anything else, was vocal jazz. And thanks to Mussolini's support, this new nationalist art form, the *canzone jazzata*, came to dominate Italian airwaves during the 1930s and 40s.

The Singers of Italian Jazz

The biggest stars in Italian jazz were its singers: Alberto Rabagliati, Natalino Otto and the Trio Lescano. The early success of figures such as these led EIAR to launch competitions in 1938/39 and 1939/40 to find even more singers to front its various in-house jazz orchestras. These competitions attracted numerous entries: 2,500 the first year, and over 3,000 the following year. One of the underlying motivations behind these vocal competitions was to build a sustainable environment for the continued development of Italian jazz, which relied heavily on native Italian singers. An article published in *Radiocorriere* at the conclusion of the second competition reveals a great deal about how the judging process functioned. Much like the popular singing competitions of recent years (*San Remo Song Festival, Eurosong, American Idol*, etc.),[59] the EIAR Singing Competitions adhered to an audition/elimination process that lasted several weeks. After multiple preliminary selection rounds held in locations across Italy, the final round was held in Turin, where it was broadcast live on EIAR.

The master of ceremonies for the final round was Riccardo Mantoni. The comedian Guido Barbarisi also participated in the broadcast. At one point, he took each singer aside and asked him or her a series of questions about his or her interests and pastimes. He also queried the singers about their personal aspirations for the future. When the finalists performed, they were accompanied either by Angelini and the Orchestra del Ballo EIAR or Barzizza and the Cetra Orchestra. As these competitions clearly demonstrated, the soundtrack of Fascism since the implementation of Italy's race laws had become dominated by the *canzone jazzata* and *canzoni sincopate* (syncopated songs), accompanied by top-notch swing bands. To promote this repertoire among the populace, a new periodical, *Il Canzoniere della Radio*, went into production in February 1940. As the second issue explained, *Il Canzoniere della Radio* supplied readers with the lyrics to "all the songs played on the radio, recorded on disc, heard in the variety theaters [and] played in the dance halls."[60]

Il Canzoniere della Radio appeared monthly, at first, in a pocket-sized format (6.5 x 4.5 inches), and its sole purpose of strengthening the popularity of new Italian tunes among the public proved instantly effective. As one contemporary listener noted: "I began listening to songs. There were already the bands, Angelini, Barzizza, I'm talking about 1939–1940 ... I was crazy about those songs, and sometimes I stood there and learned them; I learned them very easily, and I let myself go by singing them in the bathroom."[61] The earliest issues of *Il Canzoniere della Radio* contained lyrics for roughly fifty songs and information about where readers could purchase sheet music and/or recordings. There was no other content except for the occasional advertisement promoting the sale of songbooks or instrument primers. The covers of the first nineteen issues featured color illustrations that highlighted the pleasures of singing and listening to music. Contemporary political events were occasionally referenced. For example, the August 1940 cover featured a woman waving an Italian flag as uniformed soldiers marched off to war. And in December 1940, a trio of Italian men in navy uniforms donned the cover. Not surprisingly, the instrument most often featured in these illustrations was the accordion.

The demand for *Il Canzoniere della Radio* was so great that in September 1941 (issue 20) it began to appear biweekly. The content and format of the publication underwent a subtle transformation at this point. Instead of illustrations highlighting amateur performance, the covers of *Il Canzoniere della Radio* began to carry portraits of Italy's musical stars. And the content was no longer limited to song lyrics. Included also were photos, interviews and articles about the newest stars of Italian radio. In short, *Il Canzoniere della Radio* took on the guise of a fan magazine, spreading the ideal of *Italianità* so rigorously promoted at the time by EIAR.[62]

Figure 4.4 Publicity photo of Alberto Rabagliati, ca. 1941.
Source: Photographic archive of Anna Celenza.

Alberto Rabagliati was the first vocal star of Italian jazz (Figure 4.4).
Born in Milan in 1906, he lived a relatively nondescript life until 1926,
when the untimely passing of Rudolph Valentino created mass hysteria
among female fans in the United States and Europe. Hoping to discover
an equally successful replacement for the Italian heartthrob, Twentieth
Century Fox launched a worldwide lookalike contest, with the promise of
a studio contract and all the benefits that came with it: fame, money and a
Hollywood address. Over two million men entered the "New Valentino"
competition, but it was Rabagliati – tall and photogenic, with his broad
shoulders, smokey eyes and easy smile – who eventually won. His prize

included a new wardrobe, an all-expenses paid trip to Hollywood and a free screen test. "For someone like me," Rabagliati noted, "it was extraordinary to find myself aboard a luxury steamer with three cases full of clothes, a roll of dollars and grand duchesses and countesses vying for my attention."[63] Rabagliati spent the next four years in the United States. He made one silent film shortly after his arrival, but was fired on the spot when he was caught in bed with his producer's mistress. After that, his career, like that of countless other foreign actors, stalled with the arrival of the "Talkies." Despite these setbacks, Rabagliati remained in the United States, living the life of a playboy until his money ran out. During these years he familiarized himself with the newest music trends, gaining a proficiency in jazz and scat singing. When he finally returned to Italy in 1931, he established himself as a singer, first with Pippo Barzizza's Blue Star Orchestra (where he also played violin), then in 1934 with the Lecuona Cuban Boys, a traveling band from Havana founded by Ernesto Lecuona that specialized in Afro Cuban dance music. Like Al Jolson, Rabagliati regularly performed in blackface during these early years. His first big hit was a tune called "Maria la O."

But Rabagliati's major break in the music industry occurred in 1939 during a performance with the Lecuona Boys. After singing a series of popular tunes, Rabagliati was approached by Giovanni D'Anzi, one of the most notable songwriters of *musica leggera*, who recommended he audition at EIAR. As Angelini explained many years later, that first audition didn't go well.

I was passing by one of the EIAR studios where they were holding auditions, and I was struck by the voice of a young man who clearly had a considerable amount of experience. I stopped to listen to him. I learned that his name was Alberto Rabagliati, that he was from Milan, that he had failed his first audition, but refusing to give up, had returned to audition again. When he finished singing, I was amazed that the panel of judges rejected him again, claiming that his voice was not suitable for radio. At that point, I intervened and said that I thought Rabagliati had sung well. I offered to take responsibilty for him, and I took him with me to Cetra.[64]

With Angelini's sponsorship, Rabagliati secured a position singing for Italian radio, and within a year established himself as a celebrity. In 1941, he was given his own radio show, *Canta Rabagliati* (Sing Rabagliati), which aired every Monday and served as a launching pad for his most famous tunes, among them "Silenzioso slow" (Slow Silence), "Bambina inamorata" (Girl in Love) and "Ba-ba-baciami piccina" (Kiss Me Little Girl). The primary purpose of this last, somewhat nonsensical song was to show off Rabagliati's skills at singing scat. Indeed, this was one of the few recordings by Barzizza's Cetra Orchestra that did not feature an instrumental solo. The breaks between verses that would have normally gone to instrumentalists feature brief scat solos by Rabagliati instead. Rabagliati became so famous in the early 1940s that his name was continuously cited in new jazz tunes composed by Carlo Prati, namely "La famiglia canterina" (The Singing Family), "Quando la radio" (When the Radio [Plays]) and his signature tune, "Quando canta Rabagliati" (When Rabagliati Sings). This tune, recorded in 1941 with Angelini's Dance Orchestra, references the growing prominence of Italian jazz and its displacement of the more traditional singing styles associated with singers like Tito Schipa, who had established his career recording nineteenth-century opera arias.[65] The song also introduced a new verb to the Italian language: *rabagliare* (to sing in the Italian jazz style made popular by Rabagliati). And in his numerous performances of this tune, Rabagliati made the most of his ability to imitate various instruments with his voice. Indeed, the virtuosic realization of the various fast-paced passages reveals a level of competence found in only a handful of singers.

Rabagliati's fame grew exponentially with each passing year, and his female fans were especially enthusiastic. In October 1941 his portrait was featured on the cover of *Il Canzoniere della Radio*. In fact, the popularity of "il grande Raba" (the great Raba) was so strong that the Fascist government adopted one of his love songs, "C'è una Casetta Piccina" a.k.a. "Sposi" (There is a Tiny Little House, a.k.a. Newlyweds) as the theme song for a new demographic campaign. Rabagliati sang with all the popular big bands in Italy, and in 1941 he toured the peninsula with a 100-piece "super" orchestra conducted by Angelini. Touring only increased the singer's popularity. For many, it offered the first opportunity to see in person the man behind the voice from the radio and gramophone discs. Throwing roses at the stage became something of a tradition for the young women who attended his live performances, and a popular cartoon from these years showed Rabagliati dancing in the street while everyone around him, including a horse and a statue, mimicked his freewheeling style.[66] Rabagliati's popularity as a singer was so all-encompassing that the Italian film industry reached out to him. In the United States, his heavy Italian accent had undermined his career as a film star. But in Italy, his Milanese accent aligned well with the ideal of *Italianità* that was being promoted at Mussolini's Cinecittà. Rabagliati's career as a film star flourished, and not surprisingly, many of the films in which he appeared concluded with him breaking into song. One of his earliest films from this period, *Una famiglia impossibile* (1940), featured the hit tune, "Ba-ba-baciami piccina." Other films from this era included *La scuola dei timidi* (1941), *Fuga a due voci* and *Lascia cantare il cuore* (1943) and *In cerca di felicità* (1944). No doubt, one of his most iconic roles during the

Fascist era was as Count Alberto Morandi in *La Vita è Bella* (1943) with Anna Magnani.[67] Directed by Carlo Ludovico Bragaglia (younger brother of the Futurist Anton Giulio Bragaglia), the film served as a light-hearted, melody-filled distraction during the Germans' occupation of Rome.

As Rabagliati's fame grew, stories about his personal life became a popular topic in the press. In 1942, an interview with his mother appeared in *Primi piani*, a popular cinema magazine. During the interview, Mrs. Rabagliati sang the praises of her son, putting to rest any rumors that he might still be participating in the freewheeling lifestyle that had characterized his early years in the United States.[68] She also noted that, despite his appeal on the big screen, he was a singer first and foremost. This was a sentiment Rabagliati shared. Later in life, he often noted that the years he spent singing for EIAR represented the highlight of his career.

Rabagliati's greatest rival was Fonit's Natalino Otto (Figure 4.5). At the peak of his career, Otto was described as Italy's first true Italian crooner. Like Rabagliati, he was devastatingly handsome: sea green eyes, high cheekbones, and a full head of soft brown curls. He was short, but trim, and had a distinctive approach to phrasing that infused his performances with an alluring sensuality. Listening to Otto's recordings today, one cannot help but be reminded of a young Frank Sinatra: the lyrical brilliance, warm yet clear timbre, precise enunciation, liltingly fluid rhythmic sense and adept approach of using the microphone as a tool for creating subtle, intimate phrasing. These were characteristics shared by both men. Today, Otto is often referred to as the Frank Sinatra of Italy, but in truth the opposite would be more accurate. A sophisticated, chart-topping singer, Otto began singing professionally several years before Sinatra, and his earliest recordings reveal that he had already developed his distinctive phrasing and style before Sinatra made his professional debut with the Harry James Orchestra in 1939.

For most of his career, Otto carried a notebook that he used to jot down lyrics he was learning, random thoughts and special events. His daughter, Silvia Codognotto Sandon, found the notebooks shortly after his death, and in 2011 she published excerpts from them.[69] Otto's recorded memories reveal much about his life as a musician in Mussolini's Italy. They also help in demystifying some of the rumors about his career that developed after World War II.

Otto was born on Christmas Eve 1912 in a small, seaside town near Genoa called Cogoleto. He was the third of five children. His parents, Marino and Silvia Codognotto, named him Natale (Christmas), but due to his small stature – caused by a mild case of polio he contracted at age three – everyone called him Natalino. In his notebook, Otto reflected on the difficulties he faced as a child:

Natalino Otto

Figure 4.5 Publicity photo-postcard of Natalino Otto, ca. 1942.
Source: Photographic archive of Anna Celenza.

I was really little … about that there is no doubt. Yet I remember the anguish of coming and going from doctors, hospitals, specialists … My family was a family of workers, we weren't rich people. I will never forget the sacrifices they made in order to save my leg. For many years my mother told me about her anguish at seeing some nurses, who when leaving the operating room, covered in blood, showed little sensitivity as they carried in their arms the amputated limb of a child. My mother was horrified … But fate was good to me.[70]

Although Otto walked with a slight limp the rest of his life, he recovered completely from his childhood illness. So much so, that by the time he reached adolescence he had secured a job assisting the barista at the Gran

Caffè Italia in Genoa. And it was there, at this storied establishment, that he first discovered jazz. There was a small dance band that regularly played at the Gran Caffè, and every day Otto followed their performances closely. He was especially fascinated by the drummer, who served as the rhythmic pulse of the entire ensemble. At home, Otto tried to replicate the sounds he had heard at work by playing on the pots and pans in his mother's kitchen. Intrigued by her son's musical interests, she convinced Otto's father to invest in lessons for their son at a local music school. According to Otto,

I studied solfeggio, sight singing, [and] music history. I tried all the instruments, from trombone to clarinet, but my true passion was the drum. Of course, the drumset was still considered a devilry come from America. Thus, the only way to continue in music was to continue my formal study and in the meantime to work at the Gran Caffè: if for no other reason than to watch from afar and listen to the group play every Saturday and Sunday.[71]

Otto stayed late, after the cafe closed, and practiced the drums in secret. By the time he was caught, he had become quite proficient. So the bandleader let Otto fill in as his substitute, and he encouraged the teenager's interests. Eventually he gave Otto a regular paying gig.

That evening I ran home in a flash. Ten lira a night ... perhaps I could actually play ... I was chomping at the bit, but obviously, I wanted more. And in fact, after some time, I joined a real group: the Tiziana Jazz Band. Then, my real break came. It had already been a year, and our contract took us to Albissola. The summer season of 1930 had already begun; the locale was, as they say, high class [and] fashionable. One night, however, a strange thing happened ...

Otto was told that a new fashion had arrived from the United States, which required that the drummer serve as the lead singer too. At first, Otto resisted; he had never really attempted to sing before. But when he learned his job was on the line, he gave it a go, and sang "Parlami d'amore, Mariù," made famous by Vittorio Di Sica in the film *Gli Uomini, Che Mascalzoni* (What Scoundrels Men Are) in 1932.[72]

It wasn't really my style, but it was a beautiful song and the first that came into my head. While I sang I listened to myself, and what I heard wasn't bad. I would have to study some more, but I definitely wasn't out of tune ...[73]

Otto's combined talents earned him a spot in a popular Italian ensemble called the George Link Orchestra, where he remained for several months. In August 1932, Otto accepted a position as dance band musician for the Conte di Savoia, "one of the most prestigious transatlantic passenger ships of the era."[74] Over the next three years, he made a total of thirty-four crossings between Genoa and New York, and each time he arrived in the United States he "visited all the jazz locales and bought lots of gramophone discs."[75] In New York, Otto also had the experience of cutting his first record:

I entered the recording booth, followed the instructions and sang "Who?" a tune that I had heard many times [in the United States]. I didn't know all the words by heart, so for the most part I just sang the melody ... I improvised ... I had a great time. I was alone, right there in the heart of New York City, in a glass box, and I sang simply for the joy of it.[76]

"Who?" was a Jerome Kern tune, written in 1925 for the Broadway musical *Sunny*. It wasn't jazz, but for a singer just starting out, it offered a lilting melody ripe for improvisation. While working on the Conte di Savoia, Otto found his singing style – a style that made the most of his innate rhythmic sense, clear baritone voice, warm tone and impeccable enunciation. Otto had a gift for languages and could sing in Italian, English and German with little effort. The key to his performances was his attention to lyrics, their meaning and rhythmic phrasing, and his ability to use the microphone for more than just amplification. In fact, Otto belonged to the first generation of singers who embraced the microphone as a performance tool, using it as a means of creating a sense of nuanced intimacy in the recording studio and on stage. Otto was the first Italian crooner, and although he was inspired by the American singers he encountered in New York – Rudy Vallée, Bing Crosby, Russ Colombo – the sound and style he developed while working on the Conte di Savoia were all his own.

During his layovers between crossings, Otto made the most of his time in New York. In addition to connecting with the Italian American community and socializing with local musicians, he secured work singing for an Italian American radio station, most likely WOV. The WOV studios were located at 16 East 42nd Street, the center of Manhattan's entertainment district, and its broadcasts reached a listening audience that stretched as far as the Tri-State area. Established in 1928, WOV's initial programming was aimed at a general audience. But by the mid-1930s, when Otto arrived on the scene, the station had strengthened its ethnic ties and expanded its Italian-language programming to fill the daytime and primetime hours. WOV's bilingual broadcasts appealed to young and old alike, and its focus on Italian American culture created a virtual community for immigrant families in New York and New Jersey. Frank Sinatra grew up listening to WOV, and over its airwaves he no doubt encountered Natalino Otto, and countless other Italian singers, performing the characteristically Italian *musica leggera* being cultivated across the Atlantic. Indeed, much of what made Sinatra's sound so distinctive in the late 1930s was his adherence to the Northern Italian jazz style created by Otto and imitated by so many others. As Jo Stafford, a colleague of Sinatra's in the Tommy Dorsey Band, later noted, Sinatra's approach to phrasing was unlike anything she had ever heard from American singers:

Everybody up until then was sounding like Crosby, but this was a whole new sound ... Frank really loved music, and I think he loved singing ... Frank was a warm Italian boy ... I just knew it was a wonderful, great sound, and it was not Crosby. It was a new sound and a good one, a very musical sound.[77]

Stafford had no idea where Sinatra got his sound. But listening to those early recordings and comparing them to earlier performances of Italian jazz, it is clear that hearing singers like Otto over WOV had a profound effect on Sinatra's approach to singing.

In New York, Otto's closest friend and ally was Joe Venuti. As a star performer in Paul Whiteman's Orchestra and a bandleader in his own right, Venuti had established himself as one of New York's top-paid musicians, and he encouraged others, including Otto, to follow his lead. It was likely Venuti who got Otto his radio gig, and he regularly introduced the newly arrived Italian to his friends and colleagues in New York. Through Venuti, Otto met his idol, drummer Gene Krupa, in addition to Duke Ellington and the actors Douglas Fairbanks, Claudette Colbert and Hedy Lamarr. Venuti had big plans for Otto. He could see right away that the singer's good looks and innate rhythmic sense set him apart from the other crooners in New York. Consequently, he lobbied hard for Otto to stay, and for a few months it appears he was successful in his campaign. But then Mussolini invaded Ethiopia, and life for Italian immigrants became exponentially more difficult in New York. As Otto later explained, he made the decision to return to Italy. As much as he had enjoyed his life in New York, he no longer felt it was the place he needed to be. "I returned to Genoa permanently in November 1935. I had chosen my country, my land and my family, and I found all of them waiting for me on the quay."[78]

Otto didn't remain in Genoa for long. In his luggage he had carried home with him the new tools of his trade: an assortment of cymbals and woodblocks to add to his drum set, and a microphone. Within a few weeks, he found himself on the road again. "During this period a lot of things came to pass. I even went to Africa to play for the soldiers with two up-and-coming performers, Renato Rascel and Aldo Fabrizi, and with the orchestra of Maestro Franco Grassi." As Otto explained, Grassi "was the one who changed my name: from Natale Codognotto I became Natalino Otto." In Ethiopia, Otto learned how to shape his performances in a way that aligned with the current political ideologies. "During this period I learned to sing [the popular Fascist tune] 'Faccetta nera' (Little Black Face)." Although the ship that transported Otto "into the lands of the Empire" was not as luxurious as the Conte di Savoia, "it didn't matter," Otto claimed. "I was content to be doing something for my country, because I was reformed ... I felt useful to my fatherland, even if only as an artist."[79]

Like so many young Italians, Otto was swept up in the passions of war and national pride. As he admitted years later, he had assumed that his year in Ethiopia entertaining Italian troops would be rewarded with a government contract when he returned home, but such was not the case. There was no position waiting for him at EIAR, so instead he signed an exclusive recording contract with Cetra's "rival" label, Fonit, and began touring and recording with Gorni Kramer and his orchestra.

Kramer loved working with Otto, whom he found to be unlike any other artist he had ever encountered:

I had heard all kinds of singers – bad, decent, good – but when I heard Natalino I had no doubt, he was my type. He was the first, the only one in those years. There was Rabagliati, it's true, but despite his ability to sing rhythmically, he was still tied more closely to older Italian traditions. Natalino, however, was a true man of swing. He had an extraordinary sense of rhythm, perfect intonation and enthusiasm. I loved it immediately. No one else at the time was so good.[80]

Once World War II began, Kramer and Otto made several lengthy tours across Germany, entertaining the troops and building a sense of camaraderie between Germans and Italians. These tours were occasionally described in the Italian press. For example, an article that appeared in *Il Canzoniere della Radio* in June 1942 offered an account of an evening in Nuremburg, when Otto and Kramer entertained a lively group of Germans and expat Italians:

In an old tavern frequented by artists in this beautiful German city, a small crowd of Italians is gathered around a table. At the center of this group are two young men, whose facial features and gestures betray their nationality: they are Gorni Kramer and Natalino Otto, the accordion player and the singer from Fonit ... The beer contributes to the success of the evening. Kramer eventually embraces his trusty accordion and gives a *la* to Natalino, who then sings the first song. Cheers and shouts greet him at the end. At midnight Kramer and Natalino are still playing and singing ... They are far away, but their hearts remain close to the Fatherland. They socialize and get to know German friends, visiting with them in their homes, and at cafes and other venues. They might even fancy the Germans' daughters and sisters, to whom they speak of love as if they are in Venice, Naples or Florence. That said, they never pass up the occasion to express their unfailing attachment to the homeland.[81]

Figure 4.6 Advertisement for the Trio Lescano and Cetra Records, ca. 1939.
Source: Photographic archive of Anna Celenza.

During the early years of World War II, Kramer and Otto served as a unifying force for soldiers who found themselves far from home. But theirs was not the only voice of Italian jazz.

Perhaps more than anyone else, the Trio Lescano, the "three graces of the radio" represented the voice of modern Italy during Mussolini's years in power (Figure 4.6). Originally from the Netherlands, the trio was composed of three sisters – Alexandra, Judith and Katharina "Kitty" Leschan – who Italianized their names to Sandra, Giuditta and Caterinetta Lescano shortly after their arrival in Italy in 1935.

The sisters led a hardscrabble and peripatetic childhood. Their parents, Alexander Leschan and Eva De Leeuwe, were both circus performers. He was a trapeze artist from a long line of Hungarian acrobats; she was a singer who had abandoned her Jewish upbringing in Amsterdam to run away with the circus. When the couple married in 1910, Eva was eighteen years old and eight months pregnant. Alexander was thirty-three and the father of two daughters from a previous marriage. Eva and Alexander stayed together for fifteen years. Their daughters, Alexandra, Judith and Kitty were born in 1910, 1913 and 1919, respectively. In 1924, the family moved to Algeria, where a son was born. When this fourth child died in infancy, Alexander slipped into a state of depression and began to drink heavily. Frustrated by this state of affairs, Eva left her husband and returned to The Netherlands with her daughters. During their years with the circus, the sisters had trained as acrobats with their father. Once back in Europe, their mother enrolled them in dance classes. By 1929, the two oldest girls had secured positions with the Simon Dekker-Dickson dance troupe and in April traveled with the troupe to Buenos Aires under the stage names Sally and Jetje Sandro. Their mother accompanied them, but the youngest sister, Kitty, was left behind with relatives.[82]

Little is known about these early years. When interviewed about their lives before Italy, the sisters and their mother rarely offered much information, and when they did, the details of their lives were often exaggerated or changed. What we do know for sure is that it was during the tour to Buenos Aires that Eva met Enrico Portino, a dedicated Fascist who soon took over as the girls' impresario. By 1930, the sisters were performing as an acrobatic duo, called The Sunday Sisters, with various circuses and vaudeville shows, traveling from one country to the next in search of stable income. In addition to various European capitals, their travels took them to Thessaloniki, Cairo, Beirut and Ethiopia, where they may have performed for Italian troops. By late 1935, the sisters had made their way to Italy, where during a performance at a small circus outside Verona, they were discovered by Carlo Prato, EIAR's local Artistic Director. Intrigued by their stage presence and trim, athletic physiques, Prato asked if they could sing and soon discovered that they could. When he learned that there was an equally talented third sister in Amsterdam, he requested that Eva send for her as soon as possible. Prato envisioned the trio as a jazz-infused version of the trailblazing Boswell Sisters, the vocal trio from New Orleans who had been enchanting American audiences with their close harmonies for nearly a decade. With this model in mind, Prato Italianized the names of his new prodigies and set to work training them for several months before getting them their first recording contract, with Parlophon, in 1936.

Prato's primary concern upon launching the sisters' career was making sure they developed a distinctive sound that would appeal to Italian audiences. Although their mother tongue was Dutch, the sisters' years of travel had enabled them to acquire proficiency in several languages: German, French, English and Italian. This multilingualism had a prominent effect on their pronunciation, and when they sang in Italian, their subtle accent made it difficult for listeners to identify their nationality. This indistinct quality imbued their sound with a hint of exoticism that fascinated audiences and record producers alike.

The Trio Lescano's first recording was a tune called "Guarany Guaranà," a fox-trot by Farra and Chiappo that served as the title song for an Italian film. Accompanying the sisters was Cinico Angelini and his orchestra. Shortly thereafter, the sisters were paired with Barzizza's Cetra Orchestra, which facilitated their regular appearances on EIAR broadcasts. Not surprisingly, some of the Trio Lescano's earliest recordings were Italian renditions of popular songs from American films.

Beginning in the early 1930s, all foreign films imported into Italy had to be supplied with new soundtracks that were produced in Rome and featured Italian actors for the dialogue and Italian musicians for the music. In addition to employing countless actors and musicians in Italy, the establishment of the dubbing industry in Rome cost the government almost nothing. Intent on controlling the import and export of all music and film, Mussolini required that Hollywood production companies supply the financial resources needed to produce the new soundtracks for all films screened in Italy.[83] Like the dubbed dialogue, the new musical numbers were used to Italianize these films. These songs were also sung on the radio as a means of promoting the film and recorded on gramophone discs that were sold to Italian audiences. The sisters' subtle accents lent an air of foreign allure that transformed the original "American" tunes into "Italian" songs that effectively satisfied both government censors and Italian fans of jazz. Over the course of the next two years, the Trio Lescano made dozens of recordings for foreign films. In 1937 alone, they supplied music for twenty-seven separate titles. This exposure on both the radio and via the cinema made them invaluable musicians at EIAR and Cetra, where they skyrocketed to the top of the charts almost instantly. Italian newspapers dubbed them "The Three Graces of the Microphone," "The Phenomenon of the Century" and "The Sisters who Embody the Mystery of the Celestial Trinity." And among their many fans was Il Duce himself.

The Trio Lescano embodied the sound of Italian jazz. The lyricism and close harmony of their musical arrangements made whatever they sang instantly identifiable as their own. Today the Trio Lescano is often referred to as the Andrews Sisters of Italy. But such a claim is misleading, since the Lescano sisters began recording in 1936, at least a year before the Andrews Sisters had gained acclaim in the United States. Shortly after the American trio launched their recording career as Decca artists in 1937, the label's Italian partner, Fonit, began releasing their recordings in Italy as a means of competing with the already popular Trio Lescano. Not the sort to shy away from a challenge, the Lescano sisters quickly established themselves as the dominant trio in Italy by appropriating one of the Andrews Sisters' most popular numbers, "Tu-li-Tulip Time," and transforming it into their own autobiographical signature tune. Indeed, the second verse of the new lyrics, written especially for the Trio Lescano by Riccardo Morbelli, identified the "singing tulips" to be none other than the Lescano sisters themselves:

La luna di lassù
dalla cupola blu
volge gli occhi in giù
udendo questa canzon
il suo bianco faccion
si compon
– fatto strano –
di ascoltare
le Lescano
che cantano:
"tuli tuli tulipan
tuli tuli tulipan"
e nel cantar
questa canzone
le tre Lescan
ti sembreran
tre tuli tuli tulipan.

The moon up there
in the blue cupola
turns its eyes downward
upon hearing this song.
Its big, white face
Arranges itself
– Strange thing –

To listen to
The Lescanos
Singing:
"Tuli tuli tulipan
Tuli tuli tulipan."
And in singing
This song,
The three Lescans
Will seem to you to be
Three tuli tuli tulips.

No doubt, this sense of competition between the Lescano Sisters and their American rivals was fueled by the Andrews Sisters' habit of performing a wide array of "ethnic" tunes. Their first big hit came in 1938 with the Yiddish tune, "Bei Mir Bist Du Schoen."[84] Several months later, they parodied Southern Italian dialect in "Oh! Ma-Ma," a sanitized English translation of a traditional Neapolitan Song full of sexual innuendo.

Oh Ma-Ma!
Oh, catcha dat man-a for me!
Oh Ma-Ma!
How happy I will be!
Oh Ma-Ma!
I'll cheery-beery be!
Oh, if I'm gonna marry,
It's-a da butcher boy for me!

The Trio Lescano responded the following year with their own version of the tune, which was incorporated into a scene of the popular film *Ecco La Radio!* (1939/40). Produced in Rome at the new state-of-the-art Cinecittà Studios, *Ecco La Radio!* was part of a publicity campaign mounted by the Italian government in an effort to broaden radio listenership. The central purpose of the film was to show the value and ingenuity of Italian radio. The premise was to portray a "day in the life" of Italian radio, beginning with domestic programming geared towards female listeners in the morning (excercise, cooking lessons, popular love songs), followed by family content and vocational training in the afternoon (radio dramas, local announcements, weather reports, school lessons, letters to soldiers in the field) and entertainment in the evening (sports broadcasts, operas, orchestra concerts and jazz). Indeed, the transition to jazz, which occupies the final fifteen minutes of the thirty-eight-minute film, is presented via a scene showing a middle-aged man's distaste for Italian opera. Upon hearing the strains of a Donizetti aria coming from the radio, he groans: "Uff. Classical music," and then reaches for the dial and switches to a broadcast being transmitted "from the Black Cat Nightclub." For the rest of the film, the stars of *musica leggera* dominate the screen. Here jazz is portrayed in a positive light, the most popular form of Italian musical art. It is in this section of the film that the Trio Lescano's version of "Oh! Ma-Ma" appears. Cleansed of all the ethnic satire portrayed in the Andrews Sisters' version of the tune, the Lescanos' version is sung in "proper Italian" without a hint of southern dialect. The Trio Lescano also avoids any references to the song's original double-entendre, turning it instead into a harmless tune about flirting. With a swinging accompaniment supplied by Barzizza's Orchestra Cetra, the performance removes jazz from its stereotypical nocturnal setting and transforms it into an element of everyday life. The girls are shown meeting their future husbands, not in a smoky night club but rather in broad daylight while pursuing the duties of respectable young women, namely, shopping and cooking.

Ecco La Radio! highlighted the array of musical genres found on Italian radio in the early 1940s and called attention to the fact that although EIAR tried to please all tastes, preference was given to the music of the youth: Italian jazz as it was represented in the performances of the Trio Lescano, Barzizza's Cetra Orchestra and Angelini's Orchestra da Ballo dell'EIAR.

Popular songs from this era propagated a similar idea by naming outright the stars of Italian jazz. Among the most admired were "Fra tanti gusti" (Amongst our Many Tastes), also known as "La Radio" composed by Odoardo Spado in 1938, and "La famiglia canterina" (The Singing Family) by C. A. Bixio in 1941. And in a humorous radio sketch broadcast in 1940, a young Federico Fellini described the domestic turmoil occasionally caused by the continued transmission of Italian jazz:

I would like to talk with you a bit about modern songs. About those songs that greatly anger Papa and Mama. All the old and sentimental aunts, all the old and irritable uncles. "What kind of music is that?" they say, raising their arms and placing their hands on their cheeks. "Have you ever experienced such a nuisance?" they add before calling out to the maid in a very loud voice: "Mariaaa! Turn off the radio!"[85]

Italy Goes to War

The importance of the radio became all the more obvious with the outbreak of World War II. On June 10, 1940 Mussolini joined forces with Hitler and declared war on Great Britain and France.[86] Germany had taken control of The Netherlands and Belgium and begun air raids on Paris. By all indications, Mussolini believed that the war would be short. As he reportedly said to General Pietro Badoglio: "I only need a few thousand dead, so that I can sit at the peace conference as a man who has fought."[87]

Italian troops listened to the radio regularly while away from home. Indeed, it was the desires of soldiers more than any other demographic that dictated radio content during the early 1940s. The radio served as their link to life back home, and it offered a model of the Italy they were fighting for. As the writer and art critic Francesco Sapori noted in a *Radiocorriere* article in October 1941, the miraculous virtues of Italian *musica leggera* served to comfort and motivate soldiers confronting the struggles of war:

Yes. Sing and it will pass. But saying it like that does not fully describe the situation, because the soldier's song has another power that civilians do not know and can not control: it awakens dormant abilities within us, whets one's courage, inspires defiant adversity, enlivens our capabilities, increases them, makes them light and ready. If common sense and good taste will allow a comparison between the heart of a fighter and the engine of a car, I would venture to say that singing is the fuel and the lubricant of the soldier. Blessed verses! They equate nothing less than the clatter of weapons with the sighs of love; they disturb and console at the same time, arrogant and caressing, merciful and ruthless. They guess our torment, they know how to medicate it; they are crammed with domestic nostalgia, military hopes, distant promises, serene faith, stars and kisses. Each [soldier] waits for the ritornello, to raise his voice even more and contribute to the unified amplitude of the choir – the choir he knows from church, from the theater and from war.[88]

As the above quote explains, in the propaganda machine that was Italian radio in the 1940s, "soldiers' music" did not entail military tunes as much as it did upbeat jazz pieces sung by the likes of the Trio Lescano. And the audience for this programming, which was regularly identified as "Soldiers' Music," included Italians from all walks of life, from housewives and students to craftsmen, laborers and café patrons. For soldiers and civilians alike, Italian jazz was ubiquitous, the soundtrack of everyday life.

Italy's entrance into the war distressed many Americans. And the truth is that it irrevocably changed the fortunes, perceptions and careers of Italian jazz musicians. While speaking to a group of students at the University of Virginia on June 10, 1940, President Roosevelt professed his shock upon learning that Mussolini had joined Hitler in his military efforts: "The hand that held the dagger [i.e. Mussolini's] has struck it into the back of its neighbor."[89] Roosevelt hoped to assist the European democracies without having to directly involve American troops in combat. But such plans proved impossible after Japan bombed Pearl Harbor on December 7, 1941. Within twenty-four hours, Roosevelt declared War on Japan. Three days later, Japan's allies, Germany and Italy, declared war on the United States, thus bringing America into World War II. With the United States and Italy on opposite sides of the conflict, Italy's relationship with jazz grew more complicated.

Roosevelt began his third term as president in January 1941 and just over one year later the Istituto Luce released a newsreel titled "L'America del Signor Delano" (Mr. Delano's America).[90] Using stock news footage and clips from popular films, the newsreel presents the United States as a nation in decline, whose addiction to pleasure in all its guises has weakened its men and corrupted the virtues of its women. President Roosevelt and Vice President Wallace are portrayed as vainglorious figureheads, preoccupied with parties and fashion. A group of female college students is shown playing tug-of-war in the mud. Young men participating in a "fathering class" are described as weak, henpecked husbands. In another scene, Jewish and black Americans dance erratically in public to the sound of hot jazz. The film explains how social corruptions such as these have made Americans lazy and ill-prepared for war. Instead of training for combat, American soldiers are shown playing games and acting irresponsibly. The film concludes with stock footage of the bombing of Pearl Harbor. The message is clear: Italy and its new ally, Japan, are well prepared, both morally and militarily, to defeat the weak and corrupt United States. But as many Italians soon discovered, declarations such as these were little more than wishful thinking.

Ironically, Italy's alliance with Germany made the topic of Italian jazz all the more important to the Fascist government. In a public statement released to journalists on November 23, 1941, MinCulPop's Director, Alessandro Pavolini, declared:

There have been ministerial decrees in the field of *musica leggera* for the improvement of popular song. The topic is less trivial than one might believe, because popular song is as good an index as any of a population's state of mind, and to listen to this voice on occasion is helpful. In the present campaign, various workforces have helped us, among them EIAR. Conversely, one has had the impression that in commenting on this issue all of you have gradually turned against EIAR, as if it were responsible for the musical immorality in this field. This is not true. EIAR transmits popular songs because the soldiers continuously request them. As to public taste, EIAR can beneficially influence and gradually affect it, but one must do so in degrees, because if one transmits exclusively melodic music (I did not say classical), those people who have a slightly perverted taste for music that is exclusively rhythmical, or syncopated, would surely all begin listening to foreign stations. In fact, little by little our own *musica leggera* has been coming into existence, and within it a melodic vein has been resurrected over the rhythmical background that has invaded the whole world, including Germany and Japan. In this way *musica leggera* is persistently coming closer to becoming our own kind of music and one that should also be spread abroad. I testify that EIAR stands alongside us in this job and, consequently, does not deserve to be targeted.[91]

MinCulPop's goals were made even clearer during a press conference with journalists on March 9, 1942. On that occasion, Pavolini chastised reporters who continued to criticize EIAR for its jazz programming, noting that there needed to be more consideration for the desires of radio listeners, most notably, the desires of Italian enlisted men:

To be precise, the soldiers want these songs, these pop songs and also the dance tunes, and this also represents the desire of broad masses of all listeners. One has tried, little by little, to Italianize the current type of *musica leggera*, this Italian creation, which has resumed its process of expansion and gradually spread every-where, and this is controlled also by copyright. Consequently, it has moved from the syncopated music of America to music with a prevalent rhythmic character all over the world. On this rhythmic foundation a melodic vein that designates these songs as Italian was reborn in Italian *musica leggera*. One has attempted little by little to modify the method of singing, the composition of the orchestras, etc. All of this, however, has certain limits because the public is not locked up in a room and obligated to listen to what we are transmitting. Today, if this is not to one's taste, he simply turns the knob and finds his nourishment elsewhere – hopefully, from a radio broadcast by a foreign friend and not an enemy. Thus it would be much better for them simply to listen to our music, into which are interspersed our own words and ideas.[92]

The "enemy" referenced here was Radio Londra, the Italian-language broadcast produced by the British Broadcasting Company (BBC), whose programs of British and American jazz had begun to attract Italian listen-ers. As the war progressed, MinCulPop's tolerance of foreign broadcasts decreased dramatically, while its efforts to promote Italian jazz exclusively increased. Consequently, in April 1942, a new law was ratified that forbade the sale and/or radio broadcast in Italy of gramophone discs from countries that were not allies of the Fascist regime.[93]

As tolerance for the "foreign" decreased in Italy, the popularity of the Trio Lescano, and their constant promotion by EIAR, began to attract criticism in the press. It was well known that Mussolini was an ardent admirer of the Trio Lescano, so much so that he granted them Italian citizenship on March 30, 1942, despite their Jewish heritage.[94] This caused some reporters to claim that Mussolini and his government were playing favorites. In response to such accusations, Pavolini held a press conference with reporters on June 17, 1942, wherein he stressed the importance of protecting the private lives of prominent EIAR performers, most notably the Trio Lescano:

Once again, there was an incidence of referencing the private lives of certain stars from radio, film, theater, etc. [in the press]. Such references irritate our soldiers and certain segments of the general public. For example, the Italian citizenship of the Lescanos was recently discussed in the press ... I recommend trashing this news, at least for the duration of the war.[95]

EIAR and Cetra went into crisis mode as well. Realizing that there were some who now doubted the Lescano Sisters' loyalty to Italy, EIAR commissioned two of its staff, composer Gino Filippini and scriptwriter Riccardo Morbelli, to create a new tune for the trio. Titled "Addio Tulipan" (Goodbye Tulip), this song confirmed the trio's devotion to Italy. Recorded with Barzizza's Cetra Orchestra on September 24, 1942, the song commemorated their new status as Italian citizens. As the chorus clearly explained, the sisters had abandoned their previous lives for the blue skies of Italy:

Addio mulini a vento, non vi vedremo più.
Un dì vi abbiam lasciati per questo cielo blu.
È un cielo che ci ammalia e che ci fa sognar,
il cielo dell'Italia che sa farci cantar.[96]

Farewell windmills, we won't be seeing you again.
We have left you for this blue sky.
It's a sky that bewitches us and makes us dream,
The Italian sky that knows how to make us sing.

"Addio Tulipan" made several clear references, both in its music and lyrics, to one of the Trio Lescano's most popular recordings: their remake of the Andrews Sisters' "Tu-li-Tulip Time." Thus the argument could be made that with "Addio Tulipan," the Trio Lescano killed two birds with one stone. In addition to serving as a public declaration of their loyalty to Italy, "Addio Tulipan" presented a subtle rejection of their previous engagement with American culture.

If the Trio Lescano's recording of "Addio Tulipan" in September 1942 served as a public farewell to the Netherlands, their private renunciation occurred a few months earlier in a personal letter to Mussolini. Dated June

16, 1942, the letter began by thanking Mussolini for the assistance he had offered as they applied for Italian citizenship. Once this formality was out of the way, the sisters proceeded to the primary topic of their letter: another request. Now that they had secured their Italian citizenship, they wished to become official members of the PNF. They also requested that their mother's application for Italian citizenship be reconsidered, since her previous request had been denied.[97]

A series of surviving documents reveals that Mussolini and his closest advisors exerted much effort in attempting to fulfill these requests. Although Eva De Leeuwe was never granted citizenship, the Lescano sisters received official notification from the government on April 7, 1943 that their first request had been granted. They were now card-carrying members of the PNF.[98] But as the Lescano sisters soon discovered, even membership in the PNF couldn't protect them from the ravages of war.

On December 8, 1942, B52 bombers filled the blue skies of Italy as Allied forces bombed Turin. Among the various facilities targeted by the Americans were the Central Headquarters and Studios of EIAR and Cetra. No musicians lost their lives during the bombing, but the damage proved devastating nonetheless. In fact, the destruction forced Angelini and Barzizza to move their ensembles to Florence, where they began broadcasting from an affiliated station. The Allied bombing of the EIAR studios in Turin did not destroy Italian jazz, but it did mark the beginning of the end. Although Kramer and Otto continued on in Milan, the destructive forces of war dealt a heavy blow to Italy's popular music industry. Simply put, the bombing in Turin marked the first step in the gradual disintegration of Mussolini's carefully constructed ecosystem of Italian jazz.

5 | A Nation Divided

Looking back at the programming that played on Italian radio during the 1930s and early 40s, it is clear that jazz, as an instrumental genre, was never banned. Even after the race laws went into effect, jazz in its new Italianized form continued, a development largely due to the focus on the voice. MinCulPop officials weren't so concerned with the instrumental style of a composition. Rather, it was the tune's title, lyrics and the race of the composer that received the most scrutiny. As Gaetano Gimelli, a trumpet player who regularly performed on Italian radio later explained, musicians only "got into trouble" when they disregarded the MinCulPop guidelines: "Barzizza and Semprini would insert a jazz ballad into the programming and then get called into the office of the Program Director, who would give them a good scolding." But that didn't change things. "The next day, we played another jazz piece, this time with an Italianized title and the composer's name changed." And so it went, day after day. "Of course, we weren't always happy about having to accompany all those singers," Gimelli admitted, "but now and then we got the chance to play a solo."[1]

Such was the state of Italian jazz during the early years of World War II. But then American troops landed in Sicily on July 10, 1943, and Italy's political landscape underwent a dramatic change. On July 25, the Fascist Grand Council voted Mussolini out of power, and under orders of King Victor Emmanuel III, he was arrested and eventually imprisoned on Gran Sasso, in the Apennine Mountains. General Badoglio, who had led the offensive in Ethiopia, was appointed Italy's new prime minister. Badoglio dissolved Mussolini's legislative system, the *Camera dei Fasci e delle Corporazioni*, on August 2, and on September 3 he signed an armistice with the United States and its allies. Nine days later, Mussolini was liberated from Gran Sasso by German paratroopers under orders of Hitler and appointed leader of the Repubblica Sociale Italiana (RSI) – informally known as the Republic of Salò – a puppet state established by German forces in the Italian regions north of Rome. German occupation of the northern half of the peninsula sparked a civil war in Italy, and divisions between the nation's two regions deepened as the Axis-controlled North fought against the Allied-controlled South.

As far as Italy's music culture was concerned, the ecosystem that had been so carefully constructed during Mussolini's years in power proved permanently damaged. Although EIAR and Cetra reestablished their studios in Turin at the end of 1943, the national network was by then divided in two, with Mussolini and the RSI in control of Cetra and the EIAR transmitters in Turin, Florence and Milan, and the Americans in control of the EIAR stations in Palermo, Naples, Bari and eventually Rome. Additionally, all the US recording companies with offices in Turin and Milan – namely Decca, Columbia and Brunswick – were shut down, leaving only the Italian (Fonit and Cetra) and German (Grammofono and Parlophon) studios in operation. Consequently, Italy's jazz musicians were faced with two options: either remain in the North and continue to follow Mussolini in his newly strengthened alliance with the Germans, or refuse to acknowledge Mussolini's new government and face imprisonment. Carlo Prato, the director of Radio Turin and manager of the Trio Lescano, chose the latter option. He was subsequently arrested, incarcerated briefly in Italy and then transferred to a German POW camp in Limburg an der Lahn.[2] The journalist Giovanni Giovannini remembered being transported via cattle car with Prato, whom he called "the eminence grise of *musica leggera*," and several other musicians, who were allowed "to drag along with them the tools of their trade, that is [their] trumpets and trombones, saxophones, violins and cellos."[3] Prato made it through the war with his life intact. Other musicians were not so fortunate. For example, Giuseppe Funaro, who had been dismissed from EIAR in 1938 after the race laws went into effect, was arrested in Genoa on September 24, 1944 and sent to an Italian concentration camp in Bolzano. One month later, he was transferred to Auschwitz, where he died in January 1945.[4]

With the creation of RSI, efforts were made not only to reignite Italians' loyalty to Mussolini, but also to strengthen their sense of unity with German colleagues. With these goals in mind, the stars of Italian jazz were asked to perform regularly for German troops, and the previous rivalries between Fonit and Cetra and Angelini and Barzizza were abandoned. In addition, popular singers who had previously been banned from EIAR, the most notable being Natalino Otto, now found themselves welcomed on national radio as Italian jazz maintained its presence on RSI broadcasts. That said, the visibility of Italian jazz was substantially reduced in an effort to comply with new censorship guidelines established by Hitler's cultural ministers in Germany. Hardline propaganda filled much of the new radio programming created in the RSI, and as a result many Italian listeners began to lose interest. In the revamped culture that was RSI radio, innovation in the realm of jazz was no longer fueled by friendly rivalries. Instead, competition became mired in political propaganda, with the new adversaries being Radio Londra (the Italian-language program broadcast by the BBC) and the former EIAR stations in Southern Italy that had come under the control of the Anglo American Psychological Warfare Branch (PWB) and Armed Forces Radio.

Allied Control in the South

As US and British troops moved their way north from Sicily and across Italy's mainland, one of their primary objectives was to take control of each region's communication systems, including newspapers, and most importantly radio. The EIAR transmitter in Palermo was the first to be seized, on August 6, 1943. The transmitter in Bari was next, on September 23, followed by the takeover of the EIAR transmitter in Naples on October 14. In each instance, the radio stations were manned with personnel from the PWB and transformed into Anglo American communication centers. The Armed Forces Radio Service (AFRS), which had been established by the US War Department in May 1942, was given the mission of providing entertainment that simultaneously comforted soldiers and opposed propaganda broadcasts. With the overwhelming support of the entertainment industry and dedicated military members, the AFRS functioned along the lines of a professional broadcast unit. In fact, many American radio entertainers got their start by working in the Italian AFRS units during World War II.[5]

The American troops who manned the captured EIAR stations in Italy brought V-Discs, short for Victory Discs, with them. These long-playing, 12-inch 78 rpm gramophone discs were sponsored by the Music Branch of the Special Division of the War Department and manufactured by RCA and Columbia beginning in 1943. The US government's objective in sponsoring the production of these records was to boost the morale of Allied soldiers while simultaneously spreading American culture. In total, just over 905 discs, which carried upwards of 2,700 separate compositions, made their way into Italy. The range of music was broad, from spirituals, chamber music and symphonic works to popular songs and jazz. With regard to these latter categories, the soldiers fighting in Italy actually had a better selection of the latest music than listeners at home did. This was due to the fact that since July 1942 the American Federation of Musicians (AFM) had been involved in a recording strike against US recording companies over royalty payments.

The union head instigating the strike, James Caesar Petrillo, was a trumpet player from Chicago, who had led AFM with an iron fist since 1922, the same year Mussolini came to power. Petrillo was an Italian American wary of being compared to the enemy dictator. Consequently, when an Army lieutenant named George Robert Vincent proposed that Petrillo allow his union musicians to record a series of gramophone discs for the exclusive use of soldiers overseas, Petrillo was happy to oblige. From that moment on, hundreds of America's best musicians, including some of its biggest stars (i.e. Frank Sinatra, Bing Crosby, Billie Holiday, the Andrews Sisters, Louis Armstrong, Duke Ellington, Tommy Dorsey and Count Basie), made their way to recording studios in the United States and eagerly contributed to the project.[6] These V-Discs were then shipped to Italy, among other countries, where they were used to fill the programming of the EIAR radio stations controlled by the Allies, namely, those in Palermo, Bari and Naples.[7] Not surprisingly, the jazz performances proved especially popular among not just servicemen but civilians as well. In these cities, where Mussolini's push for Italian jazz over traditional Southern Italian music had been met with resistance for nearly two decades, American jazz was welcomed with open arms. Stripped of its associations with Mussolini, jazz was embraced by many Southern Italians as liberation music, a symbol of their newfound freedom from Fascist oppression.

Jazz and the RSI

In the North, Italian jazz continued to be presented as a product of youthful modernity, and the stars of Italian jazz that remained in the RSI – most notably Angelini, Barzizza, Rabagliati and the Trio Lescano – continued to record jazz-infused songs for Cetra, Fonit and foreign affiliates like Parlophon. They also returned to EIAR broadcasts, which now welcomed performances by Kramer and Otto too. As Giampiero Boneschi, a pianist for Kramer, explained, agreeing to work for the RSI was not a creative choice as much as it was a matter of survival. Working for the radio enabled one "to get a card distributed by the Germans" that made everyday life much more bearable:

The fact was that with such a card one could get something decent to eat, because the radio headquarters had a great cafeteria. To eat is a necessity ... those of you who did not live through the war can't understand the things that happened then, not just with regard to songs and records, I'm talking about life itself.[8]

As Boneschi went on to explain, it was in the cafeteria for radio employees that he first met Otto:

He sang for the radio, too, and was greatly appreciated [by the authorities] because he could also sing in German! Of course, this was because Natalino and Kramer did a lot of shows during the war in Germany, where he learned to sing in the language with some success.[9]

Otto's performances had been considered "forbidden fruit" to EIAR broadcasts before the war, but as Boneschi explained, adding him to RSI programming during the height of the war made sense. "I remember Natalino being looked upon with great respect; he was already famous, and his recordings were selling like hotcakes."[10]

Otto's popularity among Italian audiences was confirmed in an article he wrote for *Il Canzoniere della Radio* in May 1943. It was part of a series, accompanied by promotional photographs, wherein the stars of radio were asked to reveal their innermost thoughts to readers. As Otto noted, his thoughts often revolved around his own fame and popularity: "I must confess: I live for my voice, which many people, in their goodness, have judged as not being devoid of a certain value." But as Otto went on to explain, his voice wasn't the only thing that made him appealing: "Few of you know my face. Well, here it is! Does it please you?" he asked, referring to the photos accompanying the article. "It pleases me, quite a lot. In fact, no one pleases me as much as myself. Therefore, if I'm happy, everyone's happy. Right?"

Otto's early years of being banned from the radio had clearly had no ill effect on his self-confidence, and for the young ladies hoping to capture his heart, he offered little comfort. "Essentially, I only have one true love: the microphone," he claimed. "With it, I have experienced the greatest satisfactions in my life, and I am here to tell you that when the public applauds me, I am not completely content unless the microphone applauds me as well." As Otto explained, this applause was the result of his distinctive jazz-infused style. "I prefer singing lively songs wherein my imagination can delight in making fluttering swarms of improvised notes that alternate with calculated pauses. When I sing, I like to experience only the life of my sensations and my heart."[11]

As Otto reached the peak of his career during the final years of the war, Rabagliati's popularity grew at a steady pace too. He continued to appear in films and performed regularly for Italian and German troops, as did the Orchestras of Angelini and Barzizza. But living and working at EIAR was no longer as carefree as it had been. Tensions ran high in the RSI, and even though performances of Italian jazz continued to be sponsored by the government, for many artists who remained in the North, life became exponentially more difficult.

In Turin, the EIAR studios were now garrisoned with German troops, and enforcement of the race laws became increasingly more stringent. This proved especially upsetting to the Trio Lescano, whose Jewish heritage left them vulnerable under the laws of the new regime. At first, the Lescano sisters attempted to adapt to these changes with the hope of riding out the German occupation without incident. In addition to performing for the troops and recording some of their most popular tunes in German, they attempted to give themselves a more Aryan appearance by dyeing their hair blonde and chestnut. It should be noted that their mother, Eva De Leeuwe, was no longer living with them in Turin. When her second attempt to gain Italian citizenship failed in April 1942, De Leeuwe went into hiding. She moved to Valperga Canavese, a small commune about twenty miles north of Turin, where she lodged with relatives of the girls' housekeeper. Several months later, she moved again, this time to the small Alpine village of Saint-Vincent, just a few miles south of the Swiss and French borders. De Leeuwe's decision to change locations was likely motivated by news she had received from Amsterdam: in an effort to avoid capture by the Nazis, her younger brother, Aaron De Leeuwe, had committed suicide on September 20.

Despite these setbacks, the Lescano sisters continued to sing and record for Cetra.[12] In November 1943, they traveled to Genoa, where they remained for three weeks, giving concerts and performing in music revues at various theaters: first at the Teatro Grattacielo, then at the Teatro Augustus and the Politeama Sampierdarenese, where they received rave reviews. After that, they disappeared. Though they were at the height of their fame, the increasing presence of German soldiers concerned them. After the Genoa performances, the sisters packed up their belongings and joined their mother in Saint-Vincent.

Curiously, the newspapers made no mention of the Lescano sisters' disappearance, and truth be told, only those working at EIAR would have been aware of their absence. Throughout the war, recordings by the Trio Lescano continued to appear in Cetra advertisements,[13] and in 1944, several of their recordings were rereleased.[14] Thanks to the hundreds of tunes recorded by the "three graces of the radio" between 1935 and 1943, Fascist officials were able to continue featuring them on EIAR broadcasts. As far as listeners in the RSI were concerned, the Trio Lescano never went away.

Even with the continued presence of EIAR's greatest stars, radio broadcasts transformed under RSI supervision. Mussolini was no longer calling all the shots, and radio listeners sensed his weakened control right away.

His first radio broadcast as RSI Prime Minister took place on September 18, 1943. In a tired voice he announced to his followers the establishment of the RSI and confirmed that under his leadership, Italians would continue to fight side-by-side with the Germans. Giorgio Nelson Page, an American reporter living in Italy who had sided with Mussolini years before, wrote an account of this broadcast shortly after the war:

The evening Mussolini made his first radio broadcast after being liberated [by the Germans] I was at home listening to my radio. It made a sad impression on me. He told the story of his arrest at the home of the King [Victor Emmanuel III] ... His voice sounded tired and depressed ... the voice of someone who seemed to speak from beyond the grave.[15]

Little more than a puppet dictator now, Mussolini was tolerated by the Germans, but not highly respected. Consequently, EIAR programming was stuck between two contrasting agendas: the German military's demand for a propaganda machine, on the one side, and Mussolini's preference for an enticing youth-oriented media tool, on the other. This conflict confused listeners, and the effectiveness of RSI radio broadcasts waned. Mussolini was no longer the indefatigable, iron-fisted leader he had been, and as the months progressed, German officials gradually began to squeeze him out. By 1944, EIAR no longer adhered to Mussolini's original vision.

This change in style is perhaps most clearly displayed in *Segnale della Radio*, a new weekly magazine published by RSI as an accompaniment to radio broadcasts. It was intended to fill the void left by the discontinuation of *Radiocorriere*, which had ceased publication the day German paratroopers liberated Mussolini from prison. The first issue of *Segnale della Radio* appeared almost a year later, on August 27, 1944, and even a cursory look at its cover reveals the EIAR's change in focus under German control. Whereas *Radiocorriere* featured optimistic images of civilian music-making or portraits of radio's biggest stars, the covers of *Segnale della Radio* presented a barrage of racist, fear-mongering images similar to those found on the covers of *La Difesa della Razza*. For example, the cover of the first issue featured the grimacing face of a black man, with exaggerated features, wearing a US military helmet and a beaded African earring superimposed on a fragmented map of Rome. Later issues presented similar images promoting anti-Semitism.[16]

Reading through *Segnale della Radio* reveals even more clearly the changes that had occurred at EIAR under German control. As the program listings show, radio broadcasts now focused primarily on supporting the German cause. Consequently, there was an increase in newscasts and educational programming geared towards specific groups, such as soldiers, mothers, laborers and school-age children. Daily programming time was also dedicated to reading the names of RSI family members in the "enemy-occupied" South, with the hope of encouraging those Italians to join the Nazi/Fascist cause. Only broadcasts from Axis-controlled stations were included in *Segnale della Radio*. Civilians caught listening to foreign broadcasts, like the BBC's Radio Londra or the AFRS broadcasts, were punished severely. Although performances by the Orchestras conducted by Angelini, Barzizza and Kramer continued to be broadcast at night, all references to their repertoire were removed. In addition, the transmission late at night of *musica leggera* recordings was simply listed as "musica riprodotta." The titles and names of composers were no longer included. With regard to the articles in *Segnale della Radio* discussing music, these tended to focus on the "return" of Italian operettas and the artistic glories of German symphonic music. Articles discussing jazz were few and far between, but when they did occur, the goal was to describe jazz as a universal art form capable of taking on Italian characteristics ideally suited to expressing a nationalistic spirit and lifting the morale of soldiers in the field.

Not surprisingly, the changes that occurred at EIAR upset many Fascist officials loyal to Mussolini. This discontent was documented in letters of protest, such as the one from Fernando Mezzasoma (head of Mussolini's MinCulPop) to Rudolf Rahn (the German Plenipotentiary to the RSI) in January 1945:

Some misunderstanding has been caused by the rise in the RSI of propaganda agencies that are thoroughly Germanic … It would seem necessary to invoke in those responsible … a greater sense of cooperation, because their attitude is sometimes detrimental to the actual interests of common propaganda.[17]

In general, Italian listeners in the RSI disliked the heavy-handed approach to EIAR broadcasts implemented by the Germans. A report issued by the PWB at the end of 1943 revealed that a large percentage of Italians had lost confidence in official RSI news bulletins and were consequently listening more regularly to foreign broadcasts, including the BBC's Radio Londra.[18] Italian jazz could still be found on the RSI airwaves, and as Kramer later explained, he and his colleagues even found ways of getting around the Germans' ban against performing tunes by American composers:

We would announce "Fiori di prato" and then go on to improvise on "I'm confessin'," or we proposed "Strada al sole" by Giovanni Ugo and in reality we played "On the Sunny Side of the Street" by Jimmy McHugh. We had to be careful, however, about our selection of pieces: the most famous ones were recognized by too many, and thus we couldn't pass off something like "It Don't Mean a Thing" or "Caravan" by Ellington as our own stuff. Although no one admitted to listening to jazz, everyone knew all of the famous themes. But it was a good thing for us, because in a certain way, we were forced to be looking constantly for new songs. Since [American] jazz couldn't be sold openly, I spent hours in the back of the record store, rummaging through every box. I listened to everything, took notes and then went back to the studio, where I knocked out an arrangement and practiced for five minutes [before going on air].[19]

After the war, Kramer and others often recounted the effort that went into creating Italianized names for their favorite American musicians. According to popular legend, Louis Armstrong became Luigi Braccioforte, Coleman Hawkins was La Colemà, Duke Ellington took on the name Del Duca while Benny Goodman was christened Beniamino Buonuomo. It should be noted that none of these Italianized names ever appeared in advertisements, program listings or on record labels.[20] They might have been used in the dubbing of American films before the war, and during EIAR broadcasts once the Germans took control. As Kramer recalled, "When we played 'Solitude' by Duke Ellington I announced 'And now we will hear "Solitudine" by Del Duca.' "[21]

Despite the purported effectiveness of these evasive tactics, the perfor-mance of music by American composers was still rare in the RSI during the final years of the war. The truth was that with so many talented composers and arrangers on the EIAR payroll, there was little need to play anything other than the latest Italian songs. In many ways, Italian musicians believed they had little choice but to participate in EIAR broadcasts. As Virgilio Savona, a singer with the Quartetto Cetra noted, many jazz musicians in Italy did their best to avoid performing on programs strongly linked to RSI propaganda:

EIAR was always asking for new performances, but we had to be careful not to end up on Fascist propaganda broadcasts. Like everyone, we knew how things stood, and we didn't want our popularity to sustain the regime that had carried us into war. So everyone looked for excuses. I say everyone, because what we did, Kramer ... and many other musicians did, too: One said he was sick, another had a commitment, or a sick mother, or claimed that their orchestra had just dis-banded. In short, it was one excuse after another. But sometimes we just couldn't avoid the programs. And in these transmissions, while working for the Fascists, we nonetheless happened to discover things that filled us with enthusiasm.[22]

But no matter the origins of the tunes, or how distinctive the Italian style of jazz became, there were still those in the PNF who continued to object to the music, something especially true in the German-speaking regions of the RSI, where many local residents felt a closer affinity to Hitler than to Mussolini. This distaste for jazz-infused *musica leggera* was perhaps most clearly demonstrated by an incident that occurred at the height of the war in Bergamo, a city twenty-five miles northeast of Milan.

On April 22, 1944, Kramer and Otto were performing in the Teatro Duse as part of a musical revue titled *Una Notte al Madera.* The show had already enjoyed two months of success in Milan, where the press had given it positive reviews. In Bergamo, however, an altercation during the second half of the show required police intervention. Shortly after Otto's entrance, Elia Bruno, secretary of the PNF Torre dei Roveri, stormed the stage with two Italian comrades and, holding a gun to Otto's head, insisted that he sing "Giovinezza." According to firsthand reports, Kramer tried to diffuse the situation by stepping up to the microphone and explaining to the audience, which was primarily German troops, how he and Otto had spent the previous night entertaining their injured comrades in the local hospital. The anecdote received a cheer from the crowd but no assistance with regard to disarming the three men threatening Otto. Consequently, Otto gave in to Bruno's demands and sang the requested tune, accompanied by Kramer and his band.[23]

Although details of the incident were not described in the press, a reference to the interruption appeared in the *Bergamo Repubblicana* two days later in an article titled "Ritmo-mania." The reporter began by commenting, with great disdain, on the continued interest in jazz shown by many Italian youths.

It is painful to see how there are still so many young people infatuated with a certain Anglo-Americanized, saxophonized music based on wild cacophonous explosions of syncopated rhythm. One had believed that this kind of juvenile infatuation for such musical products … was a temporary phenomenon. Apparently, only in our dreams.[24]

Declaring Italian jazz to be nothing more than "idiotic manifestations" that destroy "our traditional good taste," the reporter admitted to being baffled by the "bad habit" that "continues to be fueled by the succession of certain variety shows," whose "notorious rhythms" and "instrumental acrobats … cause masses of young people to flock to the theaters and explode in beastly screams."[25]

The reference here to "certain variety shows" was a subtle dig at the tours of Italian jazz being funded by the RSI. Distressed by the fact that these performances had become popular among the youth in various parts of Italy, the Bergamo reporter took pride in announcing that in his city the audi-ence had shown what he considered to be a proper disdain for such music. "There is still a healthy group that thinks and acts in an Italian manner," he claimed. "And when faced with such manifestations of collective frenzy [no doubt a reference to the Otto incident] they could not refrain from express-ing their disapproval and disgust over such barbarisms and perversions."[26]

It should be noted that Otto's daughter, Silvia Codognotto Sandon, later claimed that her father refused to sing "Giovinezza" that night in Bergamo, and that for the duration of the war, his musical career was constantly suppressed and threatened by the RSI's Fascist and Nazi leadership. As understandable as her reasons for making such a claim might be, they none-theless represent a rewriting of history. After the Bergamo incident, Otto and Kramer continued their tour through Lombardy and Liguria without threats or impediments from RSI leadership.[27] The Bergamo incident repre-sented an atypical reaction to Otto and Kramer. In fact, one could even go so far as to argue that the establishment of the RSI in northern Italy facili-tated the launch of both men as stars on Italian radio, so much so that in February 1945 Kramer was declared "the most interesting and comprehen-sive element that modern music has conferred upon Italy" by a reporter for the popular culture magazine *L'Ora*. "Even the fiercest detractors of the new rhythmic sensibility have stopped to listen to him and have concluded that he's good," continued the reporter. "Kramer, the unsurpassed accordion-ist," was defined as an "innovator," who was destined "to travel world wide" after the war and make "his own niche in the musical history of our era." The reporter concluded by noting that "even the Americans themselves, so protective of their jazz discoveries, cite him in *Metronome* for his personal accomplishments … and innovations."[28] Kramer became the poster boy, of sorts, for the brand of Italian jazz promoted by Mussolini. Thus it should come as no surprise that as the war trudged along, Mussolini turned to the music of Kramer and his collegaues in an effort to reunite a divided nation.

Mussolini's War of the Airwaves

The continued popularity of Italian jazz among many Italian listeners no doubt influenced Mussolini to attempt, once again, to use radio as a means of garnering support from the Italian population. As the war progressed, German authorities began to censor Mussolini from EIAR broadcasts, often cutting short his speeches and sometimes going so far as eliminating them altogether. Consequently, Mussolini set out to establish his own station in the summer of 1944.[29] His original plan had been to create a channel called Radio Falco (Radio Hawk), which would have transmitted into Allied-occupied territories in an effort to regain the support of Italians living outside the RSI. Mussolini consulted with the Futurist writer Emilio Settimelli and Paolo Fabbri, a former journalist for *Gazzetta del Popolo* and *Popolo d'Italia*, about his plan. Both supported the idea in theory, but Fabbri suggested that the initiative might be more effective if listeners believed the transmission was a clandestine broadcast coming from within Rome itself. Consequently, the name was changed to Radio Tevere, after the ancient river that runs through the heart of the capital. The first broadcast took place on June 10, 1944, just one week after the capture of Rome by Allied forces.[30]

From the beginning, Radio Tevere was committed to shedding the heavy-handed propaganda that had come to characterize EIAR broadcasts in the North. Transmitted during the evening hours – from 8:00 p.m. to 1:00 a.m. – its content consisted primarily of Italian jazz, comedy sketches and short news reports read on the hour. Radio Tevere's stated purpose was to entertain listeners and take their minds off the war. Its ultimate goal, however, was to attract Italian listeners in the South and regain support for Mussolini. The tone of Radio Tevere was relatively neutral, yet its alliance with Mussolini and Italian Fascism was not difficult to recognize. Each broadcast began with a performance of Puccini's "Inno a Roma" (Hymn to Rome):

Roma divina, a te sul Campidoglio,
dove eterno verdeggia il sacro alloro,
a te, nostra fortezza e nostro orgoglio,
ascende il coro.
Salve Dea Roma! Ti sfavilla in fronte
il Sol che nasce sulla nuova storia;
fulgida in arme, all'ultimo orizzonte
sta la Vittoria.

Divine Rome, to you on the Capitoline Hill,
Where the sacred laurel forever grows green,
To you, our strength and our pride,
Ascends the chorus.
Hail Goddess Rome! Sparkling in front of you is
The sun that rises on a new [chapter of] history;
Resplendent in armor, at the final horizon,
Stands Victory.

The "Inno a Roma" featured a text by Fausto Salvatori. The composition had been commissioned by the Mayor of Rome in 1919 to celebrate Italy's victory in World War I.[31] But the Fascists eagerly adopted the hymn in the early 1920s, and its martial character and references to Rome's glorious past soon made it a musical symbol of the Fascist regime, similar in stature to "Giovinezza."[32]

This characteristic of presenting neutral material that nonetheless encouraged continued loyalty to Mussolini could also be heard in Radio Tevere's initial transmission, which began with a short speech titled "To the Italians Who are Listening:"

The voice that enters your homes for the first time this evening is a free voice. We do not speak to exalt, nor to express, nor to flatter, nor to sympathize. All this has already been done too much, and unfortunately is done still. The propagandists park themselves on the airwaves and bellow at passersby to make them clients. We're not looking for clients. We're looking for friends; we're looking for soulmates. We will never say anything deceptive simply to please. We are not frightened by the substantial ruins, the lost territory, the blows received and to be received. Time and history will heal all of this. The thing we fear, as something irreparable, is the moral ruin, the spiritual cowardliness and the yielding to foreigners, not because they are strong, but because they are rich. We notice, and thus say with brutal frankness, that this is the disaster that threatens our country.[33]

The primary content of Radio Tevere was Italian jazz. Listeners remembered hearing performances by Angelini and Barzizza, and performers, like Giampero Boneschi, remembered seeing Kramer and Otto at Radio Tevere broadcasts. The benefits of participating in the broadcasts cannot be overestimated. In addition to generous stipends and access to good meals, musicians working for Radio Tevere also received protection "from being arrested by the Germans and deported."[34]

Each Radio Tevere broadcast concluded with a performance of "Tornerai" (You Will Return), the sentimental song first made famous by the Trio Lescano and a male quartet led by Giuseppe Funaro.[35] Although anti-Semitism in the RSI had brought an end to the careers of both these ensembles, the song's emotional power continued unabated, and in 1944 it was rerecorded by Miriam Ferretti[36] with a new introductory verse by Nino Restelli that referenced the civil war dividing Italy:

Non ti ricordi quella canzon,
piena d'amore e di passion,
che dolcemente ci avvinse un dì,
e che per sempre ci unì?

Or che lontano tu sei da me,
mentre la guerra echeggia in ciel,
con un tremor io canto ancor,
Tornerai ...

Don't you remember that song,
Full of love and passion,
That once sweetly enveloped us,
And that forever unites us?
Now that you are far away from me,
While the war echoes in the sky,
With a tremor, I am still singing
You will return ...

Radio Tevere broadcasts proved popular among Italian listeners, primarily because the programming was unlike anything else on the airwaves at the time. Romano Mussolini remembered listening to the broadcasts regularly during the final months of the war (Figure 5.1). Although his father's original intent had been to fool listeners into thinking the transmission was coming from within Allied-occupied Rome, this ruse did not last long. Within a few weeks, listeners realized that the broadcast was coming from the RSI. In fact, as early as January 1945, shortwave radio enthusiasts in the United States were tracking the broadcasts of Radio Tevere, which they described as a "German-controlled station in Italy."[37]

Although Kramer later claimed that he had never participated in Radio Tevere broadcasts, witnesses said they remember him. But even if it is true that he refrained from performing live, nothing would have prevented Radio Tevere from broadcasting recordings of his performances. Either way, by the winter of 1945 jazz had become the primary weapon in a "war of the airwaves" that raged through Italy, with Allied Forces Radio broadcasting American jazz on one side and Mussolini's Radio Tevere transmitting Italian jazz on the other. Despite the growing oppression of German forces in the RSI, Italian jazz survived as a cultural symbol of Mussolini's Italy. Nowhere was this more pronounced than in an article published in the *Segnale della Radio* in December 1944. Written by Alceo Toni, a classical musician who over the years had gained an appreciation for *musica leggera* under Mussolini's guidance, the article defined jazz as a genre capable of embodying the spirit of various nations, including Fascist Italy.

Toni began by declaring that "popular song" had not "been raised to the honor of public discussion" that it deserved, and that the time had come for it to be taken seriously. Although many "superficial observers" of Italy's

Figure 5.1 Flanked by his sister Anna Maria, Romano Mussolini plays piano in the living room of their home, on the island of Ischia, near Naples, Italy. March 4, 1962. *Source*: AP Photo/Mario Torrisi.

jazz-infused singing style had recently "written much and with loud complaints," claimed Toni, no real effort had yet been made to discuss the ramifications of jazz on the development of Italian culture. "Isn't the musicality of a people manifested in the singing that it most commonly adopts to display its musical whims? Doesn't popular song follow current musical taste? Isn't it the lowest common denominator of musical culture?" Looking back over the history of popular song in Italy, Toni claimed that Italians had always been "dominated" by various "universal fashions," and that the most recent trends were simply evidence that Italians had "slipped [once again] into supine, imitation of the foreign." He then described how this fascination with the foreign had "denatured the physiological character of Italian vocality" as it once existed in opera and popular folk songs.

We no longer sing with abandonment or in a full-throated style. The beautiful swirls, and the soft, sinuous lines of the slow melodic phrasing no longer inspire nor excite our abandoned songbirds. No use denying it, the voice has bent to the vogue, which is indeed rampant around the world, of singing in an Anglo-Saxon style: a style of singing that is slow [and] funereal, whose flights rise and fall, indeed, whose bass sounds are repeated over and over like a Negro mill worker's monotonous moan.[38]

Toni described the arrival of American music in negative terms, at first, but then continued by arguing that it would have been wrong for Italians to isolate themselves from modern musical currents:

We shouldn't dream up ostracisms that evince hatred of the new. We should not lean toward avoiding the new rhythms of dance. Jazz, which comes into the picture at precisely this point, leads us into neither contradiction nor subjection. Our own musical nationalism does not suffer if we speak of it.[39]

According to Toni, because jazz was a "universal" art form, its arrival in Italy was not anathema to Italian nationalism. And even though jazz first came to light in the United States, its cultural origins were firmly rooted in European culture.

Jazz is neither an exclusive manifestation nor a typical creation of the American spirit. American music is even less than a nebula. It is a world before genesis. Although it is true that the epicenter of jazz diffusion has been and will be located in America, it is nonetheless an artistic result of universal character. Think about it. Jazz has arisen in its very substance not because of a single factor exclusive to the "Republic of many stars" [USA]. It has arisen neither from instrumentation nor from factors having to do with harmony, counterpoint, and form. Instead it owes everything to and has taken everything from European musical art. It is wholly a tributary of that art.[40]

Toni blatantly tied the origins of jazz to European culture. He then continued by returning to the topic of jazz in Italy and its connection to popular song and dance. According to Toni's definition, jazz referred not only to "a very particular type of instrumental ensemble" but also to "the compositions that came into being alongside that ensemble." In Italy, jazz had "supplanted the waltz, the polka and the mazurka, just as these in their own time had supplanted the gavotte, minuet, and sarabande." In its earliest form, jazz "was music that was derivative, decorative, and lowbrow … It was a music born in eccentric environments to support frenetic thrills of intoxication that turned everything on its head. What sort of birthright can it have had if not a spurious birthright?" Toni asked. "It doesn't matter," he responded.

Arguments about creative priority apart, the problem for us is not to avoid any and every contact with different types of jazz music, but rather to assimilate as much in them that has become "public domain." We can and we should make the different types of jazz our own, just as we did in the case of the waltz, the polka and the mazurka … It has to do with reconfiguring them in our own way: with *singing them* in an Italian way, which is a specific, personal way of singing that is our own and is tied in this respect to determinants, influences and physical characteristics of our being, something that flourishes, just as our flowers, plants and trees flourish in our own lands. Song, in the final analysis, is the music of a language. Language determines and substantiates it, even as it creates its originality. One sings in a language, in its musical sense, not in the abstract. As to what remains, in art there is no conclusion and no glory other than being oneself, in the spirit of one's own race, and in its general character. EIAR has understood all of this, and its fruits are already being observed: bringing us back to a musical flourishing that is essentially our own.[41]

The importance of this article should not be overlooked. Written by a prominent Fascist musician in the RSI, who was loyal to Mussolini and his efforts to modernize Italian musical culture, it reveals that even in the final months of the war, jazz was not rejected by Italian Fascism, but rather embraced as an essentially Italian phenomenon that was the result of a lengthy evolutionary process. In Italy, the key ingredient to the national style of jazz was "song, the music of a language." Stated simply: Italy made jazz "its own," by singing it "in an Italian way."

Jazz in Postwar Italy

Mussolini may have won his battle with the Germans in defining jazz as music fit for Fascism, but he lost the war against the Americans. As Allied forces worked their way up the Italian peninsula, more and more Italians abandoned Mussolini and the RSI. By the spring of 1945, American jazz had become the soundtrack for everything anti-Fascist – liberty, democracy, racial equality – thanks to the V-Disc. On April 26, Allied forces took control of the transmitters for Radio Tevere and EIAR Milan. The next day, Communist partisans captured Mussolini, his mistress Clara Petacci and a group of Fascist officials as they attempted to cross the border into Switzerland. Mussolini and the others were executed by gunfire the next day, then transported back to Milan, where their corpses were pelted, spat upon, kicked and disfigured by an angry mob.[42] From that day forward, the concept of jazz as a symbol of the Fascist state was willingly abandoned, and a rewriting of history began. As the war came to an end, there was a widespread "conviction that the name and very idea of Italy had been irreparably sabotaged by Fascism." This conviction tended to encourage both in public speeches and policy a rejection of Italy's immediate past and a turning outward to embrace the cultural traditions of the United States once again.[43]

General Heinrich von Vietinghoff signed the instrument of surrender on behalf of the German forces in Italy on April 29. To show their loyalty to the American and British troops, Gorni Kramer and Tata Giacobetti published a fox-trot titled "Black and Johnny" shortly thereafter. A pair of US and British flags donned the cover of the sheet music, along with the date "April 30, 1945" and the following inscription: "Ai valorosi soldati alleati gli autori dedicano" (Dedicated by the authors to the valorous Allied Soldiers). Kramer and Giacobetti also included photos of themselves on the cover, to ensure that the Americans would recognize them when they saw them. Most notable, however, was the music itself, which called for an instrumental accompaniment of accordion and mandolin, the musical symbols of Northern and Southern Italy, respectively. The lyrics celebrated the arrival of the Americans, while simultaneously poking fun at their supposed habit of heavy drinking:

Black e Johnny a passeggio vanno
per le vie della città
un soriso qua, un saluto là,
sono amici e ben lo sanno.
Ogni bar che visiteranno
mai di loro si scorderà:
sette whisky qua, venti cherry là,
e gli OK si sprecheranno.

Black and Johnny go for a walk
Through the streets of the city,
A smile here, a greeting there,
They are friends and know it well.
Each bar that they visit
Never will forget them:
Seven whiskeys here, twenty cherries there,
And to that they say OK.

Various recordings of "Black and Johnny" were released shortly after the publication of the sheet music, the most popular being those performed by Otto and Kramer in 1945 (Fonit) and by Ernesto Bonino and the Pippo Barzizza Orchestra in 1946 (Cetra). In celebration of the war's end, Kramer also recorded a new version of his 1936 hit "Crapa Pelada." Released seven months after Mussolini's assassination, the tune now included a new opening verse, sung in standardized Italian, that suggested that the identity of poor "Baldie" was none other than Il Duce himself:

A voi, miei signori, io voglio narrare
la storia che tanto mi fa disperare.

Son già sette mesi che vedo cadere
dal capo i capelli bianchi,
ormai son pelato, deluso, avvilito,
non so quali cure adottar.

To you, my gentlemen, I want to narrate
The story that drives me to despair.
For seven months now, I have watched
White hair fall from my head.
Now I'm bald, disillusioned, and sad.
I don't know which cures to adopt.

The Cetra Quartet accompanied Kramer on this revised version of the tune, which sounded noticeably more American in style than the 1936 recording. No doubt, Kramer was hoping to resurrect the idea that the tune had always been a *canzone della fronda*, designed to ridicule Mussolini and the PNF.[44] Kramer was also one of the first musicians in Italy to embrace Be-bop, a new style of jazz imported by the Americans via V-Disc just after the war's conclusion.[45] Most Italian listeners did not embrace Be-bop, and only a handful of Italian musicians attempted to assimilate the music's frenetic improvisations and dissonant harmonies into their own performances. Kramer's attempt, "Picchando in Be-bop," was released by Fonit in 1948.[46]

In general, Kramer, Rabagliati and Otto fared relatively well in postwar Italy performing American music. Having switched sides with the death of Mussolini, they eagerly entertained American troops in the months just after the war. It was during this same period that the Trio Lescano came out of hiding and returned to Cetra Studios in Turin to record two songs from Walt Disney's *Pinocchio*, which was first released in Italy in 1947.[47] One month later, they traveled to Livorno to meet their one-time rivals, the Andrews Sisters, who had come to Italy as part of a United Service Organizations (USO) tour. Two photos preserved by Sandra Lescano, which show all three Lescano sisters with blond hair, serve as documentation of the two trios' encounter.[48] But this is the only evidence. Italian newspapers offered no reports of the meeting, and the Andrews Sisters never mentioned the Trio Lescano in their accounts of traveling through Italy. In a letter written to a friend in July, however, LaVerne offered a rather frank assessment of the country as a whole: "This nation is so poor and filthy ... The only type of people here are the rich, the poor and the Pope, whose robes are gold and jewelry ... Flo, you wouldn't believe it. The Italians in Naples live like animals."[49]

After the war, the Trio Lescano floundered in Italy, where they were still recognized as the voice of Fascist Italy. On September 1, 1945, they made their final live appearance on an Italian radio broadcast. Semprini accompanied them on piano. He had just returned from London and, like the Lescano sisters, was attempting to resurrect his career. But little notice was given to the performance.[50] Although Semprini was able to rebuild his reputation, the Lescano sisters were made to feel quite unwelcome. It was at this point that Caterinetta, the youngest sister, decided to retire from singing. In March 1946, she married an antique dealer named Giulio Epicureo and settled in Turin. Intent on continuing their music careers, Sandra and Giuditta hired a replacement for their sister, the twenty-one-year-old Maria Bria, and immigrated with their mother to Argentina, where they relaunched their careers performing for an expatriate community of Fascist sympathizers.

Ezio Levi also attempted to revive a career in Italy after the war, but with similar difficulties. In Levi's case, however, it wasn't because audiences associated him with Fascism. It was because he had left. Like the Trio Lescano, he had slipped away without saying a word to anyone, and there were many who resented him for that, most notably his boyhood friend Testoni. Although Levi and Testoni had cofounded the *Circolo del Jazz Hot* and coauthored *Introduzione alla vera musica di Jazz* before the war, Testoni showed no interest in reviving their partnership. Just the year before, he had joined forces with a young writer and jazz fan named Arrigo Polillo and founded a new music journal, *Musica e Jazz*, which was underwritten by the Anglo American PWB.

The extent of American influence on the rewriting of jazz history in Italy was revealed in the introductory article penned by Testoni that appeared in the first issue. Titled "Un sogna che avvera" (A Dream Come True), it began by stating the central goals of the journal, which included building the public's interest in and understanding of jazz. Testoni then explained that the intended readership was not limited to "specialists" or "a specific social or economic class," but intended "for everyone." With these necessities out of the way Testoni then offered a retelling of the history of jazz in Italy through the lens of the *Circolo del Jazz Hot* in Milan. Like so many others after the war, Testoni revised history here, claiming that for many years "a journal" such as this, "focused on *musica leggera* and jazz" was nothing more than "an unattainable chimera." He even went so far as to claim that the new journal represented the freedom "to use the word jazz (and not giazza or musica ritmica) without any worry." The influence of the PWB was especially noticeable in the final paragraph of the article. Here Testoni defined jazz as a purely American product, "a symbol of Democracy."[51] Thus it should come as no surprise that the early issues of the journal featured the performances of American musicians almost exclusively.

In November 1955 a foreign correspondent for the *New York Times* declared that "America's secret weapon" in the Cold War was "a blue note in a minor key." Since then, countless scholars have designated the mid-1950s as the beginning of American jazz diplomacy, with the Soviet Union and Africa as primary targets. But as the early issues of *Musica e Jazz* reveal, the State Department's use of jazz as a tool for suppressing Communism began in Italy at least a decade earlier. One could even argue that the well-known Jazz Ambassadors program, launched by President Eisenhower in 1954, was simply a continuation of effective strategies first launched in Italy against the lure of Communism. It is no coincidence that the largest US Embassy in postwar Europe was, and still is, located in Italy. At the conclusion of World War II, Italy posed a particular problem, because in the minds of many Italians, the rejection of Fascism entailed an acceptance of Communism. The ideological vacuum created by the fall of Mussolini facilitated the growth of the Communist Party in Italy, a phenomenon that many US officials found troubling. In an effort to counteract the expanding red tide, the United States looked to jazz as an alluring symbol of American democracy. But here too they encountered a problem. Whereas England, France and Germany had always looked to jazz as a "foreign" art form, with indelible connections to American culture and ideals, Italy had transformed jazz, at least in part, into a "native" art form. Consequently, the United States poured money into a wide range of propaganda efforts in Italy, from V-Discs and periodicals in the 1940s to open-air jazz festivals and radio/TV programming in the following decade – all in an effort to redefine jazz as a symbol of American democracy.

With regard to *Musica e Jazz*, reading through the first dozen or so issues of the publication reveals that one of its primary purposes was to create a clear distinction between the concepts of jazz, which was presented as a definitively American style of music, and Italian *musica leggera*. These distinctions were made on the radio as well. Although broadcasting was briefly decentralized in Italy after Germany's surrender, regular broadcasts reemerged within a few months as the stations in the North were incorporated into the new national broadcast system Radio Audizioni Italiane (RAI), which facilitated the return of many former personnel.[52] Consequently, many of the musicians who worked for EIAR and Cetra during Mussolini's years returned to positions of prominence. Angelini and Barzizza took up their positions as Italy's primary bandleaders once again and happily promoted the newest music coming out of the United States. For example, on February 28, 1946, Barzizza recorded "Io t'ho incontrato a Napoli," a tune written by Hoagy Carmichael (music) and Jon Forte (lyrics) the year before, when they were stationed in Naples as musicians performing for American troops. The song was made famous in 1945 when it was featured in the Italian film *La vita ricomincia* (Life Begins Again) directed by Mario Mattòli. American listeners know the tune by its English title: "Somewhere in Via Roma." In both the Italian and English versions, the lyrics tell the ill-fated love story of a US serviceman and Neapolitan girl, with the final lines serving as a symbolic wish for future US/Italy relations:

Someday on Via Roma,
When the world is free again,
I pray that we will meet again,
Somewhere on Via Roma.

Otto also gained attention at the end of the war for a sentimental tune: "In cerca di te (Perduto amore)." This song was first recorded by Nella Colombo, and in her performance, listeners heard the story of a young girl searching in vain for a soldier who has not yet returned from the battlefield. Otto released his recording several weeks later, and for many, it was like listening to a completely different piece. Otto faced a great deal of criticism after the war for his participation in RSI programming. Thus, for many, Otto's performance offered not a tale of lost love, but rather a metaphorical longing for a world that no longer existed, an idealized image of Italy before the war.

Sola me ne vò per la città,
passo tra la folla che non sa
che non vede il mio dolore
cercando te, sognando te, che più non ho.
Ogni viso guardo, non sei tu.
Ogni voce ascolto, non sei tu.
Dove sei perduto amore?
Ti rivedrò, ti troverò, ti seguirò.

Alone I walk through the city,
I pass through the crowd that does not know,
That does not see my pain.
Searching for you, dreaming of you, the one I no longer have.
Every face I see, it is not you.

Every voice I hear, it is not you.
Where are you lost love?
I will see you, I will find you, I will follow you.

Otto was brought up on charges of colluding with the enemy, due to his performances for RSI and German troops, but these were eventually dropped,
thanks to the testimony of several members of the National Liberation
Committee (CLN), a political umbrella organization for Italian partisans
and anti-Fascists, and two patriots named "Jimmy" and "Renzo."[53] The fact
that Otto had been banned from EIAR broadcasts before the war served as
the primary evidence that he was not a Fascist supporter. Otto struggled to
overcome his past as a star in Fascist Italy, and in 1948 his former colleague
in the Kramer orchestra, Romano Alvaro, composed a song for him, titled
"No Jazz," that reflected on his musical predicament:

No, non suonare del jazz.
Ti prego non fare del jazz.
No jazz, questa sera
No jazz, per favore.
Ho nel cuore un ricordo d'amore
Che mi fa soffrir, così.
No jazz, è un tormento
No jazz, è un rimpianto.

No, don't play jazz
I beg you, please don't play jazz.
No jazz this evening,
No jazz, please.
I have a memory of love in my heart
That makes me suffer. So,
No jazz, it's a torment.
No jazz, it's a regret.

Otto waited a decade to record "No Jazz," and when he did, the melancholy
in his voice was palpable. Looking back on his years as a performer, he
noted how vulnerable life had been for artists like himself, who had lived in
the spotlight during the Fascist era:

"Ah ... Blessings on those who become artists." I heard this said to me so many
times ... An Artist! ... But an artist isn't any different from another human being.
He's just more sensitive, more vulnerable, more exposed to the will of others who
often control his life as if his opinion did not matter much.[54]

Reflecting on the Past

The luminaries of Italian jazz looked back on their years under Mussolini in different ways. Although Kramer, Otto and Rabagliati experienced some success in the early 1950s on Italian television, their performances changed. Otto and Rabagliati continued to sing, but the accompaniments that had helped define Italian jazz lost their rhythmic verve. As band-leaders, Kramer, Angelini and Barzizza continued producing swing music, but when interviewed about their early careers, they often avoided discussions of their successes during the final years of Mussolini's reign. As the years passed, the story of Italian jazz was rewritten as an era plagued by censorship and oppression – a desolate decade when jazz in all its guises was banned from Italian airwaves, and the musicians who attempted to perform it were severely punished. Late in life, Sandra Lescano even went so far as to claim – falsely – that Nazi/Fascist soldiers arrested her and her sisters during a public performance in Genoa and imprisoned them for an extended period.

Our troubles began in 1943: our mother was Jewish and had to go into hiding, in Saint-Vincent, in the home of a partisan, who we reimbursed with socks, sweaters and flags for his friends. We had been banned from the radio, but we continued to perform live shows. One night, while we were singing at the Cinema Grattacielo in Genoa, the military came to arrest us. "With such a nose you must be Jewish," a German captain said to us, and I responded to him, "If race depends on the nose, then you are a Jew as well." We were imprisoned at Marassi, in separate cells with the numbers 92, 94 and 96. We were also accused of espionage; it was probably the Trio Capinera, who, envious of our success, had denounced us. The accusation was that when singing "Tuli-Tuli-Tulipan" we had in reality sent messages to the enemy ... Those days in prison were terrible, especially because the Nazis forced my sister Judith, who knew German, to serve as an interpreter during the interrogation of prisoners – something she absolutely did not want to do. Thus she was forced to witness beatings; I remember her crying constantly in her cell.[55]

Several weeks later, Sandra retold her story, adding several details, to a reporter for *Gente* magazine:

Some government officials who hated us seized the opportunity, and while we were singing at the Grattacielo in Genoa, they arrested us on stage and carried us away in handcuffs to the Marassi prison, where our protests came to no avail.[56]

As Sandra went on to explain, she and her sisters "cried desperately" when the Germans accused them of "spying for the enemy," i.e. the Americans, and did everything they could "to explain that it wasn't true." In this version of the story, a Fascist captain told the Germans that the sisters were Italian citizens. "He explained that we weren't Jewish. That our father was not Jewish, even though our mother was." At this point, the Germans reportedly demanded information about their mother's current location, but Sandra refused to say anything:

> The SS had been searching for our mother, ... who to escape from being shot had taken refuge in the house of a partisan in Saint-Vincent. When we claimed to know nothing about our mother's whereabouts, the Fascists said that everything seemed in order and that we could be released. But the Nazis kept us in prison. They wanted to shoot us, and in the meantime they forced us to work as interpreters during interogations of detainees ... We remained incarcerated at Marassi for more than a month. I believe we were finally released from prison thanks to the direct intervention of King Umberto. We were never able to confirm this assertion in person, but we always thought that it was thanks to him.[57]

The Italians have a saying: "Se non è vero, è ben trovato" (Even if it's not true, it makes for a good story). Nowhere does this maxim ring truer than in Sandra's harrowing tale of the Trio Lescano's arrest and imprisonment. Although the details of the story changed with each telling, many in Italy embraced Sandra's account without question. In addition to being featured in countless Italian newspapers and magazines in the late 1980s, Sandra's tale sparked a documentary coproduced in The Netherlands and Italy, a trade book published in Italian and a popular miniseries for Rai Uno.[58] As engaging as Sandra's story might be, it is not true, at least not fully. Although Sandra, Giuditta and Caterinetta were likely questioned by German soldiers at some point in November 1943, there is no evidence of their arrest. Furthermore, if they had been accused of transmitting hidden messages to Allied forces through their song lyrics, it likely would not have been "Tulipan" that would have caused concern, but rather the trio's recording of "Come l'Ombra" (Like the Shadow), the haunting ballad of rejected love that was released on the same disc as "Addio Tulipan."

"Come l'Ombra" is arguably the only Trio Lescano tune still familiar to American audiences. This is because of its prominent use in the film *The Conformist* (1970), written and directed by Bernardo Bertolucci. In this song, the narrator sings of her attempts to thwart the affection of an oppressive lover who has darkened her life.

Ombra che stanca,
t'allontani da me,
nella vita cos'è
che ti manca?

Forse,
tu vai cercando l'amor,
che questo cuor
non ti sa dar?

Tired Shadow,
Turn away from me.
In life,
What is it that you're missing?
Perhaps,
You're searching for the love
That this heart
Doesn't know how to give you!

In 2013, I had the good fortune of meeting Mr. Bertolucci at the American Academy in Rome. When I asked him why he chose "Come l'Ombra," above all other songs, for the soundtrack of *The Conformist*, he noted that the song had "haunted him since childhood." He remembered listening to it during the war. He said that for him, and many of his friends, "Come l'Ombra" seemed to capture the oppressive mood brought on by the German occupation of Northern Italy in 1943.

As Bertolucci's comments suggest, the music of the Trio Lescano evoked a variety of memories and emotions for those who lived through the war. That said, none of the people who knew the Lescano sisters corroborated Sandra's story about the sisters' arrest. For example, Pippo Barzizza's daughter, Isa, who had befriended the Trio Lescano as a small girl, noted that after the war, when they were attempting to resurrect their careers in Italy, they spent countless hours with the Barzizza family and told many stories about their years in hiding. Yet, as Isa explained, there was never any talk about having been imprisoned: "When we met at the end of the war we talked about many things: we had been separated for years, and in the evening, after supper, we talked a lot. If such a thing had really happened, surely it would have been mentioned."[59]

After World War II, numerous artists from the Fascist era distanced themselves from their connections to Italian jazz. For example, Barzizza's children claimed that despite their father's success, he was censored during the 1930s and 40s due to "an exasperating nationalism" and "racism." According to them, "jazz was banned" and Barzizza was instead "invited to perform a more nationalistic music."[60] No doubt, this version of history came from their father, who late in life described his years conducting the Cetra Orchestra as "a real disaster."[61]

Otto's response was more introspective. In his diaries, he reflected on what it was like to be a star before and after the war:

In a short period of time you can become an idol, then one day "someone" decides that you are no longer in style, that your talent has become a classic, that people will esteem you, but that your talent seems no longer valid. You've been surpassed; you're finished, ready for posterity.[62]

One gets the sense from reading Otto's diaries that when looking back on the choices he made in life, he regretted his decision to leave the United States and return to Italy in 1935. In Italy, he claimed, "they do not respect you for your talent and professionalism, as they do in the United States."[63] Although Otto was given the opportunity to return to New York and restart his career there in the 1950s, he declined. Too much had happened. Too much time had passed. As he later explained in an interview, he also refused to reissue a "commemorative album" of his greatest hits from the 1930s and 40s.

It has a certain effect [on one] to find out that those songs had become [historical] documents. Truly, I am not yet ready to enter into history, even if it is only the minor history of *musica leggera* … I won't have anything to do with the idea of a commemorative recording. To put all that old stuff back into circulation doesn't make sense. It would serve no other purpose than to make everyone finally realize, without a doubt, that they are still connected to the past; and that the recordings of mine that they danced to in their youth belong to the past, just as I do.[64]

Towards the end of his life, Otto embraced the fact that he might be nothing more than "archival material," ready for posterity. He saw no purpose in bringing up old memories and putting them "back in circulation."

Rabagliati saw things differently. Unwilling to disavow his close connections with EIAR in the 1940s, he looked back on the years right after the war with a sense of sentimental melancholy and pride. For Rabagliati, his years at EIAR represented the golden age of his career, and he refused to feel shame about them. He saw the cultivation of Italian jazz as an important stage in the nation's cultural history. But then, he claimed, in the years immediately after the war, it became clear that "something had changed."

The old radio of the 40s had waned forever [like the setting sun] and taken with it all the most beautiful songs, the beautiful motives, unforgettable, simple, sweet and tender. That's when a slow and inexorable decline began for us, the old stars of the microphone. It's true, why hide it? The sunset is nothing shameful! Indeed, it is the best moment of the day. When you have shone in the sky for so many years, it is not unpleasant to set. The light during sunset is intense, full-bodied, still capable of emitting a ray of intense light.[65]

I find it interesting that Rabagliati chose to compare the end of Italian jazz to a sunset. A curious phenomenon about sunsets is the fact that pollution often intensifies their color and beauty.[66] Although Rabagliati likely was not aware of this when he reflected on the past, his description of the final years of World War II as an intense sunset seems a fitting metaphor. Let there be no doubt, Mussolini's twenty-three years in power caused great suffering, both in Italy and abroad. In many ways, he was a polluting substance in Italian culture, especially during the last decade of his reign when his pathological narcissism led to a range of disastrous decisions – from the invasion of Ethiopia and the establishment of Italy's race laws to his alignment with Germany and the founding of the RSI. And yet, it was that polluting force that facilitated the creation of a distinctly Italian style of jazz. As Rabagliati so intuitively explained, Italian jazz offered a brilliant glow in an otherwise dark and difficult era.

Shortly before he died in 1974, Rabagliati gave a final interview wherein he criticized those who had attempted to rewrite history. He was especially contemptuous of those who falsely claimed to have secretly fought against Mussolini during the 1940s.

It would be useless for me to say that I was a hero during those years. Those who today try to be clever by claiming that they were always against Fascism are liars. Back then, there were forty-five million of us, and we all believed in that man; he had charmed us all.[67]

Rabagliati had good reason to be upset. Many of the Italian musicians he had performed with on EIAR broadcasts spent the rest of their lives trying to distance themselves from their uncomfortable connections to Mussolini and his Fascist regime. And this concerted effort to rewrite history irreparably changed, perhaps more than anything else, Italy's reception and promotion of Italian jazz.

Reinvisioning the Italian Sound

As the postwar years progressed, the rejection of Italian jazz led to an inundation of American music, which troubled many in Italy, most notably those cultural and political leaders aligned with the ever strengthening Communist Party. Consequently, an effort was made in the 1950s to reclaim the concept of a specifically Italian style of *musica leggera* that was disconnected from jazz. In 1951, the song contests that had been sponsored a decade earlier by EIAR morphed into a new initiative, the *Festival della canzone italiana di Sanremo* (San Remo Festival of the Italian Song). The mastermind of the contest was a musical director at RAI named Giulio Razzi, and the primary goal was to promote Italian composers and music publishers and defend Italian song against "the rhythmic contaminations of jazz" coming out of the United States.[68] Although the San Remo Festival was, and still is, held in northwest Italy along the Riviera Coast, its original ideological focus was on the South. Indeed, traditional Neapolitan Song, the music that had been pushed aside by Italian jazz during the Fascist era, served as the preferred model for Italy's postwar national sound.

The festival was held in the ballroom of the San Remo Casino and broadcast live over the radio for three consecutive evenings. Publishers submitted a total of 250 songs, which were whittled down to twenty by a commission of music specialists. These twenty songs were then performed live by the Angelini Orchestra and various singers, so that listeners in the audience and at home could vote and select three winning songs. From the beginning, the festival drew substantial public involvement, and its popularity grew with each passing year. Most importantly, the San Remo Festival launched the careers of a new generation of Italian singers, and a new conception of Italian song. With the rise of San Remo came the decline of Italian jazz, and although singers like Otto and Rabagliati tried to adjust to the new nationalist style, they were never fully successful. San Remo became the new propagandist for Italian popular song, creating melodies and lyrics that sold thousands of records, and were repeatedly played on national radio.[69] The San Remo Festival "transformed popular song into a national sport and business," and in doing so it created a new *musica leggera* ecosystem in Italy that excluded jazz.[70]

Epilogue

The end of World War II affected the careers of Italian American artists too – perhaps none so prominent as that of Frank Sinatra. The prologue of this book began with an anecdote about Sinatra's appearance on the Major Bowes' Amateur Hour in September 1935. Accordingly, we can conclude with a brief narrative of what happened next. Sinatra and his colleagues in the Hoboken Four won the talent competition that night and were promptly sent on a nationwide tour of small-town America as part of a Major Bowes variety show.[1] Sinatra didn't last long. Mussolini's invasion of Ethiopia in October led to strong anti-Italian sentiment across much of the United States, including the small midwestern towns where Sinatra was performing. Needless to say, Sinatra encountered countless instances of racial prejudice during the tour, even suffering physical assaults on several occasions.[2] Consequently, he quit the Hoboken Four after just a few months and returned to New Jersey, where he spent the next four years developing his skills as a singer in the comfort of a close-knit Italian American community. It was during these years that Sinatra was exposed to the *musica leggera* coming out of Northern Italy. The music was imported by Decca and Columbia and marketed to communities like Sinatra's Hoboken. These tunes could be heard on the radio too, and also at rallies and fund-raisers sponsored by local politicians and Italian benevolent societies. It would have been nearly impossible for Sinatra to avoid exposure to the music, especially given his mother's ties to Hoboken's Italian American community. Dolly Sinatra was well aware of Italian jazz. And she likely would have been especially drawn to the performances of Natalino Otto, since her parents had emigrated from the same suburb in Genoa where Otto was raised.

Dolly Sinatra was a force of nature, both at home and in public. Proud and feisty, she served as a ward boss for the Democratic Party in Hoboken throughout the 1930s and 40s. Dolly was in charge of garnering votes from Hoboken's Italian American community. To do this, she not only visited her constituents regularly, but also organized local rallies and social events, which were routinely enlivened with performances of the latest hits from Italy. Like many Italian American democrats, she supported Mussolini during the 1920s and 30s. But when Italy joined forces with Germany, she changed her mind about Fascism. Indeed, Dolly was the one to instill in her son the belief that pride in one's Northern Italian heritage didn't require adherence to Mussolini's racist policies.

After his return to Hoboken, Sinatra secured a job (thanks to his mother's intervention) at the Rustic Cabin, a trendy dinner club in the Palisades with a telephone-wire hookup to WNEW, a popular New York radio station. Once a week, WNEW broadcast live from the Rustic Cabin, and it was thanks to this broadcast that Sinatra got his big break. Having heard Sinatra on the radio, the bandleader, Harry James, went to the Rustic Cabin to meet this new, young singer in person. "This very thin guy with swept-back greasy hair had been waiting tables," James recalled later. "Suddenly he took off his apron and climbed onto the stage. He'd sung only eight bars of 'Night and Day' when I felt the hairs on the back of my neck rising. I knew he was destined to be a great vocalist."[3]

Sinatra's sound was unlike anything James had ever heard. This is because James had never heard Italian jazz. He offered Sinatra a contract on the spot, but recommended that he change his name. "Sinatra is too Italian," said James, believing that the singer would have more success, with his blue eyes and light hair, distancing himself from his Italian heritage. As a bystander later explained, Sinatra refused: "You want the singer, you take the name," he supposedly said before turning his back and walking away.[4]

Needless to say, James took Sinatra on his own terms, and within just a few months, the singer found himself in a Brunswick recording studio, cutting his own iconic versions of jazz-infused love ballads with one of the best swing bands in the country. As Sinatra's fame grew, countless reporters asked him where he learned to sing. He offered a variety of answers: listening to the radio, emulating admired singers like Bing Crosby and Billie Holiday, and voice lessons with a former opera singer named John Quinlan. Sinatra even put his name on a method book with Quinlan in 1941 titled *Tips on Popular Singing*.[5] Quinlan no doubt assisted Sinatra in suppressing his heavy New Jersey accent, but even a cursory look at the exercises in the book reveals that he offered little guidance with regard to Sinatra's phrasing, keen rhythmic sense and effective use of the microphone. These are traits Sinatra claimed he picked up from closely listening to radio broadcasts. In addition to American crooners like Crosby, Sinatra also would have been listening to singers of Italian jazz, among them Otto, Rabagliati and the Trio Lescano. In fact, when Sinatra joined Harry James in 1939, he brought a new signature tune for the band, an Italian song called "Ciribiribin," which had recently been recorded by both the Trio Lescano and the Andrews Sisters.

The war years were good to Sinatra. After a year with Harry James, he moved on to the Tommy Dorsey band before breaking off on his own in 1943. Due to a punctured eardrum, Sinatra was excused from military duty. He remained in the United States, where he became a heartthrob – the surrogate voice for all the young boyfriends and husbands who had marched off to war, leaving a generation of young women behind. During the war years, Sinatra became known as "The Voice," drawing thousands of screaming young girls wherever he performed. He was the boy next door, the skinny youth with beautiful blue eyes and a velvet voice. And as much as his teenage female fans, the bobbysoxers, adored him, the boys in uniform resented him. It's no wonder that Sinatra never mentioned the early influence of Italian jazz: doing so would have only added fuel to the fire for those who called him a draft dodger and questioned his loyalty to the United States. To dispel such rumors, Sinatra became actively engaged in the war effort at home. In addition to singing for USO shows and promoting the purchase of war bonds, he gave speeches in high schools and at youth clubs against the racist policies of the Fascist and Nazi regimes. By the end of the war, Sinatra had become a national hero of sorts. He even won a special commendation at the Academy Awards for his participation in "The House I Live In," a short propaganda film that spoke out against anti-Semitism in the United States.

When World War II ended, however, Sinatra's fortunes changed. All those soldiers came home, and there was no longer any need for Sinatra's surrogate voice. In addition, Sinatra destroyed his "good guy" image when he abandoned his high-school-sweetheart wife, Nancy, and their three children for an affair in the public spotlight with Ava Gardner. With each passing year, Sinatra's career plummeted further, which is surprising, given the fact that the years after World War II featured what's commonly referred to as "the Italian decade" in American popular music.

When American soldiers returned from World War II, many of those who had been stationed in Southern Italy expressed a deep love of the region. It was in cities like Naples, Palermo, Sorrento and Salerno that American soldiers first experienced the flavors of authentic Italian cuisine and the sounds of traditional Neapolitan Song. Consequently, at the conclusion of the war, a fascination for all things Southern Italian captivated American society. Italian restaurants and pizza parlors spread across the nation, and songwriters in the United States cashed in on the latest craze. Traditional Neapolitan ballads found popularity outside of Italian American communities for the first time, and a new genre of novelty tunes, based on stereotypical images of Southern Italians and sung in Italian dialect with mandolin accompaniment, filled the playlists of radio stations across the country. Singing these songs was a new generation of crooners, Italian Americans with roots in Southern Italy: Dean Martin, Louis Prima, Tony Bennett, Perry Como and Vic Damone, to name just a few. In general, the most popular songs were the novelty tunes: "Angelina," "That's Amore," "Mambo Italiano" and a reprisal by Louis Prima of "Just a Gigolo." Dean Martin and Perry Como both found success singing songs that had first been presented as part of the San Remo Festival, namely, "Volare" and "Chee Chee Oo Chee." All of these new Italian tunes were sung in Neapolitan dialect or in a form of broken English/Italian. The success of these songs was so great that even non-Italian singers, like Rosemary Clooney, evinced a faux-Italian dialect in performances of "Mambo Italiano" and "Botch-a-Me," a crude rendition of Rabagliati's former hit "Ba-Ba-Baciami Piccina."

In an attempt to revive his career and cash in on the new Italian craze, Sinatra recorded "Torna a Surriento," a traditional ballad in Neapolitan dialect, in 1950. The result was less than gratifying. Overly slow and langorous, Sinatra struggled with the pronunciation. His ignorance of the language made his phrasing sound halting and leaden. To make things worse, Dean Martin released his own version of the tune just a few months later, as if to say to his friend and competitor: "Listen Frank, this is how you sing a Neapolitan love song."

Sinatra never sang in Italian again, and he never attempted singing novelty songs like "Angelina" or "That's Amore." Although Sinatra's grandparents on his father's side had immigrated to the United States from Sicily, it was his mother's Northern heritage that permeated the Sinatra home. Sinatra never learned to speak much Italian, and the little Italian he did know was tied to his mother's Genoese heritage. What made Sinatra different from the rest of the Italian American crooners of the mid-twentieth century was his Northern Italian style.

Sinatra only made four brief trips to Italy in his life: once in July 1945 as part of a USO show, again in 1953 when Ava Gardner was shooting a film in Milan, in 1962 for a three-day concert tour, and towards the end of his career, in 1987. This final visit was his most extensive one, and it was the first time he ever visited Genoa and Palermo. A documentarian followed Sinatra around during this final trip, recording his various interactions with local fans. Sinatra went to Sicily first, where the locals swarmed around him constantly, claiming to be a distant cousin, niece or nephew. Sinatra clearly felt uncomfortable during these encounters. Unable to understand what they were telling him, he just kept repeating time and again: "I have no family in Sicily. Everyone in my father's family is in America. They all moved to America."[6]

In Genoa, the encounters were more formal, and during the concert there, Sinatra appeared to be more at ease. For the first time, he mixed a few Italian words into his comments from the stage. At one point between songs, he even offered a little history lesson: "Two very important and wonderful people came from Genoa: one, uno. Christopher Columbus." The crowd cheered. As the applause died down Sinatra continued: "Due. Mia Mamma." The crowd went wild, clapping and shouting for nearly a full minute. Sinatra then added: "The other half was from Sicilia." Silence, and then just a smattering of applause. At this point Sinatra turned to his band and said, "I don't think they're too thrilled about the Sicilian part."[7]

Sinatra may have never admitted it publicly, but musically, he was a product of Northern Italy. Indeed, one of the things that made his approach to singing so distinctive, so different from the style of other Italian American crooners of his generation, was its foundation in the Italian jazz developed in cities like Genoa, Milan and Turin under Mussolini's watch. Although a rewriting of history nearly eliminated Italian jazz after World War II, vestiges of the music, divorced from its Fascist origins, live on in the early recordings of Frank Sinatra.

Notes

Prologue

1 The audition form for Sinatra's appearance on *Major Bowes' Amateur Hour* is currently held in Washington, DC: The Library of Congress; Motion Picture, Broadcasting & Recorded Sound Division. www.loc.gov/exhibits/treasures/trm018.html. Accessed April 7, 2014.

2 *Frank Sinatra: A Voice on Air 1935–1955*, 4-CD box-set with booklet (Columbia Records and Legacy Recordings 88875 09971 2), 2015.

3 Armstrong first released the tune with Odeon in 1931 (Odeon 36207), and then performed it again on the silver screen in *Rhapsody in Black and Blue* (1932).

4 Bing Crosby and Mills Brothers, "Shine" released in 1932 on the Brunswick label (Brunswick 6276).

5 Catherine Parsonage [Tackley], *The Evolution of Jazz in Britain 1880–1935* (Aldershot: Ashgate, 2005); Jeremy F. Lane, *Jazz and Machine-Age Imperialism: Music, "Race," and Intellectuals in France 1918–1945* (Ann Arbor, MI: University of Michigan Press, 2013); Howard Rye, "Towards a Black British Jazz: Studies in Acculturation, 1860–1935," in *Black British Jazz: Routes, Ownership and Performance*, ed. Jason Toynbee, Catherine Tackley and Mark Doffman (London and New York: Routledge, 2014), 35–42; Petrine Archer-Straw, *Negrophilia: Avant-Garde Paris and Black Culture in the 1920s* (London: Thames & Hudson, 2000); William A. Shack, *Harlem in Montmarte: A Paris Jazz Story between the Great Wars* (Berkeley, CA: University of California Press, 2001); Jeffrey H. Jackson, *Making Jazz French: Music and Modern Life in Interwar Paris* (Durham, NC: Duke University Press, 2003); Andy Fry, *Paris Blues: African American Music and French Popular Culture, 1920–1960* (Chicago, IL: University of Chicago Press, 2014); Horst J. P. Bergmeier and Rainer E. Lotz, *Hitler's Airwaves: The Inside Story of Nazi Radio Broadcasting and Propaganda Swing* (New Haven, CT: Yale University Press, 1997); Mike Zwerin, *Swing under the Nazis: Jazz as a Metaphor for Freedom* (New York: Cooper Square Press, 2000); Michael H. Kater, *Different Drummers: Jazz in the Culture of Nazi Germany* (Oxford University Press, 2003).

6 The discomfort of the connections between the name "Mussolini" and jazz were made all the more clear in February 2006, when at the funeral of Romano Mussolini, crowds shouting Fascist cheers gathered outside the church while jazz fans inside listened to a performance of "When the Saints Go Marching In."

For a description of the funeral, see Fabbio Presutti, "The Saxophone and the Pastoral. Italian Jazz in the Age of Fascist Modernity," *Italica* (Summer–Autumn, 2008): 273. For a video of the Fascist loyalists outside the church, see www .youtube.com/watch?v=xynBY85lTJ8. Accessed June 12, 2015.

1   Italians and the Origins of Jazz

1 Bruno Zuculin, "Musiche e danze americane," *La Lettura* 19/8 (August 1, 1919): 599–600.

2 According to the "New Orleans, Passenger Lists, 1813–1945" provided by Ancestry.com in association with National Archives and Records Administration, Zuculin arrived in New Orleans on the *S.S. Atenas* on June 22, 1918 from Argentina, where he had been serving as Consul to Buenos Aries.

3 Ernest Ansermet, "Sur une orchestra nègre," *La revue romande* (October 5, 1919), reprinted in Ernest Ansermet, *Écrits sur la musique* (Neuchâtel: Éditions de la Baconnière, 1971), 171–178. Andy Fry discusses this article at length in *Paris Blues: African American Music and French Popular Culture, 1920–1960* (Chicago, IL: University of Chicago Press, 2014), 220–232.

4 As Sybil Kein notes in *Creole: The History and Legacy of Louisiana's Free People of Color* (Baton Rouge, LA: Louisiana State University Press, 2009), 131, the first Louisiana document to use the term *Creole* dates from 1782 and applies the word to a slave.

5 Richard Campanella, *Geographies of New Orleans: Urban Fabrics before the Storm* (Lafayette, LA: Center for Louisiana Studies, 2006): 315. As Russell M. Magnaghi, "Louisiana's Italian Immigrants Prior to 1870," in *A Refuge for All Ages: Immigration in Louisiana History*, ed. Carl A Brasseaux (Lafayette, LA: Center for Louisiana Studies, 1996): 580–602, explains, prior to 1870, many of the Italians who came to New Orleans were from the northwestern regions of Lombardy, Liguria and Piedmont, which had "close cultural and political ties with France" (590).

6 Even at this early date, Italian musicians were not new to New Orleans. Beginning in the early 1820s, opera companies from Italy regularly included New Orleans on their tours of North and South America; and between 1828 and 1833, four operas by Gioachino Rossini received their American premieres at the Théâtre d'Orleans. In 1835 James Caldwell opened the St. Charles Theatre, an opulent space that seated upward of 400 spectators. To fill those seats, he began a vigorous campaign to import Italian performers and introduce New Orleans's audiences to the works of contemporary Italian composers. Consequently, New Orleans witnessed the American premieres of over a dozen Italian operas by Vincenzo Bellini and Gaetano Donizetti. For an excellent overview of the role Italian musicians played in New Orleans's musical culture – both in the classical/opera realm and jazz – see Bruce Boyd Raeburn, "Italian Americans

in New Orleans Jazz: Bel Canto Meets the Funk," *Italian American Review* 4/2 (Summer 2014): 87–108.

7 For example, during an interview with Dr. Edmond Souchon in New Orleans on September 29, 1956, Arnold "Deacon" Loyocano described the training that he and other New Orleans jazz musicians received from Italian members of the orchestra at the French Opera House. A transcript of the complete interview is housed in the Hogan Jazz Archive at Tulane University.

8 For a detailed study of Armstrong's connection to New Orleans opera tradition, see Joshua Berrett, "Louis Armstrong and Opera," *The Musical Quarterly* 76/2 (1992): 216–241. Additional information is also found in Raeburn, "Italian Americans in New Orleans Jazz," 88–89.

9 During the labor shortage in the nineteenth and early twentieth centuries, large landowners in Louisiana and other southern states recruited Sicilian immigrants to work as sharecroppers, but these immigrants soon left these rural areas due to the extreme anti-Italian discrimination and strict regimen, and settled in New Orleans and other urban centers in the North or on the West Coast. For a more thorough discussion of this topic, see Vincenza Scarpaci, "Walking the Color Line: Italian Immigrants in Rural Louisiana, 1880–1910," in *Are Italians White? How Race Is Made in America*, ed. Jennifer Guglielmo and Salvatore Salerno (New York: Routledge, 2003), 60–78.

10 Mark Choate, *Emigrant Nation: The Making of Italy Abroad* (Cambridge, MA: Harvard University Press, 2008), 1.

11 Ibid., 2.

12 Raeburn, "Italian Americans in New Orleans Jazz," 94.

13 Although Luigi Monti published a lengthy article about the mafia, "The Mafiusi of Sicily," in *The Atlantic Monthly* in 1876, it was relatively complimentary and only concerned the organization as it was established in Sicily. The first article about the Sicilian mafia in America appears to have been "Chief Hennessy Avenged," which appeared in the *New York Times* (March 15, 1891) and described in detail the events leading up to the lynching in New Orleans and the individuals involved. As the title indicates, this article cast New Orleans's Italian American community in a negative light; it also referred to possible "mafia" connections among those who were killed. Similar points of view appeared in "The Mafia and What Led to the Lynching," *Harper's Weekly* 35 (March 28, 1891): 602–612 and in an article penned by the Honorable Henry Cabot Lodge, Representative in Congress for Massachusetts, titled "Lynch Law and Unrestricted Immigration," *The North American Review* 152 (May 1891).

14 *Louis Armstrong in His Own Words*, ed. Thomas Brothers (Oxford: Oxford University Press, 1999), 160.

15 Robert C. Davis, *Christian Slaves, Muslim Masters: White Slavery in the Mediterranean, the Barbary Coast and Italy, 1500–1800* (London: Palgrave Macmillan, 2003); and Alessandro Triulzi, "Italian-Speaking Communities

in Early Nineteenth-Century Tunis," *Revue de l'Occident musulman et de la Méditerranée* IX/1 (1971): 155.

16 Alan Lomax, "Liner Notes," *Italian Folk Music: Naples, Campania* (Ethnic Folkways Library FE 4265), 1972. Titled "Pizzica," the lyrics of this tune, sung in the Italian dialect of the region, present a sexually suggestive call-and-response dialogue between a man nicknamed "Cavallino nero" (Little Black Horse) and the voluptuous washerwoman he is trying to seduce.

17 Adriano Mazzoletti, *Il Jazz in Italia: dalle origini alle grandi orchestre*, vol. 1 (Turin: EDT, 2004), 3. Claudio Lo Cascio, *Una Storia nel Jazz: Nick La Rocca* (Palermo: Novecento, 2003), 62–63.

18 Cf. Samuel Charters, *A Trumpet around the Corner: The Story of New Orleans Jazz* (Jackson, MS: University of Mississippi Press, 2008), 64.

19 Mazzoletti, *Il Jazz in Italia: dalle origini alle grandi orchestre*, vol. 1, 11.

20 One of the few photos we have of Joe Alexander shows him posing in his Italian army uniform, instrument in hand. For a reproduction of the photo, see Adriano Mazzoletti, *L'Italia del Jazz* (Rome: Stefano Mastruzzi, 2011), 12.

21 The film appeared in 1938, but contrary to Berlin's wishes, producers at Fox set the narrative in San Francisco.

22 Charters, *A Trumpet Around the Corner*, 76.

23 Ibid., 77.

24 New Orleans Census and World War I draft records show that he emigrated from Salaparuta, Sicily, in 1898 and became a naturalized citizen.

25 As Raeburn, "Italian Americans in New Orleans," 99–100, explains, Arnold Loyocano joined Jimmy Durante's Original New Orleans Jazz Band in New York in 1919 playing bass before moving on to the New Orleans Rhythm Kings in Chicago in 1919, and Leon Roppolo played clarinet with the Friar's Society Orchestra in 1922 and with Jelly Roll Morton and the Rhythm Kings in 1923.

26 US Census records for 1920 give his name as John Francis Sparicio and list his profession as "orchestral musician."

27 Ann Woodruff, "Society Halls in New Orleans: A Survey of Jazz Landmarks, Part II," *The Jazz Archivist* XXI (2008): 24–25.

28 "Patriotic Italians Celebrate Anniversary of Their Society," *The Daily Picayune* (October 13, 1913).

29 I would like to thank Victoria de Grazia for sharing with me the story of her grandfather, Alfred Sebastian, who played in an Italian band in New Orleans during the early 1900s and eventually became a prominent figure in the AFM union. This story led to my investigation of New Orleans's various music unions.

30 Tulane University Library Special Collections, Hogan Jazz Archive, American Federation of Musicians Local 174–496: "Collection Historical Note." http://specialcollections.tulane.edu/archon/?p=collections/findingaid&id=1713&q= Accessed June 6, 2014.

31 Ibid. Local 496 merged with 174 late in 1969. Records of Local 496 prior to 1941 are not held at the archive, and may either have been destroyed or remain in private hands.

32 For an in-depth study of the musical culture surrounding Neapolitan immigrants in New York prior to World War II, see Simona Frasca, *Italian Birds of Passage: The Diaspora of Neapolitan Musicians in New York* (New York: Palgrave McMillan, 2014).

33 David Bakish, *Jimmy Durante: His Show Business Career, with an Annotated Filmography and Discography* (Jefferson, NC: McFarland & Company, 1995), 12.

34 As Marcello Piras, "Garibaldi to Syncopation: Bruto Giannini and the Curious Case of Scott Joplin's *Magnetic Rag*," *Journal of Jazz Studies* 9/2 (Winter 2013): 107–177, has shown, the influence of Italian musicians is reflected in the works of Scott Joplin and James P. Johnson.

35 Information about many of these bands can be found in *The Encyclopedic Discography of Victor Recordings* (EDVR), an index to master recordings (matrixes) and published discs made by the Victor Talking Machine Company beginning in 1900. http://victor.library.ucsb.edu. Accessed January 27, 2014.

36 Mazzoletti, *Il Jazz in Italia: dalle origini alle grandi orchestre*, vol. 1, 4.

37 The most extensive study of Caslar's activities in the United States appears in Frasca's *Italian Birds of passage*, 109–112.

38 Advertisement in *The Billboard* (January 24, 1914), 35.

39 Laurence Bergreen, *As Thousands Cheer: The Life of Irving Berlin.* (London: Hodder and Stoughton, 1990), 26.

40 Jack Burton, "The Honor Roll of Popular Songwriters: No. 22 – Al Piantadosi," *The Billboard* (June 11, 1949), 38.

41 As Michael Wright, "The Yosco No. 2 Tenor Banjo," *Vintage Guitar Magazine* (August 2011), explains, the manufacturing business was fairly profitable, and in 1918 Lawrence Yosco was granted a patent for the "Yosco Double Rim," a double internal resonator used in banjo construction. For a reprint of the article, see www.vintageguitar.com/10981/the-yosco-no-2/. Accessed August 10, 2015.

42 Originally composed for mandolin (Yosco) and harp (Lyons), "Spaghetti Rag" was first published by Maurice Shapiro in 1910 as a piano transcription. Yosco and Lyons never recorded the tune, but in 1912 Victor released a disc featuring Vess L. Ossman on banjo accompanied by an unnamed orchestra. For a reproduction of the original publication of "Spaghetti Rag," see the University of Colorado Digital Sheet Music Collection. http://libcudl.colorado.edu/sheetmusic/brief_record.asp?oid=405479. Accessed June 18, 2014. For additional information on the Victor recording, see *Discography of American Historical Recordings*, s.v. "Victor matrix B-12148. Spaghetti rag / Vess L. Ossman," http://adp.library.ucsb.edu/index.php/matrix/detail/200012326/B-12148-Spaghetti_rag. Accessed July 29, 2014.

43 "Italian Americans in California," online exhibition presented by The Bancroft Library of the University of California, Berkeley. http://bancroft.berkeley.edu/collections/italianamericans/index.html. Accessed June 15, 2014.

44 As Ronald Flynn, Edwin Davison and Edward Chavez explain in *The Golden Age of the Accordion* (Schertz, TX: Flynn Publications, 1992), the Guerrini Musical Instrument Manufacturing Company was founded in 1903 by Paul Guerrini and Rafaelo Carbonari. They sold the company to Pasquale Petromilli and Colombo Piatanesi in 1907. In 1927 Colombo Piatanesi sold out his share to found Colombo & Sons. Guerrini Company was disbanded in 1968.

45 Full-page advertisement in *Variety* currently held in the Guido Deiro Section of the Deiro Archive, The Center for the Study of Free-Reed Instruments, The Graduate Center, The City University of New York, Part II, Scrapbook No. 1, p. 42.

46 Peter C. Muir, "Looks Like a Cash Register and Sounds Worse: The Deiro Brothers and the Rise of the Piano Accordion in American Culture 1908–1930," *Free-Reed Journal* III (2001): 55.

47 Marion Jacobson, *Squeeze This!: A Cultural History of the Accordion* (Urbana, IL: University of Illinois Press, 2012), 10, 26–39.

48 Charles Henderson, "The Call of Art and Arms," *Cleveland Plain Dealer* (September 15, 1915), 8.

49 Guido Roberto Deiro, "Guido Deiro & Mae West: The Untold Story," Liner notes to *Guido Deiro: Complete Recorded Works*, vol. 2 (Archeophone Records 5014) 2009, 12–13.

50 "Ev'rybody Shimmies Now," with lyrics by Eugene West and music by Joe Gold and Edmund J. Porray, was published by Charles K. Harris in 1918 with a photo of Mae West on the cover. For a digital copy of this publication, see http://digitalcollections.oscars.org/cdm/ref/collection/p15759coll6/id/445. Accessed July 20, 2014.

51 Richard Humphreys, *Futurism* (London: Tate Publishing, 1999), 9.

52 "Marconi's Visit to the United States," *Music Trade Review* (September 15, 1906), 40.

53 *New York Times* (August 16,1906), 14.

54 Alan Sutton gives an excellent overview of the making of the Marconi Velvetone Series in *A Phonograph in Every Home* (Denver, CO: Mainspring Press), 53–57, wherein he reproduces the patent application (US Patent #862,407) submitted by T. H. MacDonald for a "Talking Machine Record" on July 9, 1906. The patent was issued on August 6, 1907, only a few days before Marconi departed via ocean liner to New York.

55 The first manifesto of Futurist cooking, "Manifeste de la cuisine futuriste," was published by Jules Maincave (1890–1920) in the French magazine *Fantasio* in 1913. Maincave and Marinetti opened a Futurist restaurant together in Paris shortly thereafter, and in 1932 Marinetti published his own book-length manifesto, *La Cucina Futurista*. For a recent English-language edition

of Marinetti's treatise, see F. T. Marinetti, *The Futurist Cookbook*, ed. Lesley Chamberlain and trans. Suzanne Brill (London: Penguin Classic, 2015).

56 For a more detailed investigation of the link between the misinterpretation in America of Italian Futurism and its influence on early twentieth-century American painting, see Margaret Reeves Burke, "Futurism in America, 1910–1917" (PhD Dissertation, University of Delaware, 1986), 44–87.

57 "The Futurists," *The Sun* (May 23, 1909), 8. Marinetti reproduced some of the opinions in *The Sun* article and other international papers in an article about the reception of his first manifesto, "Le Futurisme et la Presse internationale," *Poesia* 5/3–6 (April–July 1909): 24.

58 John Oliver Hand, "Futurism in America: 1909–14," *Art Journal* 14/4 (Winter 1981): 337.

59 "The Futurist Movement in Italy," *Current Literature* 51/2 (August 1911): 6.

60 As Przemysław Strozek, "Futurist Responses to African American Culture," *Afromodernisms: Paris, Harlem and the Avant-garde*, ed. Fionnghuala Sweeney and Kate Marsh (Edinburgh University Press, 2013), 44, explains, the publication of Marinetti's novel *Mafarka le futuriste, roman africain* (1909) is what got him into trouble. A tale of rape, carnage and Futurist declamation set in Africa, the climax of the narrative occurs "when Mafarka-el-Bar, an Arabian king and Futurist hero, gives birth to his immortal mechanical son Gazourmah, an animated aeroplane woven from indestructible palm fibre." Throughout the novel, Marinetti focuses on the virile physicality of the black male, most notably in the figure of Mafarka, whose penis is described as being eleven meters long.

61 "The Futurist Movement in Italy," 6.

62 Ibid., 7.

63 Ibid.

64 "New Cult in Art Drapes the Nude, Bars Sentiment," *The Evening World* (December 4, 1911): 13.

65 "The New Cult of Futurism is Here," *New York Herald* (December 24, 1911): magazine section, 6.

66 Krin Gabbard, "The Word Jazz," *Cambridge Companion to Jazz*, ed. Mervyn Cooke and David Horn (Cambridge University Press, 2002), 1.

67 Clarence Major, *Juba to Jive: A Dictionary of African-American Slang* (New York, NY: Viking, 1994), 255. Bob Rigter, "Light on the Dark Etymology of JAZZ in the *Oxford English Dictionary*," in *Language Usage and Description: Studies Presented to N.E. Osselton on the Occasion of His Retirement*, ed. Ingrid Tieken-Boon van Ostade and John Frankis (Atlanta, GA: Rodopi, 1991), 91–100.

68 S. Frederick Starr, *New Orleans UnMasqued: Being a Wagwit's Affectionate Sketches of a Singular American City* (New Orleans, LA: Dedeaux Publishing, 1985), 40–41. This etymology was also presented by Wynton Marsalis in an interview included in *Jazz: A Film by Ken Burns* (2001).

69 For an excellent study of the rise of jazz in California, see Tom Stoddard, *Jazz on the Barbary Coast*, 2nd edn. (Berkeley, CA: Heyday Books, 1998).

70 "Ben's Jazz Curve," *Los Angeles Times* (April 2, 1912), III, 2. See also George Thompson, "'Jazz' in the LA Times, 1912 & 1917," *ADS-L* (a discussion list for members of the American Dialect Society), (August 4, 2003).

71 E. T. Gleason, "Sports News," *Bulletin* (March 6, 1913): 16.

72 Ernest J. Hopkins, "In Praise of Jazz: A Futurist Word Which Has Just Joined the Language," *The Bulletin* (April 5, 1913): 7.

73 Ibid.

74 Ibid.

75 Ibid.

76 Ibid.

77 Barry Popik, "Windy City (12 February 1877); Jazz notes," *ADS-L* (August 6, 2003).

78 David Wilton, *Word Myths: Debunking Linguistic Urban Legends* (New York: Oxford University Press, 2004), 116–123, gives an overview of recent research on the etymology of jazz. Walter J. Kingsley, "Jazz Has a Remarkable History as a Fad," *The Sun* (February 9, 1919), 6, claimed: "The phrase 'jazz band' was first used by Bert Kelly in Chicago in the fall of 1915, and was unknown in New Orleans."

79 Gordon Seagrove, "Blues Is Jazz and Jazz Is Blues," *Chicago Daily Tribune* (July 11, 1915), E8.

80 Ibid.

81 Ibid.

82 Cf. Burton W. Peretti, *The Creation of Jazz: Music, Race, and Culture in Urban America* (Urbana-Champaigne, IL: University of Illinois Press, 1994), 133. Nina Simone (1933–2003) once said a similar thing in a recorded interview: "Jazz is a term that was invented by white people to identify black people." *Nina Simone: The Legend* (1992). The webpage of the Nina Simone Estate www .ninasimone.com/ has released this full-length documentary, produced in France, on Vimeo: http://vimeo.com/36905801. Accessed July 15, 2014.

83 Arnold Loyocano, interview with Dr. Edmond Souchon, New Orleans, September 29, 1956. Cf. Richard M Sudhalter, *Lost Chords: White Musicians and Their Contributions to Jazz, 1915–1945* (New York: Oxford University Press, 1999), 8.

84 Sudhalter, *Lost Chords*, 7.

85 Ibid.

86 Ibid., 8.

87 Press review in *Vaudeville* (August 31, 1916). Cf. H. O. Brunn, *The Story of the Original Dixieland Jazz Band* (Baton Rouge, LA: Louisiana State University Press, 1960), 43.

88 Advertisement in the "Amusement" pages of the *New York Herald* (January 15, 1917): 6.

89 As Lynn Abbott and Doug Seroff, "Brown Skin (Who You Really For?)," *The Jazz Archivist* 15 (2001): 10–16, have revealed, LaRocca did not shy away from

cultural appropriation while establishing the ODJB's reputation in Chicago. Such practices are perhaps best shown in his alteration of the lyrics to "Brown Skin, Who You For?" composed by Clarence Williams and Armand Piron, both African Americans from New Orleans.

90 Louis Armstrong, *Swing That Music* (New York: Longmans, Green, 1936), 11–12.

91 Zuculin, "Musiche e danze americane," 599.

92 Ibid.

93 Ibid., 599–600.

94 As Raeburn, "Italian Americans in New Orleans Jazz," 100–101, reveals, this illustration first appeared in *New Orleans States* on May 11, 1919.

95 Zuculin, "Musiche e danze americane," 600.

96 Ibid.

97 Ibid.

98 Ibid.

99 Ibid.

100 Bruce Boyd Raeburn, *New Orleans Style and the Writing of American Jazz History* (Ann Arbor, MI: University of Michigan Press, 2009), 1.

2   Jazz Crosses the Atlantic

1 Petrine Archer-Straw, *Negrophilia: Avant-Garde Paris and Black Culture in the 1920s* (London: Thames & Hudson, 2000).

2 Jed Rasula, "Jazz as Decal for the Avant-Garde," in *Blackening Europe: The African American Presence*, ed. Heike Raphael-Hernandez (New York: Routledge, 2004), 13.

3 Both the Scrap-Iron Jazzerinos, which consisted of seven members of the 332nd Infantry, and the 158th Infantry Band, which was considerably larger, were stationed in France during World War I. After the Armistice, the latter ensemble was selected as President Woodrow Wilson's Honor Band at the Paris Peace Conference. For additional information on these ensembles, see Mark Miller, *"Some Hustling This!" Taking Jazz to the World, 1914–1929* (Toronto: The Mercury Press, 2005); and Lon Wolff, "Albert Ross Etzweiler: Arizona's Music Man," *The Journal of Arizona History* 50/2 (Summer 2009): 125–142.

4 For detailed information on the YMCA's activities in Europe during World War I, see William Howard Taft, ed., *Service with Fighting Men: An Account of the Work of the American Young Men's Christian Associations in the World War* (New York: Association Press, 1922); and James W. Evans and Captain Gardner L. Harding, *Entertaining the American Army: The American Stage and Lyceum in the World War* (New York: Association Press, 1921).

5 Catherine Parsonage [Tackley], *The Evolution of Jazz in Britain 1880–1935* (Aldershot: Ashgate, 2005); Jeremy F. Lane, *Jazz and Machine-Age Imerialism: Music, "Race," and Intellectuals in France 1918–1945* (Ann Arbor, MI: University of Michigan Press, 2013); Howard Rye, "Towards a Black British Jazz: Studies in Acculturation, 1860–1935," in *Black British Jazz: Routes, Ownership and Performance,* ed. Jason Toynbee, Catherine Tackley and Mark Doffman (London and New York: Routledge, 2014), 35–42.

6 Petrine Archer-Straw, *Negrophilia: Avant-Garde Paris and Black Culture in the 1920s* (London: Thames & Hudson, 2000); William A. Shack, *Harlem in Montmarte: A Paris Jazz Story between the Great Wars* (Berkeley, CA: University of California Press, 2001); Jeffrey H. Jackson, *Making Jazz French: Music and Modern Life in Interwar Paris* (Durham, NC: Duke University Press, 2003); Andy Fry, *Paris Blues: African American Music and French Popular Culture, 1920–1960* (Chicago, IL: University of Chicago Press, 2014); Horst J. P. Bergmeier and Rainer E. Lotz, *Hitler's Airwaves: The Inside Story of Nazi Radio Broadcasting and Propaganda Swing* (New Haven, CT: Yale University Press, 1997); Mike Zwerin, *Swing under the Nazis: Jazz as a Metaphor for Freedom* (New York: Cooper Square Press, 2000); Michael H. Kater, *Different Drummers: Jazz in the Culture of Nazi Germany* (Oxford University Press, 2003).

7 *Good-Bye Bill* ran for three months (March–May 1918) at the Lew Fields' 44th Street Roof Garden in New York before the Italian Contingent left for overseas; and *Let's Go* packed houses in theatres all over France in spring 1919. After the war, Hamp appeared in vaudeville, first with the popular Janet of France and later with Earl Reynolds as one of The California Blue Boys. In the mid-1920s he moved to Los Angeles, where he served as director of a local radio station. It was around this time he made his breakthrough as a "crooner" and signed a recording contract with Columbia. An article published in *Variety* in 1931 described Hamp as the highest paid individual artist in radio. In 1936, he starred in a radio show called *Rhapsody in Rhythm* that featured a jazz ensemble called The Rhythm Rascals. "CD Liner Notes," *Charles W. Hamp: A Pioneer Radio Sensation* (Take Two Records, 2012).

8 Rainer Lotz, "The United States Army Ambulance Service Band," *VJM's Jazz & Blues Mart,* 145 (Spring 2007): 2–7. www.vjm.biz/new_page_14.htm, accessed Oct 10, 2013.

9 John R. Smucker, Jr., *The History of the United States Army Ambulance Service with the French and Italian Armies, 1917, 1918, 1919* (Allentown, PA: Army Ambulance Service, 1967), e-book accessed October 15, 2014 www.ourstory .info/library/2-ww1/Smucker/usaac05.html, Chapter 6 "Armistice, Occupation, A Roman Holiday, 'Let's Go,' Home" lists the men who participated in the American Jazz Band in 1918: R. C. Mustarde, violin; Doc Neale, bass; Pat Emerick, drums; [Charles B.] Chuck Barlow, banjo; Norm Kennedy, banjo; Charlie Keck, viola; Charlie Paulik, violin; Art Decker, vocals; Allen Mattox,

ukulele; Charlie Hamp, piano, saxophone, and vocals. Hamp also served as the ensemble's bandleader.

10 Ibid. The soldier's account is confirmed in Evans and Harding, *Entertaining the American Army*, 174.

11 Smucker, Jr., *The History of the United States Army Ambulance Service with the French and Italian Armies*, Chapter 6.

12 "Jazz Band in Gondolas Delights A.E.F. Troops," *New York Herald*, Paris edn., (February 19, 1919): 2.

13 "Ambulance Jazz Band leaves for the Riviera," *New York Herald* (April 5, 1919): 2.

14 Smucker, Jr., *The History of the United States Army Ambulance Service with the French and Italian Armies*, Chapter 6.

15 In addition to the "American Jazz Band," a vocal group identified as the "Oberlin College Octette" and led by Valentine W. Gerrish contributed to the recordings as part of the "U.S.A. Army Ambulance Service."

16 Evans and Gardner, *Entertaining the American Army*, 174.

17 A copy of the catalogue can be found in the Oberlin College Archives; Henry Churchill King Papers, 1873–1934; King-Crane Commission: Printed Matter 1918–1920; RG 2/6, box 128, folder 9. For a digital facsimile see http://dcollections.oberlin.edu/cdm/ref/collection/kingcrane/id/996.

18 For a recording of "Hindustan" by the USAAS Jazz Band see www.youtube.com/watch?v=VNqyXH910CU. Accessed December 10, 2016.

19 A photo of the band recording in the Fonotipia studio is included in the commemorative catalogue, and the names of the performers are listed in the recording sessions preserved in the Fonotipia archives, which were recently published by Roger Beardsley, ed. *Fonotipia 1904–1939* [CD-ROM] (North Thoresby, Lincolnshire, England, 2003). The performers were: R. C. Mustarde, Charlie Paulik (violin); Charlie Keck (viola); Doc Neale (string bass); Charlie Hamp (piano, vocalist and bandleader); Allen Mattox (ukulele); Charles B. "Chuck" Barlow, Norm Kennedy (banjo); Pat Emerick (drums); and Art Decker (vocalist).

20 Oliver Wallace and Hugo Frey (1873–1952) both made names for themselves in later years writing film music. Wallace is perhaps best known for his work with Walt Disney, where he made his breakthrough in animated films with the score to *Dumbo* (1941). Frey was described in 1921 as "the best of the composers of so-called bad music, and therefore preferable to the bad composers of so-called good music" by the classical pianist/conductor Rudolf Ganz. Cf. Fred Edmiston, *The Coon-Sanders Nighthawks: The Band That Made Radio Famous* (Jefferson, NC: McFarland, 2009), 54.

21 "Darktown Strutters Ball" was recorded on May 30, 1917 in New York and released by Columbia Records as catalog number A-2297. This tune and "Indiana One Step" on the disc's flip side became international hits during World War I. "Oriental Jazz" (or "Jass") was recorded on November 24, 1917, and issued as Aeolian Vocalion 12097 in April 1919 with "Indigo Blues" by Ford Dabney's Band.

22 The Gramophone Company UK was also the parent organization for His Master's Voice (UK) and La Voce del Padrone (Italy) labels. "At the Jazz Band Ball" was composed by LaRocca and Larry Shields and was first recorded as "At the Jass Band Ball" on September 3, 1917 in New York and released as an Aeolian Vocalion single, A1205. It was then rerecorded on March 19, 1918, and released as Victor 18457, Matrix #B-21583/1. This second recording was reprinted shortly thereafter in Italy and released on the Grammofono label. A third version was recorded on April 16, 1919, in England and released as Columbia 735 with "Barnyard Blues" on the flip side.

23 For a complete discography of Moleti's recordings with the Orchestra del Trianon, see Mazoletti, *Il Jazz in Italia: dalle origini alle grandi orchestre*, vol. 1, 554–555.

24 Evans and Gardner, *Entertaining the American Army*, 174.

25 Smucker, Jr., *The History of the United States Army Ambulance Service with the French and Italian Armies*, Chapter 6.

26 Evans and Gardner, *Entertaining the American Army*, 174.

27 Smucker, Jr., *The History of the United States Army Ambulance Service with the French and Italian Armies*, Chapter 6.

28 A case in point was the quick tour of northern Italy in 1918 sponsored by Romeo Gallenga Stuart (1879–1938), an Italian/English nobleman serving as Italy's Under Secretary for Propaganda Abroad, that featured bands from The Royal Carabinieri (Italy), H.R.M. Coldstream Guards (United Kingdom) and The 18th Infantry Regiment (USA). This latter band was directed by Philip D'Arcy (1909–1992), who later returned to New York, where he worked as a freelance musician.

29 Taft, *Service with Fighting Men*, 92. The "Fiume Controversy" arose at the conclusion of World War I, when Italy claimed control of the Adriatic port of Fiume on the principle of self-determination. On September 12, 1919, the Italian nationalist poet Gabriele D'Annunzio and a group of militant followers occupied Fiume. D'Annunzio and his men were eventually ejected from Fiume, and after several years of negotiation, the Italo–Yugoslav treaty, which recognized Fiume as Italian, was signed in Rome on January 27, 1924. After World War II, the Treaty of Paris transferred control of Fiume to Yugoslavia. Dominique Reill, "National Histories and Rebel Cities: Fiume, a Historiographical Opportunity," paper presented at the American Academy in Rome in November 2012.

30 Spina identified Griffith as a "sailor," and in a photo taken in 1918 of Spina and Griffith, the American is wearing the uniform of a Navy Hospital Corpsman. Like the USAAS, members of the Navy Hospital Corps were sent to France and Italy during World War I to offer relief services and were often imbedded with American soldiers. As Evans and Gardner, *Entertaining the American Army*, 167, note: "The development of dormant talent in the A.E.F. had started during hostilities, but after the Armistice work on a big scale really began ... In fact,

men in every branch of the service were recruited to play before doughboy audiences."

31 Interview with Vittorio Spina conducted by Adriano Mazzoletti on December 11, 1960. Cf. Mazzoletti, *Il Jazz in Italia: dalle origini alle grandi orchestre*, vol. 1, 14.

32 Ibid.

33 This photo is reproduced in Adriano Mazzoletti, *L'Italia del Jazz* (Rome: Stefano Mastruzzi, 2011), 18.

34 Mazzoletti, *Il Jazz in Italia: dalle origini alle grandi orchestre*, vol. 1, 14. "Kay-lou-A" is no doubt a reference to the popular Jerome Kern tune "Ka-lu-a" from the musical comedy *Good Morning Dearie* (1921).

35 Enrico Pichetti, *Mezzo secolo di danza: Ricordi della mia vita e del mio insegnamento. La danza attraverso i secoli, ballerini celebri, balli antichi e moderni, comportamento in società* (Rome: Edizioni VIS, 1935), 138.

36 Mazzoletti, *Il Jazz in Italia: dalle origini alle grandi orchestre*, vol. 1, 14.

37 For a detailed discussion of Mirador's career as an impresario and his influence on Italian jazz, see Mazzoletti, *Il Jazz in Italia: dalle origini alle grandi orchestre*, vol. 1, 24–27, 38–42.

38 As Goffredo Plastino, "Jazz Napoletano: A Passion for Improvisation," *Jazz Worlds/World Jazz*, ed. Philip V. Bohlman and Geoffredo Plastino (Chicago University Press, 2016), 316, explains, although Neapolitan Song (as it was performed in the United States by immigrant musicians) played an important role in the establishment of early jazz in cities like New Orleans, the influence of jazz on Neapolitan Song (as it was sung in Southern Italy) was minimal and did not begin until the late 1920s.

39 During the two decades before World War I, numerous African American musicians and dancers performed in the theaters and concert halls of Britain, Belgium, Holland, Germany and France. These performers traveled the continent, sometimes for years at a time, exposing audiences to what was often described as the "exotic" music of the New World. But as Mazzoletti, *Il Jazz in Italia: dalle origini alle grandi orchestre*, vol. 1, 1–2, explains, only a few of these musicians crossed the Alps and traveled to Italy. These included a quartet of two men and two women from New Orleans called The Louisiana Troupe; Pete G. Hampton and his wife Laura Bradford Bowman, who advertised themselves as "Le Darktown – Duettisti negri americani;" Arabella Fields; a gospel quartet formed by Strut Payne called the Four Black Diamonds; and four former singers from the Jubilee Singers who called themselves the Black Troubadours.

40 Przemysław Strozek, "Futurist Responses to African American Culture," *Afromodernisms: Paris, Harlem and the Avant-garde*, ed. Fionnghuala Sweeney and Kate Marsh (Edinburgh University Press, 2013), 44.

41 Umberto Boccioni et al., "Technical Manifesto of Futurist Painting," quoted in Strozek, "Futurist Responses to African American Culture," 45.

42 Ibid.

43 John J. White, *Literary Futurism: Aspects of the First Avant-Garde* (Oxford University Press, 1990), 316.

44 Umberto Boccioni, *Pitture e scultura futurista* (1914). Cf. Strozek, "Futurist Responses to African American Culture," 45.

45 Ibid., 46.

46 Umberto Boccioni, "Contro il paesaggio e la vecchia estetica," *Pittura e scultura futuriste. Dinamismo plastic* (Milan, 1914); Cf. *Gli scritti editi e inediti*, ed. Zeno Birolli (Milan: Feltrinelli, 1971), 87.

47 Ibid.

48 F. T. Marinetti, "Manifesto of Futurist Dance," in *Futurism: An Anthology*, ed. Lawrence Rainey, Christine Poggi and Laura Wittman (New Haven, CT: Yale University Press, 2009), 236.

49 Matthew F. Jordan, *Le Jazz: French Cultural Identity* (Urbana, IL: University of Illinois Press, 2010), 34.

50 Matthew F. Jordan, "Jazz Changes: A History of French Discourse of Jazz from Ragtime to Be-bop" (PhD dissertation, Claremont Graduate University, 1998), 17–38.

51 George Méliès, *Complete Catalogue of Genuine and Original "Star" Films (Moving Pictures) Manufactured by Geo. Méliès of Paris* (Paris; New York: Starfilm, 1905), nos. 453–457.

52 "Una grande riunione di danze," *La Stampa* (April 23, 1915). Cf. Mazzoletti, *Il Jazz in Italia: dalle origini alle grandi orchestre*, vol. 1, 8.

53 Cf. Mazzoletti, *Il Jazz in Italia: dalle origini alle grandi orchestre*, vol. 1, 8.

54 Interview with Ugo Filippini conducted by Adriano Mazzoletti on November 27, 1960. Cf. Mazzoletti, *Il Jazz in Italia: dalle origini alle grandi orchestre*, vol. 1, 54.

55 Ibid., 56.

56 Ibid.

57 Enrico Crispolti, *Il mito della macchina e altri temi del futurism* (Trapani: Edizioni Celebes, 1969), 161. Cf. Gunther Berghaus, *Italian Futurist Theatre 1909–1944* (Oxford: Clarendon Press, 1998), 385–386.

58 "Grande Cotillon patriottico," *Il piccolo* (September 21, 1922).

59 "Al Bal Tic Tac," *Il piccolo* (August 14, 1922).

60 "Il pubblico più eletto della Capitale al Bal Tic Tac," *Il piccolo* (July 18, 1922).

61 Berghaus, *Italian Futurist Theatre*, 391.

62 "Il magnifico veglione futurista alla casa magica Depero," *Il Popolo* Trento (January 17, 1923).

63 Ibid.

64 Ibid.

65 Ibid.

66 For facsimiles of these sheet-music covers and a discussion of the intersections between popular music and Futurist art, see the exhibition catalogue edited by Claudia Salaris, *Pentagramma Elettrico: Suoni, rumori e parole in libertà*,

Rome: Auditorium Parco della Musica, April 9–May 31, 2009 (Pistoia: Gli Ori, 2009). These poems, in addition to excerpts from prose works and treatises, appear in an anthology compiled by Giorgio Rimondi, *Jazz Band: Percorsi letterari fra avanguardia consume e musica sincopata* (Milan: Mursia, 1994). Rimondi has also produced a comprehensive study of the links between jazz and Italian literature, *La scrittura sincopata: Jazz e letteratura nel Novecento italiano* (Milan: Bruno Mondadori, 1999), wherein he discusses the context of these works in great detail.

67　Alfredo Casella, "Busoni pianista," *Il Pianoforte* (June 1921). Cf. Alfredo Casella, *21 + 26* (Rome and Milan: Augustea, 1931; reprinted Florence: Leo S. Olschki, 2001), 70.

68　Carl Engel, "Jazz: A Musical Discussion," *The Atlantic Monthly* (August 1922). Cf. Karl Koenig, ed., *Jazz in Print (1856–1929): An Anthology of Selected Early Readings in Jazz History* (Hillsdale, NY: Pendragon Press, 2002), 201.

69　Felix Lamond, Report of the Professor in Charge of the Department of Music, Annual Report – 1923, New York, Offices of the American Academy in Rome, 47. Although a great deal of incredibly valuable information concerning the early years of the music program at the AAR, such as the reports of Felix Lamond, can be found in Martin Brody, ed., *Music and Musical Composition at the American Academy in Rome* (University of Rochester Press, 2014), no information concerning the program's intersections with jazz, especially with regard to Leo Sowerby, is included.

70　Alfredo Casella, "La vita musicale negli Stati Uniti," *La Critica Musicale* (April 1922), reprinted as "Casella on Jazz, *The Music Courier* (July 12, 1923). Cf. Koenig, *Jazz in Print (1856–1929)*, 245.

71　Ibid.

72　Theodore Leopold Friedman (1890–1971), known to the music world as Ted Lewis, was a Jewish clarinet player from Circleville, Ohio, who was one of the first northerners to imitate the hot jazz style coming out of New Orleans during World War I. Lewis first recorded with the Earl Fuller Jazz Band in 1917, and by 1919 he was recording with his own band under the Columbia label. Throughout the 1920s, Lewis was considered one of the leading performers of "Hot Jazz." One cannot help but wonder if Casella realized he was white.

73　Casella, "Casella on Jazz," Cf. Koenig, *Jazz in Print (1856–1929)*, 245.

74　Franco Casavola, "La musica futurista," *Il Futurismo. Rivista sintetica illustrate* 10 (1924).

75　Franco Casavola, "Difesa del Jazz Band," *L'Impero* (August 14, 1926): 4.

76　Ibid.

77　Clive Bell, "Plus de Jazz" [1921], in *Jazz in Print*, ed. Karl Koenig *(1856–1929)*, 154.

78　Piet Mondrian, "Jazz and the Neo-Plastic" [1927], in *Noise Orders: Jazz, Improvisation, and Architecture*, ed. David P. Brown (Minneapolis, MN: University of Minnesota Press, 2006), 7.

79 The primary articles rejecting jazz were: Campman, "Commenti alla vita: Ballo Jazz," *La Tribuna Illustrata* (October 5, 1919); Labb., "Jazz Band," *Il Messaggero* (January 11, 1922); Luciano Zuccoli, "Black and White," *Il Messaggero* (February 2, 1922).

80 "Ballo, digiuno e astinenza," *Corriere della Sera* (March 25, 1920).

81 As Mazzoletti, *Il Jazz in Italia: dalle origini alle grandi orchestre*, vol. 1, 90, notes, their recordings of Ernest Gillet's "Lettere de Manon" and José Serrano's "Alma de Diós" appeared on Pathé 9606.

82 Mazzoletti, *Il Jazz in Italia: dalle origini alle grandi orchestre*, vol. 1, 90–91.

83 Interview with Angelini (Angelo Cinico) conducted by Adriano Mazzoletti on April 4, 1976. Cf. Mazzoletti, *Il Jazz in Italia: dalle origini alle grandi orchestre*, vol. 1, 100.

84 Interview with Amedeo Escobar conducted by Adriano Mazzoletti on December 3, 1960. Cf. Mazzoletti, *Il Jazz in Italia: dalle origini alle grandi orchestre*, vol. 1, 57.

85 Interview with Goffredo Titti conducted by Adriano Mazzoletti on January 5, 1961. Cf. Mazzoletti, *Il Jazz in Italia: dalle origini alle grandi orchestre*, vol. 1, 68.

86 Interview with Ugo Filippini conducted by Adriano Mazzoletti on November 27, 1960. Cf. Mazzoletti, *Il Jazz in Italia: dalle origini alle grandi orchestre*, vol. 1, 69.

87 Interview with Amedeo Escobar conducted by Adriano Mazzoletti on December 3, 1960. Cf. Mazzoletti, *Il Jazz in Italia: dalle origini alle grandi orchestre*, vol. 1, 78.

88 *Discography of American Historical Recordings*, s.v. "Victor 19009 (Black label (popular) 10-in. double-faced)," http://adp.library.ucsb.edu/index.php/object/detail/13961/Victor_19009, accessed January 19, 2015. On this original recording, the flip side of the disc contained a tune called "Baby Blue Eyes" (by Jesse Greer, Walter Hirsch, George Jessel) performed by the Great White Way Orchestra (a pseudonym for the Victor house band).

89 His Master's Voice B1589; Grammofono R 7911.

90 This is perhaps most clearly shown in a note sent to Escobar in 1924 by a singer in Harl Smith's Lido-Venice Jazz Band: "Dear Mr. Escobar, I've heard most of the dance orchestras in Rome and permit me to say yours has the best rythm [*sic.*] and swing and I believe is the finest dance orchestra in Rome! David Nixon (H[arl] S[mith's])." A photograph of this note appears in Mazzoletti, *Il Jazz in Italia: dalle origini alle grandi orchestre*, vol. 1, fig. 15.

91 Interview with Potito Simone conducted by Adriano Mazzoletti on April 5, 1960. Cf. Mazzoletti, *Il Jazz in Italia: dalle origini alle grandi orchestre*, vol. 1, 88.

92 Ibid., 457–602.

93 David Forgacs and Stephen Gundle, *Mass Culture and Italian Society from Fascism to the Cold War* (Bloomington, IN: University of Indiana Press, 2007), 179.

94 Pekka Gronow and Ilpo Saunio, *An International History of the Recording Industry* (London: Cassell, 1998), 114.

95 These tunes were recorded in Columbia's Milan studio on January 18, 1930. "In chiedis" (WB 3061) and "Jeruscherlajim" (WB 3063) were released as the A and B sides of Columbia DC 24. "Yahrzeit" (WB 3066) doesn't appear to have been released. For Di Piramo's complete discography, see Mazzoletti, *Il Jazz in Italia: dalle origini alle grandi orchestre*, vol. 1, 511–514.

96 Rodolfo De Angelis, *Storia del Cafè Chantant* (Milan: Il Balcone, 1946), 61.

97 Luca Cerchiari, *Jazz e Fascismo: dalla nascita della radio a Gorni Kramer* (Palermo: L'Epos, 2003), 30.

98 Giorgio Nataletti, *1922–1962. Quarant'anni di attività di Giorgio Nataletti* (Rome: Istituto Grafico Tiberino, 1962). Cf., Mazzoletti, *Il Jazz in Italia: dalle origini alle grandi orchestre*, vol. 1, 65.

99 Gabriele Balbi, "Radio before Radio: Araldo Telefonico and the Invention of Italian Broadcasting," *Technology and Culture* 51/4 (October 2010): 797.

100 Giuseppe Richeri, "Italian Broadcasting and Fascism 1924–1937," *Media, Culture and Society* 2/1 (January 1980): 49.

3   Jazz and Fascism

1 Lilian T. Mowrer, *A Journalist's Wife* (New York: Morrow, 1937). Cf. William A. Vance, *America's Rome*, 2 vols. (New Haven, CT: Yale University Press, 1989), vol. II: *Catholic and Contemporary Rome*, 314.

2 Cf. Ibid, 315.

3 Leonard Peyton, "Rome," *The Musical Times* (January 1923): 70.

4 As Adrian R. Duran, *Painting, Politics, and the New Front of Cold War Italy* (Aldershot: Ashgate, 2014), 12, has noted: "It is essential that the years of Italian Fascism not be understood as a monolithic, unflinchingly oppressive system, particularly in relation to the arts."

5 Letter from Mussolini dated March 12, 1931. Quoted in Benito Mussolini, *Opera Omnia*, vol. XLI, ed. Emilio and Duilio Susmel (Rome: Volpe, 1979), 425.

6 Emil Ludwig, *Talks with Mussolini* (Boston: Little, Brown and Co., 1933), 158.

7 Franco Casavola, "Difesa del Jazz Band," *L'Impero* (August 14, 1926).

8 Franco Minganti, "Jukebox Boys: Postwar Italian Music and the Culture of Covering," in *Transactions, Transgressions, Transformations: American Culture in Western Europe and Japan*, ed. Heide Fehrenbach and Uta G. Poiger (New York: Berghahn Books, 2000), 149.

9 Franco Casavola, "Difesa del Jazz Band," 4.

10 Ibid.

11 Harvey Sachs, *Music in Fascist Italy* (London: Weidenfeld and Nicolson, 1987), 10.

12 In addition to ibid., two excellent books in Italian have been written about Mussolini's musical interests: Stefano Biguzzi, *L'Orchestra del Duce. Mussolini, la musica e il mito* (Turin: UTET, 2003) and Fiamma Nicolodi, *Musica e musicisti nel ventennio fascista* (Fiesole: Discanto, 1984). Unfortunately, all of these have focused exclusively on Mussolini's connection to classical music and opera. Until now, there has been little to no discussion of his early interest in popular music and jazz.

13 For examples, see Biguzzi, *L'Orchestra del Duce*, 15–16.

14 Benito Mussolini, "Da provincia rossa a provincia fascista," *Il Popolo d'Italia* (March 30, 1921).

15 Edna Richolson Sollitt, "Respighi Treads the Appian Way," *Musical America* 48/ 33 (December 1, 1928): 19. I would like to thank Dr. Davide Ceriani (Rowan University) for bringing this article to my attention.

16 Raffaello De Rensis, *Mussolini musicista* (Mantova: Edizioni Paladino, 1927), 13–14. Translation by Sachs, *Music in Fascist Italy*, 11.

17 First published in 1910 as a newspaper serial titled *Claudia Particella, l'Amante del Cardinale: Grande Romanzo dei Tempi del Cardinale Emanuel Madruzzo* in *La Vita Trentina*, this work was largely forgotten until it was reissued as a novel *L'Amante del Cardinale* (The Cardinal's Mistress) and translated into English by Hiram Motherwell (1928).

18 De Rensis, *Mussolini musicista*, 15.

19 Denis Mack Smith, *Mussolini* (New York: Knopf, 1982), 14.

20 Sachs, *Music in Fascist Italy*, 5.

21 Testimonies of those who witnessed Mussolini playing popular dance tunes on the violin at parties can be found in Stefano Biguzzi, *L'Orchestra del Duce*, 11; Paolo Monelli, *Mussolini piccolo Borghese* (Milan: Vallardi, 1983), 49, and Anita Pensotti, *Rachele e Benito: Biografia di Rachele Mussolini* (Milan: Mondadori, 1993), 22.

22 Margherita Sarfatti, *DUX* (Milan: Mondadori, 1926), 73. An example of Mussolini's lyrics is supplied by Biguzzi, *L'Orchestra del Duce*, 10: Bimba non mi guardare./ Forse tu m'ami di un affetto serio,/ Ma questo cuor che tu sognando brami/ È pieno di veleno. (Girl, don't look at me./ You might love me with serious affection,/ But this heart that you yearn for in your dreams/ Is full of poison.)

23 De Rensis, *Mussolini musicista*, 36. See also: Antonio Mambelli, *Archimede Montanelli nella vita e nell'arte. Un maestro del Duce* (Forlì: Valbonesi, 1938).

24 Cf. Biguzzi, *L'Orchestra del Duce*, 13.

25 Pensotti, *Rachele e Benito*, 28.

26 Rachele Mussolini, *Mussolini private* (Milan: Rusconi, 1980), 34. Mussolini married Rachele in a civil ceremony in 1915.

27 Luca Cerchiari, *Jazz e Fascismo: Dalla nascita della radio a Gorni Kramer* (Palermo: L'EPOS, 2003), 174.

28 Vittorio Mussolini, *Vita con mio padre* (Milan: Mondadori, 1957); Romano Mussolini, *Il duce mio padre* (Milan: Rizzoli, 2004).

29 Mazzoletti, *Il Jazz in Italia: dalle origini alle grandi orchestre*, vol. 1, 9.

30 Cf. Cerchiari, *Jazz e Fascismo*, 175.

31 Cf. Yvon de Begnac, *Palazzo Venezia: Storia di une regime* (Rome: La Rocca, 1950), 650.

32 Mazzoletti, *Il Jazz in Italia: dalle origini alle grandi orchestre*, vol. 1, 8–9.

33 For an excellent overview of Gershwin reception in Italy, see: Roberto Leydi, "Le fortune (o le sfortune) di Gershwin in Italia," in *Gershwin*, ed. Gianfranco Vinay (Turin: EDT, 1992): 305–342.

34 Jason Dovel, "The Influence of Jazz on the Solo Trumpet Compositions of Eugene Bozza" (DMA Dissertation, University of North Texas, 2007), 8–10; Lois Kuyper-Rushing, "Reassessing Eugene Bozza: Discoveries in the Bibliotheque Municipale De Valenciennes Archive," *Notes* 69/4 (June 2013): 716–717.

35 Beth Ellen Levy, *Frontier Figures: American Music and the Mythology of the American West* (Berkeley, CA: University of California Press, 2012), 160.

36 Cf. Edith Garson, *George Gershwin* (New York: Frederick Unger, 1958), 136.

37 "Gorham Phillips Stevens Addressing Visiting Fascist Members of the National Confederation of Fascist Professional Artists Unions in February 1930." AAR Archives, *Notiziario*, Misc.

38 "Nell'anniversario della nascita di Washington. S.E. Mussolini visita l'Accademia Americana in Roma," LUCE Newsreel (February 22, 1933). I would like to thank Professor Corey Brennan for bringing this newsreel to my attention.

39 On July 10, 1924, the unification of all broadcasts under a single, state-defined entity became law under the Regio Decreto Legge no. 1226.

40 Giuseppe Richieri, "Italian Broadcasting and Fascism 1924–1937," *Media, Culture and Society* 2 (1988): 49–50.

41 As Franco Monteleone noted in *Storia della radio e della televisione in Italia. Società, politica, strategie, programmi. 1922–1992* (Venice: Marsilio, 1992), 18, a primary objective for URI was to ensure there was an Italian market for radio receivers built by Italian manufacturers.

42 EIAR 1932. Cf. Franco Monteleone, *La radio italiana nel periodo fascista. Studio e documenti: 1922– 1945* (Venice: Marsilio, 1976), 27.

43 Ibid.

44 Regio Decreto Legge no. 655.

45 These goals were clearly outlined in the inaugural issue. *Radioario* 1/1 (January 1–15, 1925), 1.

46 This private/public revenue structure was outlined in the Regio Decreto Legge no. 655.

47 David Forgacs and Stephen Gundle, *Mass Culture and Italian Society, From Fascism to the Cold War* (Bloomington, IN: Indiana University Press, 2007), 3 and 173.

48 *Radioario* 1/3 (February 1–15, 1925).

49 See Mazzoletti, *Il Jazz in Italia: dalle origini alle grandi orchestre*, vol. 1, 517, for Stefano Ferruzzi's 1926 recordings.

50 "Home-Made Jazz for Italy. New Association Plans Substitute for American Product," *New York Times* (July 16, 1926): 3.

51 This point of view was made clear in the press. For example, see: "Deliberazione presa dal Consiglio dei Ministri il I° gennaio 1926," *Jazz Band* 1/2 (1926): 4.

52 Richieri, "Italian Broadcasting and Fascism 1924–1937," 51.

53 EIAR publicity letter (1937) sent to various retailers to inform them about specific initiatives and promotions targeted at the general public. Facsimile available at www.marcomanfredini.it/radio/gestione/pdf/eiar.pdf. Accessed August 11, 2015.

54 On January 20, 1927, the Fisk Jubilee Singers presented a concert in the St. Cecilia Conservatory in Rome that was greeted warmly by the Fascist press, as shown in Raffaello De Rensis, "A Santa Cecilia canzoni di negri d'America," *Il Giornale d'Italia* (January 23, 1927). And on January 7, 1931, Henry T. Burleigh, an African American classical singer and promoter of spirituals, was featured on an EIAR Italy/America broadcast. The arrival of African American musicians was also reflected in the press. For example, the cover of *La Rivista, illustrata del popolo d'Italia* 11/2 (February, 1933) featured a caricature of a black man in a white suit playing saxophone. http://digital.wolfsonian.org/l/WOLF041438/00001/12. Accessed October 17, 2015.

55 Mazzoletti, *Il Jazz in Italia: dalle origini alle grandi orchestre*, vol. 1, 1–2. From 1903 until 1913 Hampton and Bradford Bowman appeared in various European cities: upon arrival in London, they began right away to record for Edison Bell, Gramophone, Pathé, Odeon and other labels. In November 1907 they performed in Rome and Naples for fifteen days; from the 1st until 15th of December they performed in Turin (Stabilimento Romano), where they were announced as "Le Darktown, Duettisti negri americani." Arabella Fields first arrived in Europe on November 1, 1899 for an engagement in Prague with her father, James Fields. Her long career took her across most of the European continent. In 1907 she recorded various discs in Berlin, a few of which reached Italy. These included coon songs, like "Down on the Farm," and songs by Stephen Foster, like "Swannee River," sung in a lyric soprano voice. In April/May 1908 Fields performed in Genoa (Teatro Eden), Turin (also at the Eden) and Florence (Alhambra). She returned the following year and performed from July 16 through the beginning of August at the Lido d'Albaro in Genoa. She then moved to the Maffei in Turin, and from the middle of August until September 1, she was in Catania.

56 William A. Shack, *Harlem in Montmartre: A Paris Jazz Story Between the Great Wars* (Berkeley, CA: University of California Press, 2001).

57 Letter from Herb Flemming to Adriano Mazzoletti dated 1961. Cf. Mazzoletti, *Il Jazz in Italia: dalle origini alle grandi orchestre*, vol. 1, 247–249.

58 Ibid.

59 Ibid.

60 For a timeline of Sidney Bechet's European travels during 1925–1927, see Mazzoletti, *Il Jazz in Italia: dalle origini alle grandi orchestre*, vol. 1., 413–414.

61 Also spelled Flemming, but no relation to the trombonist Herb Flemming.

62 For example, "Sam Wooding and His Chocolate Kiddies" was praised as "the most celebrated orchestra of color" after a series of concerts in Milan; see "Sam Wooding all'Eden Dancing Grand Tabarin," *Corriere della Sera* (December 14, 1928).

63 Chris Albertson interview with Sam Wooding in *Official Souvenir Program of Spoleto Festival U.S.A. – 1978*. Cf. Kira Thurman, "A History of Black Musicians in Germany and Austria, 1870–1961: Race, Performance, and Reception" (PhD Dissertation, University of Rochester 2013), 89.

64 Hans Koert, "Harry Fleming," *Keep (It) Swinging Blog* (September 20, 2006) http://keepswinging.blogspot.com/search?q=Fleming. Accessed January 10, 2013; and Ronald Harringan and Hans Koert, "Harry Fleming's Band Traveled the World V.I. History Spotlight," *Virgin Island Daily News* (March 1, 2012). http://virginislandsdailynews.com/news/harry-fleming-s-band-traveled-the-world-v-i-history-spotlight-1.1279496. Accessed January 10, 2013.

65 Mazzoletti, *Il Jazz in Italia: dalle origini alle grandi orchestre*, vol. 1, 276–277, was the first to note that Fleming introduced tap dancing in Italy. He incorrectly states, however, that Fleming was born in Ethiopia.

66 Cf. Steve Jones, *Antonio Gramsci* (London: Routledge, 2006), 117.

67 Carlo Ravasio, "Fascismo e tradizione," *Il Popolo d'Italia* (March 30, 1928).

68 Ibid.

69 Ibid.

70 "Varie di musica," *Il Popolo d'Italia* (November 30, 1928).

71 Ibid.

72 "Films and Jazz Hit in Clean-Up at Rome. Products of Hollywood and New York May Be Barred in the Eternal City," *New York Times* (April 24, 1927): 22.

73 Ibid.

74 Interview with Ugo Filippini conducted by Adriano Mazzoletti on November 27, 1960. Cf. Mazzoletti, *Il Jazz in Italia: dalle origini alle grandi orchestre*, vol. 1, 71.

75 Irene Brin, *Usi e costume 1920–1940*, (Rome: Donatello De Luigi, 1944). Cf. Mazzoletti, *Il Jazz in Italia: dalle origini alle grandi orchestre*, vol. 1, 71–72.

76 "Italy Bans Hip Wiggles. Italian Police Raid Dance Halls to Save Jazz-Mad Flappers," *New York Times* (January 29, 1926): 10.

77 "Speak-Easies for Dancing Evade Italy's Ban on Jazz," *New York Times* (April 3, 1927): E23.

78 It should come as no surprise that in reaction to this conflict of interests, Pius XI reached out to Guglielmo Marconi, and with his assistance founded the Vatican's own radio broadcasting system, which began operations in February 1931. For more information, see Richieri, "Italian Broadcasting and Fascism 1924–1937," 51.

79 AAR Archives, reel 5786, March 14, 1929, letter from Stevens to Roscoe Guernsey, executive secretary of the Academy in New York.

80 "Una Nuova Iniziativa: EIAR-JAZZ," *Radiorario* 7/14 (March 31–April 7, 1929): 4.

81 Ibid.

82 Ibid.

83 "Il 'Jazz' espulso dalle … Sale da Ballo!" *Radiorario* 5/11 (March 10–17, 1929): 30.

84 "Una Nuova Iniziativa: EIAR-JAZZ," 4.

85 Ibid.

86 Franco Abbiati, "Arte negro-americana. I trucchi del jazz rivelati alla folla," *Rivista di Bergamo* VIII/12 (December 1929): 586–589. Such a claim was supported by many of the Piedegrotta posters from this time showing grotesque caricatures of African American musicians dominating local festivities. Two such images are reproduced in Goffredo Plastino, "Jazz Napoletano: A Passion for Improvisation," *Jazz Worlds/World Jazz*, ed. Philip V. Bohlman and Geoffredo Plastino (Chicago University Press, 2016), 317–318.

87 Pietro Mascagni, "L'opera ha fatto il suo tempo," *Il Popolo d'Italia* (August 3, 1929).

88 Arnaldo Mussolini, *Radiocorriere* (January 5, 1930). Arnaldo was put in charge of EIAR in 1930, and in reaction to the criticisms voiced by listeners unhappy with the new programming initiatives of 1929, he outlined the moral responsibilities of Italy's national radio system: without becoming "a pedantic moral pulpit," it must develop listeners' "awareness of their ethical and national values" and "instruct in an amusing way."

89 Emil Ludwig, *Talks with Mussolini* (Boston: Little, Brown and Co., 1933), 159–160.

90 Minganti, "Jukebox Boys: Postwar Italian Music and the Culture of Covering," 140.

91 Guido Carlo Visconti, "Fuori i Barbari!" *Il Giornale d'Italia* (September 13, 1929).

92 Ibid.

93 ibid.

94 Ibid.

95 Patrizia Veroli, "La danza e il fascismo. Anton Giulio Bragaglia e *Jazz Band* (1929)," in *L'Italia e la danza: Storie e rappresentazioni, stili e techniche tra teatro, tradizioni popolari e società*, ed. Giannandrea Poesio e Alessandro Pontremoli (Rome: ARACNE, 2008), 12.

96 Luca Cerchiari, "How to Make a Career by Writing against Jazz: Anton Giulio Bragaglia's *Jazz Band* (1929)," *Forum Italicum* 49 (2015): 462–473, discusses at length Bragaglia's new anti-jazz attitude.

97 Anton Giulio Bragaglia, *Jazz Band* (Milan: Corbaccio, 1929), 106.

98 Ibid, 38.

99 Ibid., 31–32.

100 F. T. Marinetti and Bruno Corra, "Contro il teatro morto, contro il romanzone analitico, contro il negrismo musicale," *Gazzetta del Popolo* (October 22, 1937).

101 For a wide assortment of poster illustrations, wherein "Bitter Campari" is associated with African culture and "Campari" is associated with Italian culture, see Marina Mojana and Ada Masoero (eds.), *Depero con Campari* (Rome: De Luca Editori d'Arte, 2010).

102 Alfredo Casella, "Della musica necessaria," *Italia Letteraria* 1 (April 7, 1929). Cf. Alfredo Casella, *21 + 26* (Florence: Leo S. Olschki, 2001), 49.

103 Ibid., 50.

104 Alfredo Casella, "Il Jazz," *Italia Letteraria* 1 (September 1, 1929). Cf. Alfredo Casella, *21 + 26*, 97.

105 Ibid., 102.

106 Ibid.

107 Ludwig, *Talks with Mussolini*, 218.

108 Ibid., 69–70.

109 Ibid., 70.

110 Cf. Michele Sarfatti, *The Jews in Mussolini's Italy: From Equality to Persecution*, trans. John and Anne C. Tedeschi (Milwaukee, WI: The University of Wisconsin Press, 2006), 120. Mussolini even went so far as to support the chief Rabbi in Rome, Professor Angelo Sacerdoti, in his condemnation of the atrocities brought about in the mid-1930s by Germany's sweeping anti-Semitic policies.

111 Ludwig, *Talks with Mussolini*, 143.

112 Ibid., 212–213.

113 www.openculture.com/2012/05/mussolini_sends_a_happy_message_to_ america_helps_change_history_of_cinema_1927.html. Accessed July 22, 2015.

114 Donald Crafton, *The Talkies: American Cinema's Transition to Sound, 1926–1931* (Oakland, CA: University of California Press, 1991), 525, note 8. As Crafton (567) explains, in addition to this short, Mussolini also "recorded a 900-foot address for Fox Movietone that he intended to be shown throughout Italy after his death. In it he urged the people of Italy to 'carry on the nationalistic spirit' he had fostered in them during his regime." See *Film Daily* (May 19, 1931): 8.

115 Cf. Crafton, *The Talkies*, 601, note 8.

116 The newsreel can be viewed online: www.youtube.com/watch?v=tTXhez 2mNm. Accessed April 27, 2015.

117 Cf. Raymond Fielding, *The American Newsreel: A Complete History, 1911–1967*, 2nd edn. (Jefferson, NC: McFarland & Co., 2006), 107.

118 Forgacs and Gundle, *Mass Culture and Italian Society*, 5 and 124–126.

119 Jacques Cartier danced the role of the drummer. The wealthy son of a diplomat, he made a career for himself by specializing in the "exotic" dances of Native Americans, Africans and Asians.

120 Leo Longanesi, "Film italiano," *L'Italiano* (January–February 1933). Cf. Ruth Ben-Ghiat, *Fascist Modernities: Italy, 1922–1945* (Oakland, CA: University of California Press, 2001), 70.

121 Donald Bogle, *Toms, Coons, Mulattoes, Mammies, and Bucks: An Interpretive History of Blacks in American Films*, 4th edn. (New York: The Continuum International Publishing Group, 2001), 19.

122 Ibid., 35–93.

123 Romolo Marcellini, "Film per l'Impero: I nostri negri," 20, *Lo schermo* (October 1936). Cf. Chandra M. Harris, "Who's Got the Power? Blacks in Italian Cinema and Literature, 1910–1948," (PhD Dissertation, Brown University, 2004), 99.

124 Harris, "Who's Got the Power? Blacks in Italian Cinema and Literature, 1910–1948," 117–121.

125 Antonio Papa, *Storia politica della radio in Italia*, vol. 1 (Naples: Guida, 1978), 38. For example, in 1924, only 1,314 gramophones and 10,458 discs were sold in Italy.

126 As Forgacs and Gundle, *Mass Culture and Italian Society*, 179, explain, the last of these, founded in 1904, was eventually taken over by the Lindström group.

127 Ibid.

128 Pekka Gronow and Ilpo Saunio, *An International History of the Recording Industry* (London: Cassell, 1998), 114.

129 "Radio e dischi," *Radiocorriere* 30/8 (1932): 20.

130 Cerchiari, *Jazz e Fascismo*, 24.

131 Vittorio Mussolini, "Cinque dischi hot," *Il disco*, 2 (October 1934): 10.

132 Ibid.

133 Ibid.

134 C. A., "Louis Armstrong. Il re del 'jazz hot," *La Stampa della Sera* (January 16, 1935): 1.

135 Ibid.

136 Ibid.

137 Ibid.

138 Nessim Jacques Canetti was a French talent agent who had met Armstrong in Paris. Canetti booked Armstrong on an arduous tour through France, Belgium, Italy and Switzerland, with a proposed extension to North Africa. After the concerts in Turin, Armstrong attempted to cancel the rest of the tour due to his seriously injured lip. When Canetti threatened to sue, Armstrong booked passage on an ocean liner and immediately returned to New York.

139 Alpha Smith was actually Armstrong's girlfriend at the time. They did not officially marry until 1938.

140 Giancarlo Roncaglia, "Il Jazz a Torino," *JazzItalia* www.jazzitalia.net/articoli/jazztorino01.asp#.VeoJGrT4ulI. Accessed February 20, 2013.

141 David I. Kertzer, *The Pope and Mussolini: The Secret History of Pius XI and the Rise of Fascism in Europe* (New York: Random House, 2014), 220.

142 Joseph E. Harris, *African-American Reactions to War in Ethiopia 1936–1941* (Baton Rouge, LA: Louisiana State University Press, 1994), 34–38.

143 Ibid., 93.

144 Lina Grip and John Hart, "The Use of Chemical Weapons in the 1935–36 Italo-Ethiopian War," SIPRI Arms Control and Non-proliferation Programmme (October 2009): 1–7. www.sipri.org/research/disarmament/ chemical/publications/ethiopiapaper. Accessed September 29, 2015

145 Nick LaRocca, "Jazz Stems from Whites Not Blacks, Says LaRocca," *Metronome* 52 (October 1936), 20.

146 Richard M. Sudhalter, *Lost Chords: White Musicians and Their Contribution to Jazz, 1915–1945* (New York: Oxford University Press, 1999), 16–17, is credited as one of the primary scholars to address LaRocca's racism and the negative effect it had on his legacy. As Sudhalter explains, LaRocca has been omitted from many accounts of early jazz, and when he has been mentioned, his success has been roundly dismissed as the result of "hustling and being white."

147 "Mussolini's War on Ethiopia is Praised by Josephine Baker," *Chicago Tribune* (October 2, 1935): 4.

148 Columbia DQ 1898

149 Columbia DQ 1783

150 Grammofono HN 874

151 "Concerti jazz banditi dalle radioaudizioni germaniche," *Il Messaggero* (October 13, 1935).

152 Mazzoletti, *Il Jazz in Italia: dalle origini alle grandi orchestre*, vol. 1, 327–329, 415–419.

153 For the ban issued to journalists, see http://assemblealegislativa.regione.emilia-romagna.it/wcm/studenticittadini/aapp/approfondire/approfon/storia_ memoria/p2_Esperienze/viaggio. Accessed August 10, 2015. For the quote concerning Mussolini's threat of a "March on Naples," see R. J. B. Bosworth, *Mussolini* (London: Arnold, 2002), 273.

154 "I vari gusti del pubblico: La 'Posta della Direzione'," in *EIAR, Annuario dell'anno XIII. Dieci anni di radio in Italia* (Turin: Società Editrice Torinese, 1935): 183.

155 For example, as Michele Sarfatti, *The Jews in Mussolini's Italy*, 99, explains, on May 11, 1936 Mussolini sent a telegraph to the Viceroy of Ethiopia, Pietro Badoglio, instructing him: "To avoid from the very start the frightening and not remote effects of cross-breeding" by ensuring that "no Italian – military or civilian – remain in the viceroyalty more than six months without his wife." On May 26 Galeazzo Ciano, then Minister for Press and Propaganda, declared to the Italian press: "We must have a clear separation between the dominant race and the dominated race. The Italian race must not have any sort of close contact with the Negro race and must maintain its robust purity intact."

156 As Irene Piazzoni, *La musica leggera in Italia dal dopoguerra agli anni del "boom." Cultura, consume, costume* (Milan: l'Ornitorinco, 2011), 25, has

noted: A survey of EIAR broadcasts in 1937 revealed that 40 percent of all programming was dedicated to music, and of that, 41 percent (a total of 1040 hours) was dedicated to *musica leggera* and jazz.

157 Augusto Caraceni, *Il Jazz dalle origini ad oggi* (Milan: Edizioni Suvini Zerbon, 1937), 7.

158 Ibid., 28.

159 Ibid., 95–98.

160 Ezio Levi and Giancarlo Testoni, *Introduzione alla vera musica di Jazz* (Milan: Magazzino Musicale, 1938), 44.

161 Ibid., 43.

162 Cf. Cerchiari, *Jazz e Fascismo*, 57.

4   Jazz Italian Style

1 The Manifesto was published as part of an article titled "Il Fascismo e i problemi della razza" with a byline that claimed: "L'antica purezza di sangue è il più grande titolo di nobiltà della Nazione" (The ancient purity of blood is the Nation's greatest title of nobility.) *Giornale d'Italia* (July 14, 1938): 1. For a copy of the manifesto and related documents see: http://media.accademiaxl.it/pubblicazioni/Matematica/link/venturi.pdf. Accessed October 10, 2015.

2 *Il Tevere* (August 9, 1938). Cf. Frank M. Snowden, Jr., "Race Propaganda in Italy," *Phylon* 1/2 (1940): 111.

3 Snowden, "Race Propaganda in Italy," 102.

4 Albert Viton, "Italy Under Hitler," *The Nation* (December 31, 1938): 11.

5 In the months leading up to the announcement of the new laws, a steady stream of articles rejecting the music of "inferior races" had appeared in the press. To name just a few examples, in *Il Popolo d'Italia*: "Il Lirico distrutto dal fuoco" (February 10, 1938); "Autarchia! Anche la musica costa quattrini" (March 4, 1938); "Autarchia! La musica leggera problema economico," (March 5, 1938); "In tema di gez: Chi sceglie e chi esegue" (June 10, 1938); "Cretino pubblico numero uno" (July 30, 1938); and "L'EIAR non trasmette musica dei ebrei" (September 22, 1938).

6 *Il Popolo d'Italia* (February 9, 1938). Cf. Dario Martinelli, "Da Yeah a Ueee senza passare dal MinCulPop – Strategie di coesistenza e resistenza del jazz italiano durante il fascismo," *California Italian Studies* 4/1 (2013). Retrieved from http://escholarship.org/uc/item/9fw7c793 on October 2, 2015.

7 Ibid.

8 "Cronache del Teatro e della Radio," *La Stampa* (November 7, 1937).

9 G. C. Visconti di Modrone, "Nazionalismo nella musica," *Realtà* (June 1938).

10 The damage wrought by Italy's race laws has been discussed by numerous scholars: Renzo De Felice, *Storia degli ebrei italiani sotto il fascismo* (Turin: Einaudi, 1961); Meir Michaelis, *Mussolini and the Jews: German–Italian*

Relations and the Jewish Question in Italy, 1922–1945 (New York and Oxford: Clarendon Press, 1978); Susan Zucotti, *The Italians and the Holocaust: Persecution, Rescue, and Survival* (Lincoln, NE: University of Nebraska Press, 1987); Michele Sarfatti, *Gli ebrei nell'Italia fascista. Vicende, identità, persecuzione* (Turin: Einaudi, 2000); Joshua D. Zimmerman, ed., *The Jews in Italy under Fascist and Nazi Rule, 1922–1945* (Cambridge University Press, 2005) and Michael A. Livingston, *The Fascists and the Jews of Italy: Mussolini's Race Laws, 1938–1943* (Cambridge University Press, 2014).

11 For an in-depth study of this topic, see Sandro Lopez Nuñez, *Carriere spezzate: Gli artisti ebrei colpiti dalle leggi razziale del 1938* (Milan: Mimesis, 2013).

12 Harry Fleming and his Orchestra recorded in Columbia's Milan Studios in 1933 and 1938. According to the discography compiled by Mazzoletti, *Il Jazz in Italia dalle origini alle grandi orchestre*, vol. 1, 529, his final recording engagement was April 2, 1938.

13 Hal Roach served as a mentor to Vittorio Mussolini. In September 1937, Roach invited Vittorio to New York to celebrate his twenty-first birthday. Press clippings from the time reveal that the visit served as a major social event both in New York and Los Angeles. It was during this visit that Roach and the young Mussolini began formulating a plan for the establishment of RAM Productions. Yet as several scholars have explained, anti-Fascist sentiments among some Hollywood producers eventually forced Roach to withdraw from the collaboration, a decision that resulted in him paying Vittorio Mussolini 500,000,000 lire for breach of contract. For more on Vittorio Mussolini's visit to the United States in 1937 and the rise and fall of RAM Productions, see "Life on the American Newsfront: Vittorio Teaches Hollywood the Mussolini Pose," *Life* (October 11, 1937): 31; Richard Lewis Ward, *A History of Hal Roach Studios* (Carbondale, IL: Southern Illinois University Press, 2005), 99–100; Forgacs and Gundle, *Mass Culture and Italian Society*, 133–135; Thomas Doherty, *Hollywood and Hitler, 1933–1939* (New York: Columbia University Press, 2013), 122–136, and an interview with Vittorio Mussolini conducted by Federico Scialla in Caserta in 1983. www.youtube.com/watch?v=AuJUo8OmJcs. Accessed February 2, 2015. In addition, the Istituto Luce Cinecittà released a newsreel on October 20, 1937 confirming Vittorio Mussolini's visit at various Hollywood film sets (Giornale Luce B1187). www.youtube.com/watch?v=SRQZGUb8Jds. Accessed June 27, 2015.

14 Cf. Adriano Mazzoletti, *Il Jazz in Italia, dallo swing agli anni sessanta* (Milan: EDT, 2010), vol. 2, 60.

15 Cf. Mazzoletti, *Il Jazz in Italia dalle origini alle grandi orchestre*, vol. 1, 4.

16 Cf. Mazzoletti, *Il Jazz in Italia, dallo swing agli anni sessanta*, vol. 2, 62.

17 "L'Eiar e la musica leggera," *Radiocorriere* 15/1 (1939): 5.

18 Santi Savarino, "Cronache del teatro e della radio. Altoparlante," *La Stampa* (January 7, 1939).

19 For an excellent overview of Gershwin's reception in Italy, see Leydi, Roberto, "Le fortune (o le sfortune) di Gershwin in Italia," in *Gershwin*, ed. Gianfranco Vinay (Turin: EDT, 1992), 305–342.

20 Luigi Colacicchi, "Musica leggiera," ch. 8 of *Il Libro della musica*, ed. Ferdinando Ballo, Alfredo Bonaccorsi, Enzo Borrelli, Alfedo Casella, et al. (Florence: Sansoni, 1939), 135.

21 Cerchiari, *Jazz e Fascismo*, 26.

22 Interview with Cinico Angelini conducted by Adriano Mazzoletti in Rome on April 4, 1976. Cf. Mazzoletti, *Il Jazz in Italia dalle origini alle grandi orchestre*, vol. 1, 100.

23 Ibid., 99.

24 Pippo Barzizza, Private notes, transcribed by Isa and Renzo Barzizza. Cf. "Pippo Barzizza," https://it.wikipedia.org/wiki/Pippo_Barzizza. Accessed October 25, 2014. For additional biographical details gathered from Pippo Barzizza's personal notes, see *Barzizza Channel*, an audio/video archive of the Barzizza Family managed and curated by Eros D'Antona, Mauro Giuliani and Renzo Barzizza. www.youtube.com/channel/UCtowQ1nkkggC-weMFzl7Bdg/featured. Accessed December 28, 2015.

25 Pippo and Isa Barzizza appeared as guests of Giancarlo Magalli on the television show *Pronto, è la Rai?* in 1987. http://datab.us/0u0K7RnqKjI#Pippo%20 e%20Isa%20Barzizza%20ospiti%20di%20Giancarlo%20Magalli%20a%20 "Pronto,%20è%20la%20Rai?"%20(1987). Accessed November 5, 2015.

26 Ibid.

27 Pippo Barzizza, Private notes, transcribed by Isa and Renzo Barzizza. Cf. "Pippo Barzizza," https://it.wikipedia.org/wiki/Pippo_Barzizza. Accessed October 25, 2014.

28 Interview with Pippo Barzizza conducted by Adriano Mazzoletti in San Remo on September 14, 1984. Cf. Mazzoletti, *Il Jazz in Italia dalle origini alle grandi orchestre*, vol. 1, 194.

29 For an excellent overview of the British jazz scene around this time, see Catherine Parsonage [Tackley], *The Evolution of Jazz in Britain, 1800–1935* (Aldershot: Ashgate, 2005).

30 Interview with Pippo Barzizza conducted by Adriano Mazzoletti in San Remo on September 14, 1984. Cf. Mazzoletti, *Il Jazz in Italia dalle origini alle grandi orchestre*, vol. 1, 194.

31 Ibid.

32 Cf. Mazzoletti, *Il Jazz in Italia dalle origini alle grandi orchestre*, 196.

33 Interview with Potito Simone conducted by Adriano Mazzoletti in Rome on April 5, 1960. Cf. Mazzoletti, *Il Jazz in Italia dalle origini alle grandi orchestre*, vol. 1, 197.

34 Ibid.

35 Dan Caslar enjoyed relative success in the United States as a songwriter and music impresario during the 1920s, but with the stock market crash of 1929,

he lost everything. It was at this point he returned to Naples with the hope of starting again. In Naples, Caslar befriended Michele Galdieri, who was then manager of the Curci Publishing House. Caslar convinced Galdieri to expand its repertoire, and with Caslar's help Curci began to publish Italian versions of popular songs tied to American films. In 1932, the central office transferred from Naples to Milan, with a branch office in Rome, the center of Italy's film industry. "Tempi Moderni" is an example of the style of music Caslar composed for Italian bands.

36 Interview with Pippo Barzizza conducted by Adriano Mazzoletti in San Remo on September 14, 1984. Cf. Mazzoletti, *Il Jazz in Italia dalle origini alle grandi orchestre*, vol. 1, 331.

37 S. Bonagura, "Liner notes" to CD anthology *La bacchetta di Barzizza* (Selezione del Reader's Digest/Comuzzi, RDCD 228), 2002.

38 Ibid.

39 Interview with Gorni Kramer conducted by Adriano Mazzoletti in Milan on January 23, 1979. Cf. Mazzoletti, *Il Jazz in Italia, dallo swing agli anni sessanti*, vol. 2, 2.

40 See Mazzoletti, *Il Jazz in Italia: dalle origini alle grandi orchestre*, vol. 1, 504–505, for a list of recordings by Guido Deiro released in Italy between 1911 and 1920.

41 Mazzoletti, *Il Jazz in Italia, dallo swing agli anni sessanti*, vol. 2, 2.

42 Ibid., 3.

43 Ibid.

44 Vittorio Franchini, *Gorni Kramer. Una vita per la musica* (Rivarolo Mantovano: Fondazione Sanguanini Rivarolo, 1996), 43.

45 Mazzoletti, *Il Jazz in Italia, dallo swing agli anni sessanti*, vol. 2, 3.

46 Ibid.

47 Franchini, *Gorni Kramer*, 47–49.

48 "Ja-Da" was originally a novelty song, with lyrics that emulated scat singing. Carleton had been a member of the US Navy Relief Forces deployed to Italy and France during the final months of the war, thus it is likely that "Ja-Da" was performed in Italy during this time. The cover of the original sheet music, published by Leo Feist in New York, shows the Ja-Da Trio (Carleton, Edward Sobol and Chester Rosenberg) in uniform and declares in bold print: "The sale of this song will be for the benefit of the Navy Relief Society. The society that guards the home of the men who guard the seas."

49 Franchini, *Gorni Kramer*, 49.

50 Adriano Mazzoletti, "Liner Notes" for *40 anni di Jazz in Italia* (Ricordi MRJ 8007/8), 1963.

51 Mazzoletti, *Il Jazz in Italia, dallo swing agli anni sessanti*, vol. 2, 4.

52 Ibid., 10.

53 Ibid., 4.

54 Ezio Levi, "Musica incise," *Il disco* (April/May 1936): 17. Cf. Mazzoletti, *Il Jazz in Italia, dallo swing agli anni sessanta*, vol. 2, 20–21.

55 Here Vittorio Mussolini is likely referring to "Some of these Days" from the MGM film *Broadway Melody of 1938*, released in Italy as *Follie di Broadway 1938* and "Bugle Call Rag," which was included in Paramount's *The Big Broadcast of 1937*.

56 Vittorio Mussolini, "Semprini e Kramer," *Cinema* (January 25, 1941).

57 As Mazzoletti, *Il Jazz in Italia, dallo swing agli anni sessanti*, vol. 2, 38–39, explains, the trio recorded a series of American tunes on September 7 and 16, 1938: "Sweet Sue, Just You" by Victor Young; "Japanese Sandman" by Richard A. Whiting; Jimmy McHugh's "I Can't Give You Anything But Love"; and Hoagy Carmichael's "Stardust."

58 Although the name still referenced only three members, there were in fact five in the band. Pietro Spairani (alto saxophone and clarinet) and Giuseppe "Pinùn" Ruggeri (drums) joined the band in 1939.

59 It should be noted that *American Idol* was based on the British *Pop Idol* (2001–2003), which was in turn inspired by the New Zealand television singing competition *Popstars* (launched in 1999).

60 *Il Canzoniere della radio*, 1 (March 1940): 2.

61 Forgacs and Gundle, *Mass Culture and Italian Society*, 54–55.

62 As World War II progressed, the government's ties to *Il Canzoniere della Radio* became all the more obvious. For example, in the 49th issue (December 1, 1942), a notice began to appear on the cover of each issue, requesting that readers send their used issues to the MinCulPop offices in Rome, so that they could be distributed to soldiers, since "Song is appreciated by our combatants!"

63 Alberto Rabagliati, *Quattro anni fra le stelle* (Milan: Bolla, 1932).

64 Interview with Cinico Angelini conducted by Adriano Mazzoletti in Rome on April 4, 1976. Cf. Mazzoletti, *Il Jazz in Italia: dalle origini alle grandi orchestre*, vol. 1, 345.

65 Schipa also appeared frequently in early sound films produced in Italy. A performance of him singing "Una furtiva lagrima" from Donizetti's *L'elisir D'amore* is available on YouTube: www.youtube.com/watch?v= pGKp78ZEGVE. Accessed February 27, 2016.

66 Alfredo Bonavera, Gilbert Rolle and Frank Ponzio, "Concert-Conference: Homage to Alberto Rabagliati," at NYU's Casa Italiana Zerilli-Marimo (May 7, 2010).

67 Not to be confused with Roberto Benigni's 1997 film of the same name.

68 Vincenzo Baggioli, "Quattro chiacchiere con una 'cara signora'," *Primi piani* (April 1942): 22.

69 Silvia Codognotto Sandon, *Vendo Ritmo: Natalino Otto 40 +1 anni dopo …* (Canatalupo in Sabina: Edizioni Sabinae, 2011).

70 Ibid., 12–13.

71 Ibid., 56–57.

72 Composed by Cesare Andrea Bixio and Ennio Neri.

73 Codognotto Sandon, *Vendo Ritmo*, 58.

74 Ibid., 59.

75 Ibid., 59.

76 Ibid., 60.

77 James Kaplan, *Frank: The Voice* (New York: Anchor Books, 2011), 94–97.

78 Codognotto Sandon, *Vendo Ritmo*, 61.

79 Ibid., 62.

80 Franchini, *Gorni Kramer*, 86.

81 "Natalino Otto," *Il Canzoniere della Radio* 37 (June 1, 1942): 4–5.

82 Unless otherwise noted, all biographical information about the Lescano family comes from the online archive, *Ricordando il Trio Lescano* (www .trio-lescano.it), compiled and curated by Angelo Zaniol. Over the years, many unsubstantiated legends have been published about the Trio Lescano. At present, the only reliable source for biographical information, not to mention facsimiles of primary sources related to the lives and careers of the Lescano sisters, is Professor Zaniol's extensive, meticulously curated online archive.

83 For an excellent overview of these practices, see Carla Mereu Keating, "'100% Italian:' The Coming of Sound Cinema in Italy and State Regulation on Dubbing," *California Italian Studies* 4 (2013): 1–24. http://escholarship.org/uc/item/7f86023v. Accessed May 21, 2015.

84 Written in 1932, "Bei Mir Bist Du Schön" (translation: "To Me You Are Beautiful") was part of a Yiddish operetta called *I Would if I Could*, written by Abraham Bloom, with music by Sholom Secunda and lyrics by Jacob Jacobs.

85 Cf. Gianni Isola, *L'ha scritto la radio: Storia e testi della radio durante il fascismo (1924–1944)* (Milan: Mondadori, 1998), 301.

86 One of the most distressing outcomes of this strengthened collaboration with Hitler was Mussolini's establishment of the Campagna Internment Camp in Southern Italy in 1940.

87 Pietro Badoglio, *L'Italia nella seconda guerra mondiale* (Milan: Mondadori, 1946): 37.

88 Francesco Sapori, "Canta che ti passa," *Radiocorriere* 14 (October 18, 1941).

89 Cf. www.archives.gov/research/military/ww2/sound-recordings.html#40. Accessed October 15, 2015.

90 "L'America del Signor Delano," D005201, Istituto Nazionale Luce (1941) www .archivioluce.com/archivio/. Accessed August 20, 2015.

91 Cf. Nicola Tranfaglia, *Ministri e giornalisti. La guerra e il Minculpop (1939–1943)* (Turin: Einaudi, 2005), 202–203.

92 Ibid., 238.

93 The new law was legge 615. Pietro Cavallo, *Vincere. Vincere. Vincere. Fascismo e società italiana nelle canzoni e nelle riviste di varietà. 1935–1943* (Rome: Ianua, 1981), 47.

94 "Concessione della cittadinanza italiana alle Sorelle Lescano," dated March 30, 1942. Private Collection of Giorgio Bozzo. This document is also available

online: www.trio-lescano.it/archivio_documenti/ cittadinanza_italiana_alle_
leschan.pdf. Accessed June 28, 2014.

95 Tranfaglia, *Ministri e giornalisti*, 266–267.

96 I would like to offer my sincere thanks to Angelo Zaniol and Manuel Carrera
for supplying me with a recording of this song and for their assistance in
transcribing the lyrics.

97 Virgilio Zanolla, "Storia anno per anno delle sorelle Leschan/Lescano:
Compendio dei fatti salienti," last updated September 2015. www.trio-lescano
.it/pdf/storia_sorelle_lescano.pdf. Accessed October 10, 2015.

98 The letter also informed the sisters that their membership had been backdated
several months, to October 29, 1942. This letter and the accompanying
documentation are now held in the Archivio di Stato di Roma. These documents
are also available online: www.trio-lescano.it/archivio_documenti/iscrizione_
al_pnf.pdf. Accessed June 28, 2014.

5   A Nation Divided

1 Interview with Gaetano Gimelli conducted by Adriano Mazzoletti in Turin
on January 21, 1980. Cf. Mazzoletti, *Il Jazz in Italia: dalle origini alle grandi
orchestre*, vol. 1, 344.

2 According to Virgilio Zanolla, "Carlo Alberto Prato, il Pigmalione delle
Lescano," www.trio-lescano.it/pdf/Carlo_Alberto_Prato,_il_Pigmalione_
delle_Lescano.pdf (p. 8). Accessed December 17, 2015, Prato was transferred
to a camp in Mannheim in early 1944, where he spent the rest of the war
"writing long letters to his wife wherein he inquired, with painstaking yet
understandable meticulousness, if his piano was being maintained, and
asked for news about his friends, the Lescano sisters, whom he believed were
still in Turin." Zanolla describes both the camp in Limburg and the camp in
Mannheim as "German concentration camps," but they were not. Both were
Prisoner of War camps.

3 Giovanni Giovannini, *Il Quaderno nero. Settembre 1943–Aprile 1945* (Milan:
Scheiwiller, 2005).

4 According to the testimony of Rosetta Nulli, another prisoner in Bolzano,
while Funaro was there he tried to keep the other inmates' spirits up by writing
new lyrics to popular tunes. See "Rosetta Nulli," in *Testimonianze dai Lager*,
www.testimonianzedailager.rai.it/testimoni/pdf/test_34.pdf. Accessed October
11, 2015.

5 "Historical Summary: American Forces Radio and Television Service (AFRTS),"
http://afrts.dodmedia.osd.mil/facts/1.pdf. Accessed March 23, 2014.

6 It should be noted that when Petrillo agreed to let union members participate
in the government's V-Disc project, it was under one condition: the recordings
could not be offered for purchase in the United States or played on commercial

radio. When the V-Disc program ended after the war, the Armed Services tried to honor the original AFM request that the records not be used for commercial purposes. Original masters and stampers were destroyed, leftover V-Discs were discarded, and V-Discs smuggled home by servicemen were confiscated and destroyed. An employee at a Los Angeles record company even served a prison sentence for the illegal possession of over 2,500 V-Discs. http://www.chuckthewriter.com/vdisc.html.

7 Irene Piazzoni, *La musica leggera in Italia dal dopoguerra agli anni del "boom". Cultura consumo costume* (Milano: l'Ornitorinco, 2011), 35–36.

8 Cf. Silvia Codognotto Sandon, *Vendo Ritmo*, 20.

9 Ibid.

10 Ibid.

11 Natalino Otto, "Confidenze lampo di Natalino Otto," *Canzoniere della Radio* 59 (May 1, 1943): 28–29.

12 Although the Trio Lescano made their final recordings for Cetra in April 1943, their discs remained in the catalogue and continued to be advertised in *Radiocorriere.*

13 In February 1944 Cetra was still advertising recordings by the Trio Lescano with both the Angelini and Barzizza orchestras in popular magazines. For example, see *Il Dramma* (February 1–15, 1944): 2–3.

14 The Trio's Italianized versions of the US tunes "St. Louis Blues" and "Pagan Love Song" accompanied by the Angelini Orchestra (Cetra AA 361) appeared in 1944, as did their rendition with Rabagliati of the Italian tune "Brilla una stella in cielo," accompanied by Barzizza's Cetra Orchestra (Cetra AA 366).

15 Giorgio Nelson Page, *L'americano di Roma* (Milan: Longanesi, 1950), 698. For the complete text of Mussolini's speech, see Benito Mussolini, "La Reppublica sociale italiana," in *Opera Omnia di Benito Mussolini XXIII* (Florence, IT: La Fenice, 1960), 1–5.

16 PDFs of all issues of *Radiorario*, *Radiocorriere* and *Segnale della Radio* are available online: www.radiocorriere.teche.rai.it/Default.aspx. Accessed April 10, 2013.

17 Rome: Archivo Centrale dello Stato, Ministero della Cultura Popolare, b. 67, f. 640, sf. 12, Posta Civile 361, 3.

18 Gianni Isola, "Il microfono conteso. La guerra delle onde nella lotta di liberazione nazionale (1943–1945)," *Mélanges de l'Ecole française de Rome. Italie et Méditerranée* 108/1 (1996): 92, and Luisa Quartermaine, *Propaganda and Politics in the Italian Social Republic (R.S.I.) 1943–45* (Exeter, UK: Elm Bank Publications, 2000), 72.

19 Cf. Franchini, *Gorni Kramer*, 89–90.

20 As Mazzoletti, *Il Jazz in Italia, dallo swing agli anni sessanta*, vol. 2, 1124, has noted, the use of the "Italianized" names during the Fascist era appears to be an urban legend that took root after World War II. As he noted in personal correspondence with me in March 2016, in all his years of extensive research,

he has never come across any of these names in print. And only the name "Del Duca" for Duke Ellington was mentioned in an interview with Gorni Kramer.

21 Mazzoletti, *Il Jazz in Italia, dallo swing agli anni sessanta*, 217.

22 Cf. Franchini, *Gorni Kramer*, 94–95.

23 Riccardo Schwamenthal, "Jazz a Bergamo: Ricordi testimonianze documenti dagli anni trenta agli anni settanta," *Archivio storico Bergamasco* XV/2 (1995): www.archiviobergamasco.it/wp-content/uploads/2014/01/Rivista-2.0 .pdf. Accessed January 27, 2016.

24 "Ritmo-mania," *Bergamo Repubblicana* (April 26, 1944): 2.

25 Ibid.

26 Ibid.

27 Giancarlo Dosselli, "Natalino Otto e il fascismo," *Bresciaoggi.it* (September 29, 2011), www.bresciaoggi.it/stories/Lettere/292467_natalino_otto_e_il_fascismo/. Accessed April 19, 2014; Online Catalogue of Jazz Sources in Bergamo: Riproduzione della locandina pubblicitaria dello spettacolo "Una notte al Madera" sul quotidiano Bergamo Repubblicana del 22/04/1944. Lo spettacolo fu interrotto dai fascisti e Natalino Otto fu obbligato a cantare "Giovinezza." Negativo mancante. www.bibliotecamai.org/cataloghi_inventari/ fotografie/ fondi_fotografici/ catalogo_jazz.html#17 Bergamo, 1994. Accessed March 19, 2014. See also R. Schwamenthal, "Chi ha paura di Natalino Otto," in *Studi e ricerche di storia contemporanea, rassegna dell'Istituto bergamasco per la Storia della Resistenza e dell'età contemporanea* 53 (June 2000): 63–70.

28 "Kramer è un inventore," *L'Ora* (February 18, 1945): 10.

29 Gianni Isola, "Il microfono conteso," 110. See also Clemente Galligani, *L'Europa e il mondo nella tormenta. Guerra, nazifascismo, collaborazionismo, resistenza* (Rome: Armando, 2012), 170–171.

30 Radio Tevere should not be confused with the English-language program, "Jerry's Front Calling," transmitted by the Germans from Rome (1943) and then Como (1944–45). Hosted by Rita Louisa Zucca, the Italian "Axis Sally," this broadcast was aimed at Allied soldiers. The music performed was American swing and the commentary was propaganda aimed at weakening the morale of Allied troops. For more information on Zucca and these broadcasts, see "Americans Seize Axis Sally in Italy; Fascist Broadcaster Born Here; Military Police Find Rita Louisa Zucca in Turin – Relatives in New York Deny She Served Foe Willingly Family Denies Voluntary Talks," *New York Times* (June 8, 1945): 9; Richard Lucas, "Axis Sally: The Americans Behind That Alluring Voice," *Historynet* (November 23, 2009) www.historynet.com/axis-sally.htm. Accessed November 15, 2015.

31 Julian Budden, *Puccini: His Life and Works* (Oxford University Press, 2005), 417–418.

32 Additionally, German filmmakers regularly used "Inno a Roma" as background music for propaganda newsreels featuring Mussolini. "Mussolini an der französchinen Front" (*Deutsche Wochenschau* 516–522) is a typical

example. Recorded on July 22, 1940, it presents "Inno a Roma" as a symbol of Fascist strength. For a clip of this newsreel, see www.youtube.com/watch?v=MJS0FbxnQu0. Accessed November 30, 2015.

33 Cf. "In RSI," *ACTA dell'Istituto storico Repubblica Sociale Italiana* 16/1 (January–March 2002): 7.

34 Giampero Boneschi later described his connection to Radio Tevere and the benefit of participating in its broadcasts: "I joined a covert band that performed on the radio. It was composed of Masetti on clarinet and alto saxophone, Papurello on bass, Gambarelli on drums and me on piano. They [Mussolini and his officials] also gave us a card that protected us from being arrested by the Germans and deported. Performances transmitted from Via Rovani and also in the Palazzo featured a group led by Kramer, with Otto singing. Otto knew a little German and he could perform his songs in that language." Cf. Franchini, *Gorni Kramer*, 97.

35 Massimo Zannoni, "L'EIAR," *ACTA dell'Istituto storico Repubblica Sociale Italiana* 16/1 (January–March 2002): 6.

36 Ferretti was a popular opera singer in the RSI, who also recorded a number of popular tunes in 1944. Her recording of "Tornerai" (Columbia D13041) is fittingly sentimental, but not syncopated in the least.

37 *Radio News* 33 (January 1945): 84.

38 Alceo Toni, "Ancora della canzone popolare," *Segno della Radio*, I/17 (December 17, 1944): 11.

39 Ibid.

40 Ibid.

41 Ibid.

42 Sergio Luzzatto, *The Body of Il Duce: Mussolini's Corpse and the Fortunes of Italy* (New York: Henry Holt and Company, 2014), 68–71.

43 Silvio Lanaro, *Storia della Repubblica italiana. Dalla fine della Guerra agli anni novanta* (Venice: Marsilio, 1992), 18.

44 American audiences became acquainted with this version of "Crapa Pelada" in 2010 when it was featured in season 3, episode 13 of the television series *Breaking Bad* when Gale (David Costabile) is shown singing along to the tune right before he is murdered.

45 Guido Salvetti and Bianca Maria Antolini, *Italia Millenovecentocinquanta* (Milan: Edizioni Angelo Guerini e Associati Spa, 1999), 312.

46 "Picciando in Be-bop," Fonit 12957 B, recorded in Turin on November 1, 1948. In addition to Gorni Kramer on accordion, this recording featured a stunning performance by Enrico Cuomo on drums.

47 When *Pinocchio* was first released in the United States in 1940 it did poorly at the box office. It was not screened in Italy then because Paolo Lorenzini, the nephew of author Carlo Collodi, formally requested MinCulPop to sue Disney for its "Americanization" of his uncle's novel: "Pinocchio's adventures are an Italian work of art and must not be distorted to make it American," he stated.

"Government authorities should intervene." For a US report of Lorenzini's complaint, see Maxine Garrison, "Poor Pinocchio Runs Afoul of The Law," *The Pittsburgh Press* (January 20, 1941): 14.

48 For reproductions of these photos see www.trio-lescano.it/fototeca/trio_ lescano_in_privato.pdf. Figures 49 and 50. Accessed December 9, 2015.

49 H. Arlo Nimmo, *The Andrews Sisters: A Biography and Career Record* (Jefferson, NC: McFarland & Company, 2004), 219.

50 Piero Vacca Cavalotto, "Il Trio Lescano in Canavese," originally published in *Canavèis* 12 (Winter 2007). Reproduction available at www.trio-lescano .it/aggiornamenti/Il_Trio_Lescano_in_Canavese.pdf.   Accessed   December 10, 2015.

51 Giancarlo Testoni, "Un Sogno che si avvera," *Music e Jazz* 1/1 (August 15– September 1, 1945): 1–2, 15.

52 Forgacs and Gundle, *Mass Culture and Italian Society*, 177.

53 Daniele Biello, "E lo swing venne dal mare. La canzone italiana e l'età dei transatlantici. Il caso di Natalino Otto," *Parlami d'amore Mariù: Cultura, società e costume nella canzone italiana*. ed. Elvira Bonfati (San Cessario di Lecce: Piero Manni, 2005), 53–54.

54 Codognotto Sandon, *Vendo Ritmo*, 55.

55 Natalia Aspesi, "Sfogliando i Tuli-Tuli Tulipan," *La Repubblica* (October 26, 1985): 26. It should be noted that Adriano Mazzoletti was the first to interview Sandra Lescano, in Salsomaggiore Terme on April 3, 1980, and it is interesting to note that when he asked about the RSI years, she made no mention of an arrest or imprisonment: "We were constrained to hide our mother; then there was someone, who for personal reasons, denounced us to the Germans, even though we were Catholic, had Italianized our name to Lescano and had become citizens in the country that had made us celebrities. There were three young girls who had formed a vocal trio and wanted to take our place. We were forced to run away and hide ourselves." Cf. Mazzoletti, *Il Jazz in Italia: dalle origini alle grandi orchestre*, vol. 1, 333.

56 Luciano Verre, "Ero la regina del Trio Lescano, adesso vivo sola e sono in miseria," *Gente* 29/47 (November 22, 1985): 106–109.

57 Ibid.

58 *Tulip Time: The Rise and Fall of the Trio Lescano* (2008), directed by Tonino Boniotti and Marco De Stefanis and produced by Memphis Film in The Netherlands; Gabriele Eschenazi, *Le regine dello swing, Il Trio Lescano: una storia fra cronaca e costume* (Turin: Einaudi, 2010). The fictionalized miniseries, *Le Ragazze dello Swing*, directed by Maurizio Zaccaro and produced by Casanova Multimedia, aired on Rai Uno in September 2010. For the most accurate archive-based study of the Trio Lescano in 1943 see: Virgilio Zanolla, "Una leggenda da sfattare, 1943: le Lescano a Genoa," www.trio-lescano.it. Accessed November 14, 2014.

59 Interview with Isa Barzizza conducted by Manuel Carrera in Rome on November 8, 2010. Posted online: www.trio-lescano.it/archivio_documenti/intervista_a_ isa_barzizza.pdf. Accessed on November 5, 2015.

60 S. Bonagura, "Liner notes" to CD anthology *La bacchetta di Barzizza* (Selezione del Readrer's Digesr/Comuzzi, RDCD 228), 2002.

61 Ibid.

62 Codognoto Sandon, *Vendo Ritmo*, 55.

63 Ibid.

64 Cf. Pierluigi "Piji" Siciliani, *La Canzone Jazzata: L'Italia che canta sotto le stelle del jazz* (Arezzo: ZONA, 2007), 44–45.

65 Transcription of a radio broadcast "Special oggi" in July 1973 on RAI. Cf. La trascrizione del racconto che lo stesso "Raba" ha fatto di se stesso durante la trasmissione radiofonica *Special oggi* nel luglio del 1973, alle soglie della propria esistenza. www.albertorabagliati.com/biografia/. Accessed November 12, 2015.

66 Coco Ballantyne, "Fact or Fiction?: Smog Creates Beautiful Sunsets," *Scientific American* (July 12, 2007) www.scientificamerican.com/article/fact-or-fiction-smog-creates-beautiful-sunsets/. Accessed May 1, 2016.

67 Cf. "Alberto Rabagliati la voce de Milano," www.storiaradiotv.it/ALBERTO%20 RABAGLIATI.htm. Accessed May 2, 2016.

68 Forgacs and Gundle, *Mass Culture and Italian Society*, 186.

69 Ibid.

70 Gianfranco Baldazzi, *La canzone italiana del Novecento* (Rome: Newton Compton, 1989), 83.

Epilogue

1 As James Kaplan, *Frank: The Voice* (New York: Anchor Books, 2010), 44, explains, The Hoboken Four joined the Major Bowes Number Five Touring Unit.

2 Ibid. 47.

3 Cf. ibid., 74.

4 Ibid.

5 Frank Sinatra in collaboration with John Quinlan, *Tips on Popular Singing* (New York: Embassy Music Corp., 1941).

6 Cf. the documentary directed by Daniele Segre and aired on RAITRE in 1987: *"Dall'Italia con amore ..." Frank Sinatra*.

7 Ibid.

Bibliography

Abbiati, Franco. "Arte negro-americana. I trucchi del jazz rivelati alla folla," *Rivista di Bergamo VIII*, 12 (December 1929): 586–589.

Abbott, Lynn and Doug Seroff. "Brown Skin (Who You Really For?)," *The Jazz Archivist* 15 (2001): 10–16.

"Ambulance Jazz Band Leaves for the Riviera," *New York Herald* (April 5, 1919): 2.

"Americans Seize Axis Sally in Italy; Fascist Broadcaster Born Here; Military Police Find Rita Louisa Zucca in Turin – Relatives in New York Deny She Served Foe Willingly Family Denies Voluntary Talks," *New York Times* (June 8, 1945): 9.

Amori, Silvio. "Jazz in Italy: From Its Origins to the Second World War," *Columbia Journal of American Studies* 9 (Fall 2009): 306–325.

Ansermet, Ernest. "Sur une orchestra nègre," *La revue romande* (October 5, 1919), reprinted in Ernest Ansermet, *Écrits sur la musique* (Neuchâtel: Éditions de la Baconnière, 1971), 171–178.

Archer-Straw, Petrine. *Negrophilia: Avant-Garde Paris and Black Culture in the 1920s* (London: Thames & Hudson, 2000).

Armstrong, Louis. *Louis Armstrong in His Own Words*, ed. Thomas Brothers (Oxford University Press, 1999), 160.

   Swing That Music (New York: Longmans, Green, 1936).

Aspesi, Natalia. "Sfogliando i Tuli-Tuli Tulipan," *La Repubblica* (October 26, 1985).

"Autarchia! Anche la musica costa quattrini," *Il Popolo d'Italia* (March 4, 1938).

"Autarchia! La musica leggera problema economico," *Il Popolo d'Italia* (March 5, 1938).

Badoglio, Pietro. *L'Italia nella seconda guerra mondiale* (Milan: Mondadori, 1946).

Baggioli, Vincenzo. "Quattro chiacchiere con una 'cara signora'," *Primi piani* (April 1942): 22.

Bakish, David. *Jimmy Durante: His Show Business Career, with an Annotated Filmography and Discography* (Jefferson, NC: McFarland, 1995).

Balbi, Gabriele. "Radio before Radio: Araldo Telefonico and the Invention of Italian Broadcasting," *Technology and Culture* 51/ 4 (October 2010): 786–808.

Baldazzi, Gianfranco. *La canzone italiano del Novecento* (Rome: Newton Compton, 1989).

"Ballo, digiuno e astinenza," *Corriere della Sera* (March 25, 1920).

Beardsley, Roger. (ed.). *Fonotipia 1904-1939* [CD-ROM] (North Thoresby, Lincolnshire, England, 2003).

Begnac, Yvon de. *Palazzo Venezia: Storia di une regime* (Rome: La Rocca, 1950).

Ben-Ghiat, Ruth. *Fascist Modernities: Italy, 1922–1945* (Oakland, CA: University of California Press, 2001).

"Ben's Jazz Curve," *Los Angeles Times* (April 2, 1912): III, 2.

Berghaus, Günther. *Futurism and Politics: Between Anarchist Rebellion and Fascist Reaction, 1909-1944* (Providence, RI: Berghahn Books, 1996).

  Italian Futurist Theatre 1909–1944 (Oxford: Clarendon Press, 1998).

Bergmeier, Horst J. P. and Rainer E. Lotz. *Hitler's Airwaves: The Inside Story of Nazi Radio Broadcasting and Propaganda Swing* (New Haven, CT: Yale University Press, 1997).

Bergreen, Laurence. *As Thousands Cheer: The Life of Irving Berlin* (London: Hodder and Stoughton, 1990).

Berrett, Joshua. "Louis Armstrong and Opera," *The Musical Quarterly* 76/2 (1992): 216–241.

Biello, Daniele. "E lo swing venne dal mare. La canzone italiana e l'età dei trans-atlantici. Il caso di Natalino Otto," *Parlami d'amore Mariù: Cultura, società e costume nella canzone italiana*, ed. Elvira Bonfati (San Cessario di Lecce: Piero Manni, 2005), 43–56.

Biguzzi, Stefano. *L'Orchestra del Duce. Mussolini, la musica e il mito* (Turin: UTET, 2003).

Boccioni, Umberto. "Contro il paesaggio e la vecchia estetica," *Pittura e scultura futuriste. Dinamismo plastic* (Milan, 1914).

  Gli scritti editi e inediti, ed. Zeno Birolli (Milan: Feltrinelli, 1971).

Bogle, Donald. *Toms, Coons, Mulattoes, Mammies, and Bucks: An Interpretive History of Blacks in American Films*, 4th edn (New York: The Continuum International Publishing Group, 2001).

Bonagura, S. "Liner Notes" to CD anthology *La bacchetta di Barzizza* (Selezione del Reader's Digest/Comuzzi, RDCD 228), 2002.

Bragaglia, Anton Giulio. *Jazz Band* (Milan: Corbaccio, 1929).

Brin, Irene. *Usi e costume 1920–1940* (Rome: Donatello De Luigi, 1944).

Brody, Martin (ed.). *Music and Musical Composition at the American Academy in Rome* (University of Rochester Press, 2014).

Brothers, Thomas. *Louis Armstrong's New Orleans* (New York: Norton, 2007).

Brown, David P. (ed.). *Noise Orders: Jazz, Improvisation, and Architecture* (Minneapolis, MN: University of Minnesota Press, 2006).

Brunn, H. O. *The Story of the Original Dixieland Jazz Band* (Baton Rouge, LA: Louisiana State University Press, 1960).

Budden, Julian. *Puccini: His Life and Works* (Oxford University Press, 2005).

Burke, Margaret Reeves. "Futurism in America, 1910–1917" (PhD Dissertation, University of Delaware, 1986).

Burton, Jack. "The Honor Roll of Popular Songwriters: No. 22 – Al Piantadosi," *The Billboard* (June 11, 1949): 38.

C. A., "Louis Armstrong. Il re del 'jazz hot,'" *La Stampa della Sera* (January 16, 1935): 1.

Cabot Lodge, Henry. "Lynch Law and Unrestricted Immigration," *The North American Review* 152 (May 1891).

Campanella, Richard. *Geographies of New Orleans: Urban Fabrics before the Storm* (Lafayette, LA: Center for Louisiana Studies, 2006).

Campman, "Commenti alla vita: Ballo Jazz," *La Tribuna Illustrata* (October 5, 1919).

Caraceni, Augusto. *Il Jazz dalle origini ad oggi* (Milan: Edizioni Suvini Zerbon, 1937).

Casavola, Franco. "Difesa del Jazz Band," *L'Impero* (August 14, 1926): 4.

"La musica futurista," *Il Futurismo. Rivista sintetica illustrate* 10 (1924).

Casella, Alfredo. *21 + 26* (Rome and Milan: Augustea, 1931; reprinted Florence: Leo S. Olschki, 2001).

"Casella on Jazz," *The Music Courier* (July 12, 1923).

"Della musica necessaria," *Italia Letteraria* 1 (April 7, 1929).

"Il Jazz," *Italia Letteraria* 1 (September 1, 1929).

"La vita musicale negli Stati Uniti," *La Critica Musicale* (April 1922).

Cavallo, Pietro. *Vincere. Vincere. Vincere. Fascismo e società italiana nelle canzoni e nelle riviste di varietà. 1935–1943* (Rome: Ianua, 1981).

Cerchiari, Luca. "How to Make a Career by Writing against Jazz: Anton Giulio Bragaglia's Jazz Band (1929)," *Forum Italicum* 49 (2015): 462–473.

Jazz e Fascismo: dalla nascita della radio a Gorni Kramer (Palermo: L'Epos, 2003).

Charters, Samuel. *A Trumpet around the Corner: The Story of New Orleans Jazz* (Jackson, MS: University of Mississippi Press, 2008).

"Chief Hennessy Avenged," *New York Times* (March 15, 1891).

Choate, Mark. *Emigrant Nation: The Making of Italy Abroad* (Cambridge, MA: Harvard University Press, 2008).

Codognotto Sandon, Silvia. *Vendo Ritmo: Natalino Otto 40 +1 anni dopo …* (Canatalupo in Sabina: Edizioni Sabinae, 2011).

Colacicchi, Luigi. "Musica leggiera," in *Il Libro della musica*, ed. Ferdinando Ballo, Alfredo Bonaccorsi, Enzo Borrelli, Alfedo Casella, et al. (Florence: Sansoni, 1939).

"Concerti jazz banditi dalle radioaudizioni germaniche," *Il Messaggero* (October 13, 1935).

Crafton, Donald. *The Talkies: American Cinema's Transition to Sound, 1926–1931* (Oakland, CA: University of California Press, 1991).

"Cretino pubblico numero uno," *Il Popolo d'Italia* (July 30, 1938).

Crispolti, Enrico. *Il mito della macchina e altri temi del futurism* (Trapani: Edizioni Celebes, 1969).

"Cronache del Teatro e della Radio," *La Stampa* (November 7, 1937).

Davis, Robert C. *Christian Slaves, Muslim Masters: White Slavery in the Mediterranean, the Barbary Coast and Italy, 1500–1800* (London: Palgrave Macmillan, 2003).

De Angelis, Rodolfo. *Storia del Cafè Chantant* (Milan: Il Balcone, 1946).

De Felice, Renzo. *Storia degli ebrei italiani sotto il fascismo* (Turin: Einaudi, 1961).

De Grazia, Victoria. *The Culture of Consent: Mass Organization of Leisure in Fascist Italy* (Cambridge University Press, 1981).

Deiro, Guido Roberto. "Guido Deiro & Mae West: The Untold Story," Liner notes to *Guido Deiro: Complete Recorded Works*, vol. 2 (Archeophone Records 5014) 2009, 12–13.

"Deliberazione presa dal Consiglio dei Ministri il I° gennaio 1926," *Jazz Band* 1/2 (1926): 4.

De Rensis, Raffaello. "A Santa Cecilia canzoni di negri d'America," *Il Giornale d'Italia* (January 23, 1927).

    Mussolini musicista (Mantova: Edizioni Paladino, 1927).

Doherty, Thomas. *Hollywood and Hitler, 1933–1939* (New York: Columbia University Press, 2013).

Dosselli, Giancarlo. "Natalino Otto e il fascismo," *Bresciaoggi.it* (September 29, 2011).

Dovel, Jason. "The Influence of Jazz on the Solo Trumpet Compositions of Eugene Bozza" (DMA Dissertation, University of North Texas, 2007).

Duran, Adrian R. *Painting, Politics, and the New Front of Cold War Italy* (Aldershot: Ashgate, 2014).

Edmiston, Fred. *The Coon-Sanders Nighthawks: The Band That Made Radio Famous* (Jefferson, NC: McFarland, 2009).

Engel, Carl. "Jazz: A Musical Discussion," *The Atlantic Monthly* (August 1922).

Eschenazi, Gabriele. *Le regine dello swing, Il Trio Lescano: una storia fra cronaca e costume* (Turin: Einaudi, 2010).

Evans, James W. and Captain Gardner L. Harding. *Entertaining the American Army: The American Stage and Lyceum in the World War* (New York: Association Press, 1921).

Fielding, Raymond. *The American Newsreel: A Complete History, 1911–1967*, 2nd edn. (Jefferson, NC: McFarland, 2006).

"Films and Jazz Hit in Clean-Up at Rome. Products of Hollywood and New York May Be Barred in the Eternal City," *New York Times* (April 24, 1927): 22.

Flynn, Ronald. *The Golden Age of the Accordion* (Schertz, TX: Flynn Publications, 1992).

Forgacs, David and Stephen Gundle. *Mass Culture and Italian Society from Fascism to the Cold War* (Bloomington, IN: University of Indiana Press, 2007).

Franchini, Vittorio. *Gorni Kramer. Una vita per la musica* (Rivarolo Mantovano: Fondazione Sanguanini Rivarolo, 1996).

Frasca, Simona. *Italian Birds of Passage: The Diaspora of Neapolitan Musicians in New York* (New York: Palgrave McMillan, 2014).

Friedwald, Will. *Sinatra! The Song is You: A Singer's Art* (New York: Scribner, 1995).

Fry, Andy. *Paris Blues: African American Music and French Popular Culture, 1920–1960* (Chicago, IL: University of Chicago Press, 2014).

"The Futurist Movement in Italy," *Current Literature* 51/2 (August 1911): 6–7.

"The Futurists," *The Sun* (May 23, 1909): 8.

Gabbard, Krin. "The Word Jazz," *Cambridge Companion to Jazz*, ed. Mervyn Cooke and David Horn (Cambridge University Press, 2002).

Galligani, Clemente. *L'Europa e il mondo nella tormenta. Guerra, nazifascismo, collaborazionismo, resistenza* (Rome: Armando, 2012).

Garrison, Maxine. "Poor Pinocchio Runs Afoul of the Law," *The Pittsburgh Press* (January 20, 1941): 14.

Garson, Edith. *George Gershwin* (New York: Frederick Unger, 1958).

Giovannini, Giovanni. *Il Quaderno nero. Settembre 1943–Aprile 1945* (Milan: Scheiwiller, 2005).

Gleason, E. T. "Sports News," *Bulletin* (March 6, 1913): 16.

Gracyk, Tim. *Popular American Recording Pioneers: 1895-1925* (Binghamton, NY: The Hawthorn Press, 2000).

Gronow, Pekka and Ilpo Saunio. *An International History of the Recording Industry* (London: Cassell, 1998).

Gundle, Stephen. *Mussolini's Dream Factory: Film Stardom in Fascist Italy* (New York: Berghahn, 2013).

Hand, John Oliver. "Futurism in America: 1909–14," *Art Journal*, 14/4 (Winter 1981): 337–342.

Harris, Chandra M. "Who's Got the Power? Blacks in Italian Cinema and Literature, 1910–1948" (PhD Dissertation, Brown University, 2004).

Harris, Joseph E. *African-American Reactions to War in Ethiopia 1936–1941* (Baton Rouge, LA: Louisiana State University Press, 1994).

Harrison, Max. "The Violin in Jazz," *Cambridge Companion to the Violin*, ed. Robin Stowell (Cambridge University Press, 1992), 249–256.

Henderson, Charles. "The Call of Art and Arms," *Cleveland Plain Dealer* (September 15, 1915): 8.

"Home-Made Jazz for Italy. New Association Plans Substitute for American Product," *New York Times* (July 16, 1926): 3.

Hopkins, Ernest J. "In Praise of Jazz: A Futurist Word Which Has Just Joined the Language," *The Bulletin* (April 5, 1913): 7.

Humphreys, Richard. *Futurism* (London: Tate Publishing, 1999).

"I vari gusti del pubblico: La 'Posta della Direzione'," in *EIAR, Annuario dell'anno XIII. Dieci anni di radio in Italia* (Turin: Società Editrice Torinese, 1935), 183.

"Il 'Jazz' espulso dalle ... Sale da Ballo!" *Radiorario* 5/11 (March 10–17, 1929): 30.

"Il Lirico distrutto dal fuoco," *Il Popolo d'Italia* (February 10, 1938).

"Il magnifico veglione futurista alla casa magica Depero," *Il Popolo* Trento (January 17, 1923).

"In tema di gez: Chi sceglie e chi esegue," *Il Popolo d'Italia* (June 10, 1938).

Isola, Gianni. *L'ha scritto la radio: Storia e testi della radio durante il fascismo (1924-1944)* (Milan: Mondadori, 1998).

"Il microfono conteso. La guerra delle onde nella lotta di liberazione nazionale (1943–1945)," *Mélanges de l'Ecole française de Rome. Italie et Méditerranée* 108/1 (1996): 83–124.

"Italy Bans Hip Wiggles. Italian Police Raid Dance Halls to Save Jazz-Mad Flappers," *New York Times* (January 29, 1926): 10.

Jackson, Jeffrey H. *Making Jazz French: Music and Modern Life in Interwar Paris* (Durham, NC: Duke University Press, 2003).

Jacobson, Marion. *Squeeze This!: A Cultural History of the Accordion* (Urbana, IL: University of Illinois Press, 2012).

Jaker, Bill, Frank Sulek and Peter Kanze (eds.). *The Airwaves of New York: Illustrated Histories of 156 AM Stations in the Metropolitan Area, 1921-1996* (Jefferson, NC: MacFarland, 1998).

"Jazz Band in Gondolas Delights A.E.F. Troops," *New York Herald*, Paris edn. (February 19, 1919): 2.

Jones, Steve. *Antonio Gramsci* (London: Routledge, 2006).

Jordan, Matthew F. "Jazz Changes: A History of French Discourse of Jazz from Ragtime to Be-bop"(PhD dissertation, Claremont Graduate University, 1998).
Le Jazz: French Cultural Identity (Urbana, IL: University of Illinois Press, 2010).

Kaplan, James. *Frank: The Voice* (New York: Anchor Books, 2011).

Kater, Michael H. *Different Drummers: Jazz in the Culture of Nazi Germany* (Oxford University Press, 2003).

Keating, Carla Mereu. "'100% Italian:' The Coming of Sound Cinema in Italy and State Regulation on Dubbing," *California Italian Studies* 4 (2013): 1–24.

Kein, Sybil. *Creole: The History and Legacy of Louisiana's Free People of Color* (Baton Rouge, LA: Louisiana State University Press, 2009).

Kertzer, David I. *The Pope and Mussolini: The Secret History of Pius XI and the Rise of Fascism in Europe* (New York: Random House, 2014).

Kingsley, Walter J. "Jazz Has a Remarkable History as a Fad," *The Sun* (February 9, 1919): 6.

Koenig, Karl (ed.). *Jazz in Print (1856–1929): An Anthology of Selected Early Readings in Jazz History* (Hillsdale, NY: Pendragon Press, 2002).

"Kramer è un inventore," *L'Ora* (February 18, 1945): 10.

Kuyper-Rushing, Lois. "Reassessing Eugene Bozza: Discoveries in the Bibliotheque Municipale De Valenciennes Archive," *Notes* 69/4 (June 2013): 706–721.

Labb. "Jazz Band," *Il Messaggero* (January 11, 1922).

Lanaro, Silvio. *Storia della Repubblica italiana. Dalla fine della Guerra agli anni novanta* (Venice: Marsilio, 1992).

Lane, Jeremy F. *Jazz and Machine-Age Imperialism: Music, "Race," and Intellectuals in France 1918–1945* (Ann Arbor, MI: University of Michigan Press, 2013).

LaRocca, Nick. "Jazz Stems from Whites Not Blacks, Says LaRocca," *Metronome* 52 (October 1936): 20.

"L'Eiar e la musica leggera," *Radiocorriere* 15/1 (1939): 5.

"L'EIAR non trasmette musica dei ebrei," *Il Popolo d'Italia* (September 22, 1938).

Levi, Ezio. "Musica incise," *Il disco* (April/May 1936): 17.

Levi, Ezio and Giancarlo Testoni. *Introduzione alla vera musica di Jazz* (Milan: Magazzino Musicale, 1938).

Levy, Beth Ellen. *Frontier Figures: American Music and the Mythology of the American West* (Berkeley, CA: University of California Press, 2012).

Leydi, Roberto. "Le fortune (o le sfortune) di Gershwin in Italia," *Gershwin*, ed. Gianfranco Vinay (Turin: EDT, 1992), 305–342.

Librando, Diego. *Il jazz a Napoli: dal dopoguerra agli anni Sessanta* (Naples: Alfredo Guida, 2004).

"Life on the American Newsfront: Vittorio Teaches Hollywood the Mussolini Pose," *Life* (October 11, 1937): 31.

Livingston, Michael A. *The Fascists and the Jews of Italy: Mussolini's Race Laws, 1938–1943* (Cambridge University Press, 2014).

Lo Cascio, Claudio. *Una Storia nel Jazz: Nick La Rocca* (Palermo: Novecento, 2003).

Lomax, Alan. "Liner Notes," *Italian Folk Music: Naples Campania* (Ethnic Folkways Library FE 4265), 1972.

Lombardi, Giorgio (ed.). *Genova e il Jazz* (Genoa: GGallery Publishing, 2013).

Longanesi, Leo. "Film italiano," *L'Italiano* (January–February 1933).

Lotz, Rainer. "The United States Army Ambulance Service Band," *VJM's Jazz & Blues Mart*, 145 (Spring 2007): 2–7.

Ludwig, Emil. *Talks with Mussolini* (Boston: Little, Brown and Co., 1933).

Luzzatto, Sergio. *The Body of Il Duce: Mussolini's Corpse and the Fortunes of Italy* (New York: Henry Holt and Company, 2014).

"The Mafia and What Led to the Lynching," *Harper's Weekly* 35 (March 28, 1891): 602–612.

Magnaghi, Russell M. "Louisiana's Italian Immigrants Prior to 1870," in *A Refuge for All Ages: Immigration in Louisiana History*, ed. Carl A Brasseauk (Lafayette, LA: Center for Louisiana Studies, 1996), 580–602.

Major, Clarence. *Juba to Jive: A Dictionary of African-American Slang* (New York: Viking, 1994).

Mambelli, Antonio. *Archimede Montanelli nella vita e nell'arte. Un maestro del Duce* (Forlì: Valbonesi, 1938).

Marcellini, Romolo. "Film per l'Impero: I nostri negri," 20, *Lo schermo* (October 1936).

"Marconi's Visit to the United States," *Music Trade Review* (September 15, 1906): 40.

Marinetti, F. T. *The Futurist Cookbook*, ed. Lesley Chamberlain and trans. Suzanne Brill (London: Penguin Classic, 2015).

   "Le Futurisme et la Presse internationale," *Poesia* 5/3–6 (April–July 1909): 24.

Marinetti F. T. and Bruno Corra. "Contro il teatro morto, contro il romanzone analitico, contro il negrismo musicale," *Gazzetta del Popolo* (October 22, 1937).

Martinelli, Dario. "Da Yeah a Ueee senza passare dal MinCulPop – Strategie di coe-sistenza e resistenza del jazz italiano durante il fascismo," *California Italian Studies* 4/1 (2013): 1–15.

Mascagni, Pietro. "L'Opera ha fatto il suo tempo," *Il Popolo d'Italia* (August 3, 1929).

Mazzoletti, Adriano. *Eddie Lang: Stringin' the Blues* (Rome: Pantheon, 1997).

    L'Italia del Jazz (Rome, Italy: Stefano Mastruzzi, 2011).

    Il Jazz in Italia: dalle origini alle grandi orchestre, vol. 1 (Turin: EDT, 2004).

    Il Jazz in Italia: dallo swing agli anni sessanta vol. 2 (Milan: EDT, 2010).

    "Liner Notes" for *40 anni di Jazz in Italia* (Ricordi MRJ 8007/8), 1963.

Meli, Francesco. *Frank Sinatra semplicemente il migliore* (Bologna: Odoya, 2014).

Méliès, George. *Complete Catalogue of Genuine and Original "Star" Films (Moving Pictures) Manufactured by Geo. Méliès of Paris* (Paris; New York: Starfilm, 1905).

Michaelis, Meir. *Mussolini and the Jews: German–Italian Relations and the Jewish Question in Italy, 1922–1945* (New York and Oxford: Clarendon Press, 1978).

Miletti, Vladimiro. *Aria di jazz. Parole in libertà* (Trieste: Edizioni dell'Alabarda, 1934).

Miller, Mark. *"Some Hustling This!" Taking Jazz to the World, 1914–1929* (Toronto: The Mercury Press, 2005).

Mojana, Marina and Ada Masoero (eds.). *Depero con Campari* (Rome: De Luca Editori d'Arte, 2010).

Monelli, Paolo. *Mussolini piccolo Borghese* (Milan: Vallardi, 1983).

Monteleone, Franco. *Storia della radio e della televisione in Italia. Società, politica, strategie, programmi. 1922–1992* (Venice: Marsilio, 1992).

    La radio italiana nel periodo fascista. Studio e documenti. 1922–1945 (Venice: Marsillio, 1976).

Monti, Luigi. "The Mafiusi of Sicily," *The Atlantic Monthly* 37 (January 1876): 58–76.

Mowrer, Lilian T. *A Journalist's Wife* (New York: Morrow, 1937).

Muir, Peter C. "Looks Like a Cash Register and Sounds Worse: The Deiro Brothers and the Rise of the Piano Accordion in American Culture 1908–1930," *Free-Reed Journal* 3 (2001): 55–79.

"Mussolini's War on Ethiopia is Praised by Josephine Baker," *Chicago Tribune* (October 2, 1935): 4.

Mussolini, Benito. *The Cardinal's Mistress*, trans. Hiram Motherwell (London: Cassell, 1928).

    "Da provincia rossa a provincia fascista," *Il Popolo d'Italia* (March 30, 1921).

    "La Reppublica sociale italiana," in *Opera Omnia di Benito Mussolini* XXIII (Florence, IT: La Fenice, 1960), 1–5.

    Opera Omnia, vol. XLI, ed. Emilio and Duilio Susmel (Rome: Volpe, 1979).

Mussolini, Rachele. *Mussolini private* (Milan: Rusconi, 1980).

Mussolini, Romano. *Il duce mio padre* (Milan: Rizzoli, 2004).

Mussolini, Vittorio. "Semprini e Kramer," *Cinema* (January 25, 1941).

    "Cinque dischi hot," *Il Disco 2* (October 1934): 10.

    Vita con mio padre (Milan: Mondadori, 1957).

Nataletti, Giorgio. *1922–1962. Quarant'anni di attività di Giorgio Nataletti* (Rome: Istituto Grafico Tiberino, 1962).

"Natalino Otto," *Il Canzoniere della Radio* 37 (June 1, 1942): 4–5.

"New Cult in Art Drapes the Nude, Bars Sentiment," *The Evening World* (December 4, 1911): 13.

"The New Cult of Futurism is Here," *New York Herald* (December 24, 1911): magazine section.

Nicolodi, Fiamma. *Musica e musicisti nel ventennio fascista* (Fiesole: Discanto, 1984).

Nimmo, H. Arlo. *The Andrews Sisters: A Biography and Career Record* (Jefferson, NC: McFarland, 2004).

Nuñez, Sandro Lopez. *Carriere spezzate: Gli artisti ebrei colpiti dalle leggi razziale del 1938* (Milan: Mimesis, 2013).

Otto, Natalino. "Confidenze lampo di Natalino Otto," *Canzoniere della Radio* 59 (May 1, 1943): 28–29.

Padovani, Cinzia. *A Fatal Attraction: Public Television and Politics in Italy.* (Lanham, MD: Rowman & Littlefield, 2005).

Page, Giorgio Nelson. *L'americano di Roma* (Milan: Longanesi, 1950).

Papa, Antonio (ed.). *Storia politica della radio in Italia*, 2 vols. (Naples: Guida, 1978).

"Patriotic Italians Celebrate Anniversary of Their Society," *The Daily Picayune* (October 13, 1913).

Pensotti, Anita. *Rachele e Benito: Biografia di Rachele Mussolini* (Milan: Mondadori, 1993).

Peretti, Burton W. *The Creation of Jazz: Music, Race, and Culture in Urban America* (Urbana-Champagne, IL: University of Illinois Press, 1994).

Peyton, Leonard. "Rome," *The Musical Times* (January 1923): 70.

Piazzoni, Irene. *La musica leggera in Italia dal dopoguerra agli anni del "boom." Cultura, consume, costume* (Milan: l'Ornitorinco, 2011).

Pichetti, Enrico. *Mezzo secolo di danza: Ricordi della mia vita e del mio insegnamento. La danza attraverso i secoli, ballerini celebri, balli antichi e moderni, comportamento in società* (Rome: Edizioni VIS, 1935).

Piras, Marcello. *Dentro le note: Il jazz al microscopio* (Rome: Arcana, 2015).

"Garibaldi to Syncopation: Bruto Giannini and the Curious Case of Scott Joplin's *Magnetic Rag*," *Journal of Jazz Studies* 9/2 (Winter 2013): 107–177.

Plastino, Goffredo. "Jazz Napoletano: A Passion for Improvisation," *Jazz Worlds/World Jazz*, ed. Philip V. Bohlman and Geoffredo Plastino (Chicago University Press, 2016), 309–337.

Popik, Barry. "Windy City (12 February 1877); Jazz notes," *ADS-L* (August 6, 2003).

Presutti, Fabbio. "The Saxophone and the Pastoral. Italian Jazz in the Age of Fascist Modernity," *Italica* (Summer–Autumn 2008): 273–294.

Quartermaine, Luisa. *Propaganda and Politics in the Italian Social Republic (R.S.I.) 1943–45* (Exeter, UK: Elm Bank Publications, 2000).

Rabagliati, Alberto. *Quattro anni fra le stelle* (Milan: Bolla, 1932).

"Radio e dischi," *Radiocorriere* 30/8 (1932): 20.

Raeburn, Bruce Boyd. "Italian Americans in New Orleans Jazz: Bel Canto Meets the Funk," *Italian American Review* 4/2 (Summer 2014): 87–108.

New Orleans Style and the Writing of American Jazz History (Ann Arbor, MI: University of Michigan Press, 2009).

Ragnetta, Massimo. "Radio Broadcasting in Fascist Italy: Between Censorship, Total Control, Jazz and Futurism," *Broadcasting in the Modernist Era*, ed. Matthew Feldman, Erik Tonning and Henry Mead (London: Bloomsbury, 2014), 195–211.

Rainey, Lawrence, Christine Poggi and Laura Wittman (eds.). *Futurism: An Anthology* (New Haven, CT: Yale University Press, 2009).

Rasula, Jed. "Jazz as Decal for the Avant-Garde," in *Blackening Europe: The African American Presence*, ed. Heike Raphael-Hernandez (New York: Routledge, 2004).

Ravasio, Carlo. "Fascismo e tradizione," *Il Popolo d'Italia* (March 30, 1928).

Richieri, Giuseppe. "Italian Broadcasting and Fascism 1924–1937," *Media, Culture and Society* 2 (1988): 49–56.

Rigter, Bob. "Light on the Dark Etymology of JAZZ in the *Oxford English Dictionary*," in *Language Usage and Description: Studies Presented to N. E. Osselton on the Occasion of His Retirement*, ed. Ingrid Tieken-Boon van Ostade and John Frankis (Atlanta, GA: Rodopi, 1991), 91–100.

Rimondi, Giorgio (ed.). *Jazz Band: Percorsi letterari fra avanguardia consume e musica sincopata* (Milan: Mursia, 1994).

"Ritmo-mania," *Bergamo Repubblicana* (April 26, 1944): 2.

Rye, Howard. "Towards a Black British Jazz: Studies in Acculturation, 1860–1935," in *Black British Jazz: Routes, Ownership and Performance*, ed. Jason Toynbee, Catherine Tackley and Mark Doffman (London and New York: Routledge, 2014), 35–42.

Sachs, Harvey. *Music in Fascist Italy* (London: Weidenfeld and Nicolson, 1987).

Salaris, Claudia (ed.). *Pentagramma Elettrico: Suoni, rumori e parole in libertà*, Rome: Auditorium Parco della Musica, April 9–May 31, 2009 (Pistoia: Gli Ori, 2009).

Salvetti, Guido and Bianca Maria Antolini. *Italia Millenovecentocinquanta* (Milan: Edizioni Angelo Guerini e Associati Spa, 1999).

"Sam Wooding all'Eden Dancing Grand Tabarin," *Corriere della Sera* (December 14, 1928).

Sapori, Francesco. "Canta che ti passa," *Radiocorriere* 14 (October 18, 1941).

Sarfatti, Margherita. *DUX* (Milan: Mondadori, 1926).

Sarfatti, Michele. *The Jews in Mussolini's Italy: From Equality to Persecution*, trans. John and Anne C. Tedeschi (Milwaukee, WI: The University of Wisconsin Press, 2006).

Savarino, Santi. "Cronache del teatro e della radio. Altoparlante," *La Stampa* (January 7, 1939).

Scarpaci, Vincenza. "Walking the Color Line: Italian Immigrants in Rural Louisiana, 1880–1910," in *Are Italians White? How Race Is Made in America*, ed. Jennifer Guglielmo and Salvatore Salerno (New York: Routledge, 2003), 60–78.

Schwamenthal, Riccardo. "Jazz a Bergamo: Ricordi testimonianze documenti dagli anni trenta agli anni settanta," *Archivio storico Bergamasco* XV/2 (1995): 18–57.

Seagrove, Gordon. "Blues Is Jazz and Jazz Is Blues," *Chicago Daily Tribune* (July 11, 1915): E8.

Segrave, Kerry. *American Films Abroad: Hollywood's Domination of the World's Movie Screens* (Jefferson, NC: McFarland, 1997).

Shack, William A. *Harlem in Montmartre: A Paris Jazz Story between the Great Wars* (Berkeley, CA: University of California Press, 2001).

Siciliani, Pierluigi "Piji." *La Canzone Jazzata: L'Italia che canta sotto le stelle del jazz* (Arezzo: ZONA, 2007).

Sinatra, Frank in collaboration with John Quinlan, *Tips on Popular Singing* (New York: Embassy Music Corp., 1941).

Smith, Denis Mack. *Mussolini* (New York: Knopf, 1982).

Smucker, John R. Jr. *The History of the United States Army Ambulance Service with the French and Italian Armies, 1917, 1918, 1919* (Allentown, PA: Army Ambulance Service, 1967).

Snowden, Frank M. Jr. "Race Propaganda in Italy," *Phylon* 1/2 (1940): 103–111.

Sollitt, Edna Richolson. "Respighi Treads the Appian Way," *Musical America* 48/33 (December 1, 1928): 19.

"Speak-Easies for Dancing Evade Italy's Ban on Jazz," *New York Times* (April 3, 1927): E23.

Starr, S. Frederick. *New Orleans UnMasqued: Being a Wagwit's Affectionate Sketches of a Singular American City* (New Orleans, LA: Dedeaux Publishing, 1985).

Stoddard, Tom. *Jazz on the Barbary Coast*, 2nd edn. (Berkeley, CA: Heyday Books, 1998).

Strozek, Przemysław. "Futurist Responses to African American Culture," *Afromodernisms: Paris, Harlem and the Avant-garde*, ed. Fionnghuala Sweeney and Kate Marsh (Edinburgh University Press, 2013), 43–61.

Sudhalter, Richard M. *Lost Chords: White Musicians and Their Contributions to Jazz, 1915–1945* (New York: Oxford University Press, 1999).

Sutton, Alan. *A Phonograph in Every Home: The Evolution of the American Recording Industry, 1900–19* (Denver, CO: Mainspring Press, 2010).

[Tackley], Catherine Parsonage. *The Evolution of Jazz in Britain 1880–1935* (Aldershot: Ashgate, 2005).

Taft, William Howard (ed.). *Service with Fighting Men: An Account of the Work of the American Young Men's Christian Associations in the World War* (New York: Association Press, 1922).

Tarli, Tiziano. *Op Op Trotta Cavallino: Epopea dello swing italiano* (Rome: Curcio Musica, 2013).

Testoni, Giancarlo. "Un Sogno che si avvera," *Music e Jazz* 1/1 (August 15–September 1, 1945): 1–2, 15.

Thompson, George. "'Jazz' in the LA Times, 1912 & 1917," *ADS-L* (a discussion list for members of the American Dialect Society) (August 4, 2003).

Thurman, Kira. "A History of Black Musicians in Germany and Austria, 1870–1961: Race, Performance, and Reception" (PhD Dissertation, University of Rochester, 2013).

Toni, Alceo. "Ancora della canzone popolare," *Segno della Radio* I/17 (December 17, 1944): 11.

Toynbee, Jason, Catherine Tackley and Mark Doffman (eds.). *Black British Jazz: Routes, Ownership and Performance* (London and New York: Routledge, 2014).

Tranfaglia, Nicola. *Ministri e giornalisti. La guerra e il Minculpop (1939–1943)* (Turin: Einaudi, 2005).

Triulzi, Alessandro. "Italian-Speaking Communities in Early Nineteenth-Century Tunis," *Revue de l'Occident musulman et de la Méditerranée* IX/1 (1971): 153–184.

"Una Nuova Iniziativa: EIAR-JAZZ," *Radiorario* 7/14 (March 31–April 7, 1929): 4.

Vance, William A. *America's Rome*, vol. 2 *Catholic and Contemporary Rome* (New Haven, CT: Yale University Press, 1989).

"Varie di musica," *Il Popolo d'Italia* (November 30, 1928).

Veroli, Patrizia. "La danza e il fascismo. Anton Giulio Bragaglia e *Jazz Band* (1929)," in *L'Italia e la danza: Storie e rappresentazioni, stili e techniche tra teatro, tradizioni popolari e società*, ed. Giannandrea Poesio e Alessandro Pontremoli (Rome: ARACNE, 2008).

Verre, Luciano. "Ero la regina del Trio Lescano, adesso vivo sola e sono in miseria," *Gente* 29/47 (November 22, 1985): 106–109.

Visconti, Guido Carlo. "Fuori I Barbari!" *Il Giornale d'Italia* (September 13, 1929).
  "Nazionalismo nella musica," *Realtà* (June 1938).

Viton, Albert. "Italy under Hitler," *The Nation* (December 31, 1938): 7–11.

Ward, Richard Lewis. *A History of Hal Roach Studios* (Carbondale, IL: Southern Illinois University Press, 2005).

White, John J. *Literary Futurism: Aspects of the First Avant-Garde* (Oxford University Press, 1990).

Wilton, David. *Word Myths: Debunking Linguistic Urban Legends* (New York: Oxford University Press, 2004).

Wolff, Lon. "Albert Ross Etzweiler: Arizona's Music Man," *The Journal of Arizona History* 50/2 (Summer 2009): 125–142.

Woodruff, Ann. "Society Halls in New Orleans: A Survey of Jazz Landmarks, Part II," *The Jazz Archivist* XXI (2008): 19–36.

Wright, Michael. "The Yosco No. 2 Tenor Banjo," *Vintage Guitar* Magazine (August 2011) www.vintageguitar.com/10981/the-yosco-no-2/

Zannoni, Massimo. "L'EIAR," *ACTA dell'Istituto storico Repubblica Sociale Italiana* 16/1 (January–March 2002): 6.

Zimmerman, Joshua D. (ed.). *The Jews in Italy under Fascist and Nazi Rule, 1922–1945* (Cambridge: Cambridge University Press, 2005).

Zuccoli, Luciano. "Black and White," *Il Messaggero* (February 2, 1922).

Zucotti, Susan. *The Italians and the Holocaust: Persecution, Rescue, and Survival* (Lincoln, NE: University of Nebraska Press, 1987).

Zuculin, Bruno. "Musiche e danze americane," *La Lettura* 19/ 8 (August 1, 1919): 599–600.

Zwerin, Mike. *Swing under the Nazis: Jazz as a Metaphor for Freedom* (New York, NY: Cooper Square Press, 2000).

Online Archives

The Encyclopedic Discography of Victor Recordings. http://victor.library .ucsb.edu.

Radiocorriere TV RAI 1925–1995. www.radiocorriere.teche.rai.it

Ricordando Alberto Rabagliati. www.albertorabagliati.com

Ricordando il Trio Lescano. www.trio-lescano.it

Tulane University Hogan Jazz Archive. https://jazz.tulane.edu

University of Colorado Digital Sheet Music Collection. http://libcudl .colorado.edu/sheetmusic

The Wolfsonian-Florida International Library. www.wolfsonian.org

Index